The Politics of Central Banks

This book is a study of power. In particular, it is a study of governmental power in Britain and France. Its focus is the changing relationship between the government and the central bank in the two countries, and it examines the politics of this relationship since the time when the Bank of England and the Bank of France were first created.

The book begins by considering the issue of governmental control in general. It then focuses on monetary policy making, and asks what has been the role of governments in this area and what freedom have central banks enjoyed. After a detailed historical analysis of this issue in Britain and France, the authors conclude by considering the likely role of the European Central Bank.

The main observations are that the relationship between governments and central banks has been subject to great variation over time. In the contemporary context we see increasingly independent central banks, European monetary integration and globalised economic markets. Consequently, the politics of monetary policy has become increasingly complex and national governments appear to be losing control over monetary policy. And yet, this study shows that core issues concerning the political control of economic life are as salient as ever.

Robert Elgie is Lecturer in Politics at the University of Limerick and author of *The Role of the Prime Minister in France* and *Political Leadership in Liberal Democracies*. **Helen Thompson** is University Lecturer in Politics at Cambridge University and author of *The British Conservatives and the Exchange Rate Mechanism*.

Routledge Advances in International Relations and Politics

1 **Foreign Policy and Discourse Analysis**
France, Britain and Europe
Henrik Larsen

2 **Agency, Structure and International Politics**
From Ontology to Empirical Enquiry
Gil Friedman and Harvey Starr

3 **The Political Economy of Regional Co-operation in the Middle East**
Ali Carkoglu, Mine Eder, Kemal Kirisci

4 **Peace Maintenance**
The Evolution of International Political Authority
Jarat Chopra

5 **International Relations and Historical Sociology**
Breaking Down Boundaries?
Stephen Hobden

6 **Equivalence in Comparative Politics**
Edited by Jan W. van Deth

7 **The Politics of Central Banks**
Robert Elgie and Helen Thompson

The Politics of Central Banks

Robert Elgie and
Helen Thompson

Routledge
Taylor & Francis Group
LONDON AND NEW YORK

First published 1998 by Routledge

2 Park Square, Milton Park, Abingdon, Oxon OX14 4RN
711 Third Avenue, New York, NY 10017, USA

Routledge is an imprint of the Taylor & Francis Group, an informa business

First issued in paperback 2016

Typeset in Baskerville by Routledge

British Library Cataloguing in Publication Data
A catalogue record for this book is available from the British Library

Library of Congress Cataloguing in Publication Data
Elgie, Robert.
The politics of central banks / Robert Elgie and Helen Thompson.
p. cm.
Includes bibliographical references and index.
1. Banks and banking, Central–Great Britain–History. 2. Banks and banking, Central–France–History. 3. Monetary policy–Great Britain–History. 4. Monetary policy–France–History. 5. European Central Bank. I. Thompson, Helen, 1966– . II. Title.
HG2995.E44 1998
332.1'1'0941–dc21 98-4866
CIP

ISBN 978-0-415-14422-3 (hbk)
ISBN 978-1-138-97900-0 (pbk)

Contents

Preface

John Mackintosh once stated that 'the student of government is chiefly interested in power. His [sic] task is to discover where power lies in any society and to describe the government's share in its operation' (Mackintosh 1968: 3). This is a book about government. It is a book about the power of government, and about the government's share in the operation of power.

This is a study of executive power. More particularly, it is a study of executive power in Britain and France. More particularly still, it is a study of the government's share of power in the domain of monetary policy in each of these two countries. It examines the relationship between the executive branch of government and the central bank. It examines the politics of government/central bank relations in Britain and France. Finally, it examines the extent to which members of the British and French core executives have been able to control the process of monetary policy making in their respective systems.

By virtue of this focus, the book is able to establish the scope of core executive influence over monetary policy in Britain and France. Moreover, it does so from the time when the Bank of England and the Bank of France were first created, in 1694 and 1800 respectively. Its main observations are threefold: it demonstrates that in these two countries this relationship has been subject to great variation over time; it argues that recently the politics of monetary policy, or the politics of core executive/central bank control, has become increasingly complex; and it asserts that, even in the contemporary context of increasingly independent central banks, long-standing issues concerning the political control of economic life are still as salient as ever.

The result is a study which examines government–central bank relations from a political science perspective. Its concern is for the politics of monetary policy. That said, it draws heavily upon some of the most recent literature on central banking in the discipline of economics. In particular, it adapts the methodology proposed by Alex Cukierman so as to measure the degree of central bank independence from the executive. Similarly, it draws equally heavily upon archival sources and the academic literature on central banking in the discipline of history. In itself this book does not constitute a history or a simple narrative of government–central bank relations in Britain and France, but it is a study which places government–central bank relations in these two countries in their appropriate historical context.

The result is also a book which approaches the study of government–central bank relations from the perspective of domestic politics. It goes without saying that international events have frequently impinged upon government–central bank relations over the years and continue to do so. The power to shape monetary policy within any given system has always been affected by international trade flows, and increasingly it has been determined by the role of global financial markets as well as by issues related to regional economic and political systems, such as the European Union. This book takes account of such factors when and where appropriate, but its focus is firmly and squarely on the politics within states rather than the politics between them. In short, this book is in the tradition of the recent work on government by such people as Rhodes and Dunleavy (1995) and it provides a modest contribution to some of the issues which are addressed in this work.

The first chapter introduces the concept of the core executive and examines some of the ways in which the issue of core executive control may be studied. The second chapter focuses very generally on the relationship between core executives and central banks and, notably, proposes both quantitative and qualitative methods of studying core executive/central bank relations. The third and fourth chapters analyse in some detail the relationship between the core executive and the Bank of England since 1694, including the most recent reform of the Bank's statutes in 1997. The fifth and sixth chapters investigate in equal detail the relationship between the core executive and the Bank of France since 1800, and consider the relationship between the government and the Bank since the latter became independent in January 1994. The final chapter places the politics of core executive control in its contemporary context. In particular, this chapter examines the likely role of the European Central Bank and considers the changing nature of political control over economic life.

In preparing this book, the authors have relied heavily upon personal interviews with senior figures in both Britain and France. In total, over thirty interviews were conducted. Those interviewed comprised elected representatives, their policy advisers, top civil servants and some of the most senior central bank officials, including former and incumbent members of the most senior decision-making institutions in the two countries. All of these interviews were sought, and were granted, on the basis that they would be non-attributable. Consequently, in the text which follows direct quotations from these interviews are used but the source is not specified.

Robert Elgie would like to thank the University of Limerick for an award under the 'Seed' Funding for Research scheme.

The authors would also like to thank Patrick Proctor and John Dixon at Routledge for their time and comments.

1 The politics of core executive control

The core executive may be defined as 'all those organizations and structures which primarily serve to pull together and integrate central government policies, or act as final arbiters within the executive of conflicts between different elements of the government machine' (Dunleavy and Rhodes 1990: 4). The core executive corresponds to 'the heart of the machine', and consists of a 'complex web of institutions, networks and practices' (Rhodes 1995: 12) which incorporates all the significant policy-making and co-ordinating actors in the executive branch of government, heads of state, heads of government, ministers and senior civil servants as well as central co-ordinating agencies, secretariats, committees and services. The term 'core executive' is one which has no normative connotations and which permits comparative analysis. It is the term which will be used in this book to examine both the politics of core executive control in general, and the politics of monetary policy in particular.

This chapter consists of two main parts. The first part examines the study of core executive control. In so doing, it sets the scene for Chapter 2, which explores the particularities of core executive/central bank control. The second part considers the changing patterns of core executive control over the last three centuries. In this way, it provides the background for Chapters 3–6 inclusive, which place core executive/central bank relations in Britain and France in an historical perspective. Overall, this chapter serves as an introduction to the politics of monetary policy and to the problem of core executive control in this area.

The study of core executive control

There are two sets of relationships that feature in the study of core executive control. The first set concerns those that occur within the core executive. This set reflects the relationships between the various actors within the core executive and the resources and constraints that they possess. For example, is the relationship structured so that the prime minister controls the decision-making process and exercises a form of individual leadership, or alternatively, is it structured so that the prime minister is obliged to share power within the cabinet and exercise a form of collective leadership? In this set of relationships, the issue of core executive control is concerned with the internal politics of the core executive. By contrast, the second set of relationships concerns those which occur between the core executive and external forces. This set reflects the relationships between the core executive and the various actors in the wider political process, such as trade unions, business groups and political parties. For example, does the core executive have the capacity to shape the demands of the actors in the general environment within which it operates, or does it simply respond to the demands generated by those actors within that environment? In this set of relationships, the issue of core executive control is concerned with the external 'reach' of the core executive.

Just as there are two sets of relationships in the study of core executive control, so there are two main methodological approaches to the study of core executive control. The first is a qualitative approach. This involves a careful unpacking of the formal and informal powers of the different actors both inside and outside the core executive. It identifies the context within which the core executive operates and examines the attitudes and behaviour of individuals and groups who operate within that context. It is an essentially descriptive approach, and represents the traditional way of studying the issue of core executive control. The second is a quantitative approach (or at least a semi-quantitative approach). This only rarely involves the measurement of objectively identifiable criteria; instead, more often than not, it consists of calculations based on subjectively manufactured scales, tables and rankings derived from ordinal data. It provides a numerical indication of the respective powers of the players concerned. It is an essentially analytical approach, and is to be found in some of the more recent studies of core executive control.

The identification of two sets of relationships in the study of core executive control and two distinct approaches to the study of core executive control generates a matrix, which is shown in Table 1. This matrix provides an indication of the various different types of core executive studies that can and have been undertaken. Cell 1 corresponds to a qualitative study of power relationships within the core executive, whereas Cell 3 corresponds to a quantitative study of those same power relationships. Similarly, Cell 2 signifies a qualitative study of power relationships between the core executive and the other players in the political process, and Cell 4 signifies a quantitative study of the same. It is useful to identify and briefly examine examples of each of the four types of core executive studies so as to show the various issues involved in the politics of core executive control, and so as to set the scene for subsequent chapters in which both qualitative and quantitative methods are used.

The first type of core executive studies, corresponding to those in Cell 1, comprises qualitative studies of power relationships within the core executive. In the main, this type of core executive studies concerns in-depth accounts of internal core executive power relations in individual countries. In a British context, for example, this work is to be found in the long-running debate about the relative powers of the prime minister and cabinet. This debate produced two mutually exclusive schools of thought: the prime ministerial government school and the cabinet government school. On the one hand, Richard Crossman famously declared that the 'post-war epoch has seen the final transformation of Cabinet Government into Prime Ministerial Government' (Crossman 1972: 51), whereas on the other hand, Patrick Gordon Walker argued that a 'Prime Minister who habitually ignored the Cabinet, who behaved as if Prime Ministerial government were a reality – such a Prime Minister could rapidly come to grief (Walker 1970: 95). Supporters of both sides provided evidence to back up their argument based on their own experience of core executive operations and/or on interviews with others with such experience. In particular, Crossman emphasised the importance of the centralisation of political parties and the growth of a centralised bureaucracy (Crossman 1972: 51–2), while Walker argued that 'neither of [these points] is as novel nor as significant as is sometimes made out' (Walker 1970: 86).

If, for the most part, this type of core executive studies has focused on core executive power relations in individual countries, then there are still some qualitative studies which examine internal core executive power

Table 1 Types of core executive studies

	Qualitative	Quantitative
Internal	1 qualitative study of power relationships within the core executive	3 quantitative study of power relationships within the core executive
External	2 qualitative study of power relationships between the core executive and the other players in the political process	4 quantitative study of power relationships between the core executive and the other players in the political process

relations comparatively. Perhaps most notably, Anthony King has studied the relative influence of prime ministers 'within their own systems of government' (King 1994: 151). By focusing on whether prime ministers head single-party or multi-party governments, the degree of control that prime ministers wield over the careers of other politicians within the government, the public visibility of prime ministers and the legacy of history, King establishes a ranking of prime ministers according to the degree of their influence within government (King 1994: 151–61) (see Table 2). This table is based on secondary information rather than interviews with primary sources, but it still provides an interpretation of the comparative strength of these political leaders within their own systems of government which is derived from an essentially qualitative approach.

The advantage of this type of study is that it can provide a full description of the complexities of political life. As one writer notes about the merits of another similar type of study, it can 'proffer a highly sophisticated account of the power relationships' (Devine 1995: 148) between actors within the core executive.

The second type of core executive studies, corresponding to those in Cell 2, comprises qualitative studies of power relationships between the core executive and the other actors in the political system. One such study, even though it calls upon certain figures to back up its points, has been conducted by Richard Rose (1985). This is a comparative study of selected Western governments and, in particular, of the power of the US president in comparison to European presidents and prime ministers. Rose begins by describing some of the resources that these political leaders can mobilise in the context of their own core executive. In this sense, he is engaging in the same type of study as King above. However, Rose then goes on to examine the 'total amount of resources mobilized by government' (Rose 1985: 10).

Rose identifies three factors which serve to indicate the position of the government, or core executive, within the wider system. First, there is the proportion of gross domestic product claimed by government as tax

Table 2 King's ranking of prime ministers according to their degree of influence within government

High	*Medium*	*Low*
Germany	Austria	Italy
UK	Belgium	Netherlands
Greece	Denmark	Norway
Ireland	Sweden	
Portugal		
Spain		

Source: King (1994): 153

revenue. Needless to say, some governments command a larger portion of their natural resources than others, and some governments collect more government revenue centrally than others. These indicators point to the comparative centralisation of the core executive and, therefore, to the extent of its reach. Second, there is the extent of centralisation of public employment. For Rose, public employment is a major resource of government because 'insofar as a leader requires followers, then public employees are reliable followers, being bureaucrats paid by the state to follow rules laid down from above' (Rose 1985: 11). Again, some governments employ a larger number of employees than others and so the reach of certain core executives is greater than others in this respect. Third, there is the proportion of laws sponsored by governments annually. For Rose, this is another indication of the core executive's ability to influence the political system. Once again, there are cross-national variations in the amount of government-sponsored legislation which is passed annually, and so there are also cross-national variations in the relative influence of core executives.

It scarcely needs to be said that there are certain problems with Rose's analysis. For example, the assumption that core executive influence increases proportionally to the level of public employment is highly questionable. After all, the larger the bureaucracy the more unwieldy it may become and the more interests it may generate to which the chief executive is obliged to respond. Nevertheless, it remains that Rose's article is a good example of a qualitative approach to the study of the position of the core executive in relation to the wider political system. In this respect, it benefits from the general advantages of this type of approach that were identified above.

The third type of core executive studies, corresponding to those in Cell 3, comprises quantitative studies of power relationships within the core executive. The most imaginative study in this category is by Patrick Dunleavy (1995), who measures the relative importance of the different actors within the British core executive under the prime ministership of John Major. He does so by examining the functioning and membership of cabinet committees and subcommittees. He assumes that committees are more important than subcommittees, that cabinet ministers are more important than non-cabinet ministers and that committee chairs are more important than committee members (Dunleavy 1995: 306–7). He then proposes a formula which indicates the relative importance (or weighted score) of each committee and subcommittee. On the basis of this formula, he calculates the relative influence of each committee and subcommittee member by dividing the committee or subcommittee's weighted score by the total number of members plus one for the position of the chair and then calculates the relative influence of the chair by doubling this figure.

Dunleavy's formula for measuring the relative importance of the actors within the British core executive

The proposed formula is:

100*S*(C/N)

where:

S is the status of the committee with a committee counting as 1.0 and a subcommittee counting as 0.5;
C is the number of cabinet members who sit on the committee or subcommittee;
N is the total number of people who sit on the committee or subcommittee.

Source: Dunleavy, 1995, pp. 306–7.

When the calculations are made for all cabinet and non-cabinet members across all committees and subcommittees, the findings are both striking and yet intuitively correct. The prime minister scores far higher (256 points or 14.9 per cent of the total share) than any other cabinet member, reflecting his/her multiple positions of influence throughout the committee structure. There is then a first-ranked group of three ministers, the Foreign Secretary, the Secretary of State for Defence and the Chancellor of the Exchequer, who score significantly higher (155, 138 and 110 points respectively) than other cabinet members and who are well placed to shape the decision-making process. There are then second, third and fourth-ranked groups of ministers corresponding to the scores that they achieve and the relative degree of influence that they possess. In the article, Dunleavy then goes on to discuss these findings. In particular, he examines the linkages that occur across committees and the appointments that the prime minister needs to make in order to ensure that politically 'friendly' ministers control the most central positions in the cabinet decision-making process.

As Dunleavy himself notes, there are good reasons to be 'cautious in interpreting the numerical estimates' (Dunleavy 1995: 319). Indeed, he states that these scores 'should not be fetished, nor should any fine or precise significance be attached to them' (ibid.). They are, after all, simply calculations based on a number of limiting, subjective and contestable assumptions. However, this approach to the study of control within the core executive has its merits. Most notably, it provides the opportunity for systematic cross-temporal and comparative research. In this respect, though, as Dunleavy again notes, its value is still primarily heuristic in that it provides an indication of the sorts of research questions that need to be asked rather than an answer to those self-same questions.

The final type of core executive studies, corresponding to those in Cell 4, comprises quantitative studies of power relationships between the core executive and the other actors in the political system. One useful study in this respect has been suggested by Lane and Ersson (1991: 264–7). They establish what they call the central government influence index. This gives a numerical indication of the degree to which citizens and collectivities are able to influence political decision-making within the polity. In so doing, it provides a way of measuring the general reach of the core executive comparatively.

Lane and Ersson's index is derived from an examination of three influence mechanisms. Each mechanism is classified ordinally and then the scores for each country are simply totalled. The higher the total, the greater the extent to which citizens are able to influence policy making and so, arguably, the smaller the reach of the core executive. First, Lane and Ersson examine the capacity of citizens to influence policy makers by way of the frequency of referendums and the degree of proportionality in electoral formulae. So, for example, Switzerland scores 4/4 in this category because there is frequent recourse to referendums and because there is a proportional electoral system. Second, they consider the capacity of elites to influence policy making by way of the propensity towards both consociationalism and corporatism. Here, for example, the Netherlands and Norway both score 2/2 because they have highly developed consociational and/or corporatist procedures. Finally, they assess the importance of citizen influence by way of the presence of minimum-winning cabinets which are 'conducive to effective translation of citizen preferences into policies' (Lane and Ersson 1991: 265). According to this category, the UK scores 4/4 and Italy scores 0/4. By summing the various scores, citizens appear most able to influence policy in Norway (7/10) and least able to do so in Greece, Portugal and Spain (3/10). It might be argued, then, that the core executive reaches least far in Norway and furthest in this latter set of countries.

The same caution is needed when interpreting these results as was needed when interpreting the results produced by Dunleavy above. Indeed, perhaps a greater degree of caution is needed in the case of the central government influence index because of its extremely broad range and the rather simplistic method of classification. At the same time, though, this index has the same general advantages as the methodology identified by Dunleavy in that it permits comparisons both across time and across countries, and that it highlights certain features of the politics of core executive control which may then be explored more fully.

This book adopts both a qualitative and a semi-quantitative approach to the study of core executive/central bank relations in Britain and France. It describes both the historical and the contemporary relationship between the two institutions in the two countries and uses primary and secondary material in order to do so. It also establishes a means by which the degree of core executive control over the central bank can be measured and applies this methodology to the changing relationship between the two institutions across time. In this way, this study benefits from the advantages of both types of core executive studies outlined above and provides a full and comprehensive account of core executive/central bank relations in Britain and France. Before embarking on this account, however, it is necessary briefly to outline the changing role of governments during the course of the last three centuries.

The scope of government: an historical overview

S.E. Finer defines the term 'government' as 'a standardized arrangement for taking decisions affecting the group and for giving effect to them' (Finer 1970: 37). For Finer, government is a ubiquitous phenomenon. It arises in all instances where rival group members advocate policies which are mutually exclusive. He notes that 'the mutually exclusive policies of these groupings are, precisely, what generate the demand for a common public policy and formulate its alternatives . . . ' (Finer 1970: 38). It is this demand which makes 'public government', or the government of the territorial state, a 'necessary or at least desirable' (ibid.) aspect of all political life. In this sense, government occurs everywhere. However, even if this is the case, Finer also notes that 'the form, the procedures, the scope of government differ from one society to another, often very widely' (ibid.). So, for example, on the basis of the criteria identified in his posthumously published work, *History of Government from the Earliest Times*, Finer distinguishes between ten main types of polity. These range from Palace, or Court, government where 'interpersonal intriguing, plotting, feuding and faction fighting exemplifies the pathology of government' to the Forum government where '"the people", to whom the government is accountable, debate and vote' (Hayward 1997: 125). More parsimoniously, in his study of contemporary comparative government, Finer distinguishes between five types of government: military regimes, dynasties, façade democracies, quasi-democracies and liberal democracies (Finer 1970: 56–9).

Liberal democratic government through the modern state originated in Europe, primarily in Britain and France, between the middle of the sixteenth and seventeenth centuries amid the horrors of more than a century of domestic and international religious warfare. What distinguished the modern state, as a form of social and political control, from the immediate past was its claim to a monopoly of legislation, jurisdiction and the deployment of violence over a large territory. It created national centralised government in order to stop human societies across Europe destroying themselves, and each other, in the aftermath of the Reformation and Counter-Reformation. In this sense, the primary purpose of modern government was, as Thomas Hobbes conceived, to provide security to societies which could no longer be trusted to manage interpersonal conflict between either groups, or individuals, without frequent resort to violence (for a discussion of the idea of the modern state, see Skinner (1989)). In practice, this meant that the first modern governments created for themselves, above all else, a formidable apparatus of control. To provide their citizens with security, governments deemed it necessary not only to deploy force against external threats and internal challenges to their authority but often to control most aspects of national life including, for example, the publication of books and movement in and out of the territory over which they held sovereign power (for further discussion see Tilly (1975); Grew (1978)).

At the beginning of the nineteenth century the primary focus of European governments remained on security and jurisprudence, backed by central taxation and standing armies. Through the second half of the century and the years leading up to the First World War, the ambitions of governments grew in two broad directions. First, in the wake of the vast social and economic changes precipitated by industrialisation, governments began to commit themselves to greater regulation of parts of economic and social life. In part – for example in the creation of police forces and the supervision of prisons – this new control was exercised to strengthen the capacity of governments to do what they had long done in what were, for them, more threatening circumstances (Bayley 1975). At the same time, however, by taking decisions about such matters as employment conditions, railway building and public health, governments were acting in a qualitatively new manner. Except largely in Prussia and France, until around the 1870s government activism in these areas was primarily limited to simply instructing, through executive action or legislation, local agencies to act and administer control. Thereafter, in order to rationalise and centralise public administration, governments began to construct for themselves a bureaucratic apparatus subject to their own direct authority. With the creation of modern bureaucracies, the institutional capacity of governments to act was massively increased (for a discussion of some of the political implications, see Skowronek (1982)). Second, two European governments, in Germany in the 1880s and in Britain after 1906, began to provide practical economic services to their citizens in the form of transfer payments financed by taxation and insurance contributions. This represented the first attempt to exercise some political control over, if not economic life itself, some of the social and political consequences of industrial market economies (Flora and Heidenheimer 1995). Yet, despite the expansion of the scope of government during the nineteenth century, the prevailing political discourse about the purposes and responsibilities of government, as manifested in the preoccupations of those who engaged in high politics, remained firmly tied to the provision of internal and external security and all that meant in the context of European imperialism. Governments were interested in neither the production and distribution of goods, nor the economic consequences of the outcomes, in this respect, produced by markets.

During the course of the First World War the scope of government increased again, as most governments across Europe increased the level of control over their economies. After the cessation of hostilities, governments moved quickly to restore markets as the primary means of resource allocation. Thereafter, what was historically significant in broad political terms about the early interwar years was that, outside the Soviet Union, representative democracy was grafted on to the modern state. As a result, the demands placed on government, and the incentives for governments to act politically, substantially grew. In particular, governments became more anxious to provide welfare services and to try to secure high levels of employment. Yet, however necessary such political action seemed to governments in the prevailing international economic circumstances, the relationship between bigger government and representative democracy on the basis of a full franchise became increasingly problematic as the interwar years progressed. Most significantly, in Italy between 1918 and 1922 and in Germany during the Weimar Republic, the more ambitious governments grew in delivering services to certain groups of citizens, usually the relatively poor, the more they undermined the legitimacy of representative democracy. Indeed, only in Scandinavia did government effectively get substantially larger without endangering democracy.

By the end of the 1930s, 'government' had clearly triumphed over representative democracy in most of Europe. Ironically, if initially it was the demands that representative democracy placed on governments to do more that caused political resentment and instability, the eventual success of fascism in various states led to the extension of government authority into virtually all aspects of society and the economy. At the same time, in those states where representative democracy survived, such as Britain and France, governments still sought to extend their control over particular aspects of life, including trade, investment and credit, and strengthened the national bureaucracies over which they presided to do so (for a general discussion, see Polanyi (1944)). Nonetheless, after the authority of government over economic life in the remaining representative democracies had expanded during the previous decade, by 1940 almost all of these governments found themselves without the resources, or perhaps in some cases the will, to fulfil the primary task of the modern state, namely the provision of security to its citizens.

In the aftermath of the Second World War, governments in Western Europe redefined the role of government. In part, of course, this required them to reconstruct their capacity to provide security, but just as importantly, they chose to extend their authority over social and economic life including the international economy itself (Ruggie 1982). For around thirty years, until the mid-1970s, governments sought to exercise sufficient overall control to guarantee all citizens a minimum standard of living, both materially and qualitatively in terms of opportunities, and to ensure that market economies operated as rationally and effectively as possible (Milward 1992: chapter 2). Such control meant not only a huge increase in the peacetime financial resources of government, but also a massive expansion in the administrative structures of government (Shonfeld 1965: part iv). In explicit contrast to the experience of the interwar years, governments endeavoured to maintain a broad political consensus around representative democracy as they assumed this new authority for themselves. Governments did not simply act instrumentally, but created a public discourse in which these newly-provided services were deemed public goods, the provision for which they assumed moral responsibility as the servants of representative democracy. Although alienated impersonal authority remained the core of the contemporary modern state, citizens had now been told to expect that government would act as a buffer between themselves and misfortune and the competitive game of the market economy.

By the 1990s this particular model of government had clearly been superseded. What government now means in its wake is, of course, fiercely contested in contemporary analysis of politics. For some, the transformation has been profound. Some argue that the challenge of recent decades has been to the modern state itself and that we are now witnessing the replacement of the coercive authority of the state, both within the international (Held 1995; Rosenau and Czempiel 1992) and domestic (Rhodes 1996; Kooiman 1993) spheres, by more diffuse and less impersonal forms of control shared between government and civil society. Others, from a somewhat different perspective, argue that government in a more practical sense is in retreat in the wake of the globalisation, or at least the liberalisation, of the world economy, effectively 'privatising the public space' (Wallace 1993) it colonised during the interwar years and after the Second World War (see for example Strange 1996; Cerny 1990).

Certainly the drive towards privatisation, deregulation of markets and the introduction of market principles into the provision of particular public services can plausibly be characterised as a retreat by government from areas where it chose in the recent past to exercise some control. Equally, however, it is misleading to conclude that, for either reason, government is somehow in demise. There is simply no evidence that governments in the 1990s have any inclination to share the means of violence with either their own citizens or international organisations, let alone 'the empire of [global] civil society'. Neither is it easy to see how the dangers posed to human life by giving free rein to competitive human judgment can be resolved in any other way than through coercive impersonal authority, however brutal and imaginatively uncompelling Hobbes' premises remain (Dunn 1996a: chapter 4). Just as importantly, the retreat of government from economic life is on close inspection a more complicated phenomenon than is often suggested. The pursuit of economic liberalisation might well mean that governments can no longer 'take full responsibility for the economic welfare of a given population through the deft exercise of [their power]' (Dunn 1996a: 206), but it does not mean that governments are not trying to use their practical authority to secure relative prosperity for still significant numbers of their citizens. Keynesian demand management and *dirigisme*, for example, may no longer be part of the tools of government, but in their place governments are seeking to use the financial, administrative and legal resources of the state to compete for investment and international comparative economic advantage (Hirst and Thompson 1996). What is different about this form of government control is the political consequences, and their potential long-term implications in terms of representative democracy when the economic benefits it yields are so unequally distributed between citizens.

At the same time, governments in Europe have increasingly sought different means to exercise the kind of control that was more easily achieved in the first decades after the Second World War. Obviously, the pursuit of economic liberalisation, particularly as it has related to international capital and currency markets, has led governments to reappraise their welfare state commitments. Nonetheless, outside the United States there is no evidence that governments wish to disinvest themselves of responsibility for the welfare state. Rather, they have sought to place their welfare states on a sounder fiscal footing, which may in the short term require cuts in expenditure so as to defend their long-term viability (Pierson 1991). Meanwhile, the member-state governments of the European Union have tried to reconstitute some of the practical foundations of government authority, in particular as it relates to economic life, at the supra-national level while keeping an unquestioned national grip on the coercive powers of the state (Milward 1992; Milward *et al.* 1993). Seen in the appropriate context, therefore, the ambitions of government to govern and control are still profoundly politically relevant today. It is the form which those ambitions have taken, and their consequences for electoral competition, that are somewhat different from the immediate past. Against this background, it is now necessary to examine the politics of core executive/central bank control in more detail.

2 Core executive/central bank relations

The relationship between the core executive and the central bank has become an increasingly salient economic and political issue over the last twenty years. Indeed, during this time the relationship between the two institutions has been altered or even transformed in many parts of the world; in New Zealand, for example, the 1989 Reserve Bank Act fundamentally changed the statutory relationship between the Bank and the core executive. As a result, according to Dowd and Baker, 'the Reserve Bank went from being one of the two least independent central banks in the developed world to become of the most independent ones' (Dowd and Baker 1994: 857). Similarly, in the European Union the issue of core executive/central bank relations has been placed firmly and squarely on the legislative agenda. In particular, the specific obligations of the Maastricht Treaty recently encouraged the Belgian, French and Spanish governments, among others, to increase the formal autonomy of their respective central banks. Finally, in Eastern Europe the collapse of communism has brought about a general realignment of core executive/central bank relations. In these countries, it is certainly the case that central banks still remain 'vulnerable to government pressure' (Semler 1994: 51). However, it is also the case that certain central banks now exhibit a quite considerable degree of independence and, needless to say, all exhibit a greater degree of independence than under the previous regime.

This chapter explores the foundations of core executive/central bank relations. The first part charts the development of central banking, providing a brief historical overview of the changing relationship between core executives and central banks. The second and third parts identify the economic and political rationales for central bank independence. The fourth part presents a quantitative approach to the study of core executive/central bank relations, and proposes a comprehensive scale by which the degree of central bank independence can be calculated. The final part presents a qualitative approach to the study of core executive/central bank relations and briefly examines the current state of the relationship in three countries, Germany, the United States and Brazil. This chapter thus sets the scene for the detailed case studies of core executive/central bank relations in Britain and France which form the core of this book and which follow in the next four chapters.

The development of core executive/central bank relations

Central banking dates back to the seventeenth century (for an overview, see de Kock (1974: 1–17)). The oldest central bank, the Swedish Riksbank, was formed in 1668 and the next oldest, the Bank of England, was formed in 1694. However, central banking only began to emerge more widely in the early nineteenth century. For example, the Bank of France was founded in 1800, the Bank of the Netherlands in 1814, the National Bank of Austria and the Bank of Norway both in 1816, and the forerunners of the Danish National Bank and the Bank of Spain in 1818 and 1829 respectively. The next wave of central bank formation came in the late nineteenth and early twentieth centuries. The Bank of Russia was created in 1860, the German Reichsbank in 1875, the Bank of Japan in 1882, the Bank of Italy in 1893, the Swiss National Bank in 1905 and the US Federal Reserve System in 1914. In fact, though, it was only in the aftermath of the First World War and, in particular, as a result of the International Financial Conference in Brussels in 1920 that central banking came to be considered as an essential element of statehood (de Kock 1974: 9). Consequently, there followed a worldwide move towards central banking in many former British colonies, such as South Africa (1921), Australia (1924), New Zealand (1933), Canada (1935) and Ireland (1942), as well as in many South American countries, including Peru (1922), Colombia (1923), Chile (1926), Ecuador (1927), Bolivia (1928) and Argentina (1935), and more generally thereafter in newly-independent states such as Pakistan (1948), Israel (1954), Morocco (1959), Kenya, Tanzania and Uganda (all in 1966). Currently, then, even though there is still some debate as to whether a central bank is a necessary component of a sound economic system (see for example Goodhart 1991), it is apparent that in practice central banking is an almost ubiquitous phenomenon.

Despite its long history, the nature of central banking has altered over time. For at least one observer there was 'no clearly defined concept of central banking' (de Kock 1974: 1) prior to the beginning of the twentieth century. Whether or not this is the case, it is certainly true that the first central banks performed a relatively limited set of functions. They were formed mainly as banks of note issue, either for a particular area of a country or for the country as a whole. Governments tended to grant such banks an exclusive right of issue in return for certain privileges such as additional finance (Goodhart 1995: 211). Only gradually were the functions of central banks extended. By the early twentieth century, however, they were widely established as non-profit maximising, non-competitive organisations which were able 'to stand above the commercial fray' (Goodhart 1995: 210). They acted both as the bankers' banker, with the centralisation of the commercial banks' reserves, and as the government's banker, by managing domestic and foreign currency reserves on the government's behalf.

Just as the nature of central banking has altered over time, so too has the relationship between core executives and central banks. Each central bank has an individual history. Each bank was formed under a certain set of circumstances, has operated in a particular context since its formation and has enjoyed a specific relationship with its respective core executive. Consequently, the degree of central bank independence has always varied from one country to another. At the same time, however, it may be argued that there have been certain trends which have structured the general relationship between core executives and central banks. These trends mean that it is possible to categorise the changing relationship between the two institutions into certain periods. In particular, it is possible to identify three periods during which core executive/central bank relations resembled each other across a large range of countries (Goodhart *et al.* 1994: 50–5; Goodhart 1995: 211–15).

The first period extended from the time when the first central banks were formed through to the early twentieth century. As Goodhart *et al.* (1994: 51) note: '[f]or those institutions founded in the nineteenth century and gradually emerging as central banks in the course of the century there was relative independence'. This 'relative independence' stemmed only indirectly from the fact that the stock of most central banks was privately owned during this period. Instead, it was a result of the fact that, first, this was the period of *laissez-faire* economics and, second, the international monetary system was regulated by the gold standard. The importance of the *laissez-faire* period was that the domestic state was not expected to intervene to any great extent in the management of the economy. Consequently, governments only rarely tried to manipulate monetary policy for their own ends. The importance of the gold standard was that the primary responsibility of central banks was to maintain the convertibility of the domestic currency. However, the rules of the game were such that central bank adjustments were considered to be largely automatic. In short, during this first period economies were believed to be self-stabilising and governments were not expected to engage in counter-cyclical policy interventions. Only during times of exceptional fiscal stress, usually caused by war, did governments try to intervene in the business of central banks. As a result, central banks tended to maintain an arm's length relationship from core executives.

The second period began with the outbreak of the First World War and continued until the late 1960s. During this period, 'the links between Central Banks and Governments . . . [became] very much closer' (Goodhart 1995: 212). Consistent with the experience of the previous period, the start of the First World War marked a general increase in the role of the state in the economy, including the manipulation of central bank policy instruments. In contrast to the previous period, however, the consequences of the war were such that afterwards, core executive control was either maintained or gradually reintroduced. The effect of the Depression, the abandonment of the gold standard and increasing public and political calls for the greater accountability of economic and monetary policy meant that by the 1930s there was a 'pronounced and persistent trend towards the extension of State ownership and control of central banks . . .' (de Kock 1974: 316). The experience of the Second World War only increased this general trend. In particular, the widespread adoption of Keynesian demand management policies ensured that monetary policy was no longer considered to be separable from overall economic policy objectives. Governments were expected to manipulate the former in order to pursue the latter. As a result, therefore, many central bank reforms occurred during this second period. Most notably, central banks in a number of countries, such as Canada, Denmark, England, France, the Netherlands, New Zealand and Norway, were nationalised. Although nationalisation was perhaps not the most significant operational change in these countries during this second period, it was certainly the most symbolically important.

The third period began in the late 1960s. Since this time there has been a general desire for more central bank independence (Goodhart *et al.* 1994: 55). The next two parts of this chapter outline the economic and political rationales for greater central bank independence. Suffice it to say here that, for one observer at least, by 1993 it was quite reasonable to assert that central bank independence was 'now an idea whose time has most certainly come' (Goodhart 1995: 60).

The economic rationale for central bank independence

The economic rationale for central bank independence is both theoretical and empirical. The theoretical case for central bank independence is a result of the work on the so-called 'expectations-augmented Phillips curve' in the late 1960s and 1970s. Prior to this time, it was argued that there was a trade-off between unemployment and inflation. The Phillips curve purported to show that when unemployment was low then inflation would be high and *vice versa*. This was because when, for example, unemployment was low the demand for scarce resources meant that wages would tend to rise and costs would tend to increase. In this situation, the way to bring down inflation was to reduce the level of demand in the economy. Therefore, governments could supposedly manipulate the economy so as to bring about an optimum trade-off between unemployment and inflation.

By the 1970s, however, the notion that there was a trade-off between the two phenomena was challenged. In particular, it was argued that the public remembered the adverse effects that previous bouts of inflation had had on their real wages and profits, and reacted rationally to the prospect of future bouts by constantly revising their inflationary expectations upwards. The result was that whenever unemployment was below its natural level the public would continue to demand higher and higher wage, or price, increases and so inflation would accelerate. In other words, in the long-run the expectations-augmented Phillips curve was vertical. In this situation, the only way to bring down inflation was to reduce the level of inflationary expectations amongst the public. The best way to do this, it was subsequently argued, was by the adoption of a rule-based monetary regime (Barro and Gordon 1983). In such a regime, there would be clear monetary targets and publicly announced medium-term financial strategies. The announcement of these targets and strategies would show that decision makers were serious about reducing inflation which would, in turn, reduce the level of inflationary expectations amongst the public.

The corollary of this work was the argument that responsibility for managing the rule-based regime, and hence for setting monetary policy, should be transferred from governments to independent central banks. This argument was at least partly derived from the work on political business cycles. For example, William Nordhaus (1975) argued that there was a short-term opportunistic political business cycle in the USA. He argued that in the period immediately prior to an election, presidential incumbents had an incentive to try to manipulate the economy in order to win voter support. This would engender higher growth, lower unemployment and an increase in inflation just before the election, but then after the election presidents would be obliged to contract the economy so as to reduce the inflationary effects of the pre-electoral boom. The literature of political business cycles (for an overview, see Alesina and Roubini (1992)) suggested that the public soon became sceptical of the claims made by electorally sensitive politicians that they were serious about beating inflation. Politicians were not sufficiently credible to be able to reduce the level of inflation. They were likely to cheat on their promises. They sacrificed the need to keep to medium-term inflationary targets in order to boost their short-term electoral needs (the so-called time-consistency problem). Consequently, the level of inflationary expectations remained high.

In this context, attention increasingly shifted to central bankers. In an influential article, Kenneth Rogoff argued that there were inflation gains to be made by entrusting responsibility for monetary policy to an independent, conservative, inflation-averse central bank (Rogoff 1985: 1177–80). Over time, the central bank will establish a reputation for sound money. It will not accommodate short-term expansionary government policy; it will not cheat on its promises. Instead, it will demonstrate that it is serious about meeting its monetary targets in both the short and the medium term. All in all, it will resolve the time-consistency problem which will drive inflationary expectations down.

The empirical case for central bank independence is a result of the studies that have established a positive correlation between a high degree of central bank independence and a low level of inflation. One of the earliest studies of this sort was conducted by Michael Parkin (1978). Parkin found that central banks which were formally committed to maintaining low inflation were associated with countries where the level of inflation was indeed low. This finding led him to state that 'there is a positive association between the legislation of a price stability objective and the achievement of a relatively non-inflationary and low variability monetary policy' (Parkin 1978: 182). In a slightly later and equally influential study, a group of authors reached a more general conclusion that 'independent central banks have conducted monetary policies over the years that have been less accommodative to outside pressures than the policies of their less autonomous counterparts; consequently, their countries have experienced substantially lower rates of inflation' (Banaian *et al.* 1983: 13). More recently still, another set of authors confirmed this conclusion in even more unequivocal terms: '[i]n general, central bank independence leads to low inflation, irrespective of political institutions and budgetary problems' (Grilli *et al.* 1991: 375).

The empirical case for central bank independence was strengthened by the fact that there seemed to be no particular correlation between central bank independence and low growth. In his theoretical treatment of the subject, Rogoff argued that:

> by having the central bank place an infinite weight on inflation stabilization, society could succeed in bringing inflation down to its socially optimal level. But the central bank would also end up responding very inappropriately to supply shocks, allowing them to pass entirely through to employment.
>
> (Rogoff 1985: 1187)

In other words, independent central banks might bring low inflation at the cost of high unemployment. However, various studies have found that in practice this has not happened. For example, in their empirical study Grilli *et al.* conclude that:

> if central bank independence is on average associated with lower inflation, there is no systematic impact on real output growth. Thus having an independent central bank is almost like having a free lunch: there are benefits but no apparent costs in terms of macroeconomic performance.
>
> (Grilli *et al.* 1991: 375)

A similar conclusion based on empirical evidence was reached by Alesina and Summers who state that: 'the monetary discipline associated with central bank independence reduces the level and variability of inflation but does not have either large benefits or costs in terms of real macroeconomic performance' (Alesina and Summers 1993: 159). In turn, this empirical evidence was reinforced with a formal model which suggested that in theory too an independent inflation-averse central bank 'eliminates "politically induced" output variability, since monetary policy is not under the direct control of governments with changing preferences' (Alesina and Gatti 1995: 200). Finally, there is even some evidence to suggest that central bank independence not only does not have a negative effect on economic growth it may even be associated with positive growth (De Long and Summers 1992: 14).

Despite this evidence, there is still a certain degree of scepticism in the academic community about the economic rationale for central bank independence (see Fuhrer 1997). Indeed, one of the most respected writers on central banking states that there is 'a delightful, but not notably conclusive, academic literature' (Goodhart 1995: 218) about the link between independence and low inflation. For example, questions might be raised concerning the way in which the degree of central bank independence is measured (see below). Flawed measurements may produce flawed correlations (see, for example, the criticism in Woolley (1994: 63)). Questions might also be raised concerning the way in which economic performance is measured. Different performance indicators may produce different results (Epstein 1992). Finally, even if there is a correlation between central bank independence and low inflation, questions might be raised concerning the line of causality from one to the other. Do countries such as Germany actually adopt independent central banks because they are already more inflation-averse?

To summarise, whatever the validity of the economic rationale for central bank independence, it is apparent that it has been promoted by an increasingly large number of people in the professional and political classes over the course of the last couple of decades.

The political rationale for central bank independence

Whatever the economic rationale for central bank independence, the political rationale seems, initially at least, to be less well grounded. This is because, as Goodman notes, 'independence remains something of a paradox. For, if independence enables a central bank to resist pressures from its government, why do governments establish independent central banks in the first place?' (Goodman 1992: 7). Why should any government acting rationally want to cede responsibility for monetary policy to an independent central bank? In fact, there are various reasons why it might wish to do so.

First, central bank independence may allow governments to make short-term political gains or avoid short-term political costs. Gains may be made if the economic advantages of central bank independence can be reaped sufficiently quickly so as to be translated into an increase in electoral support. If the bank quickly establishes its credibility, then inflationary expectations may fall. This will help to shore up the value of the currency and allow interest rates to fall. In turn, this will encourage businesses to invest and will help consumers who are in debt. Needless to say, the government is likely to take the credit for the ensuing economic feel-good factor which can only increase its chances at the next electoral contest.

By contrast, costs may be avoided if the government can blame the central bank for an unpopular economic performance. Perhaps the most extreme version of this argument is presented by Semler in the context of Eastern Europe. He argues that there is an incentive for responsibility for monetary policy to be shifted out of the political process 'because it is a political liability' (Semler 1994: 51) and states that 'so long as [monetary policy] is in the hands of a central bank, legislators have a very convenient scapegoat when facing an electorate, angry over economic conditions' (ibid.). In a different context, Woolley states that in the US 'incentives for scapegoating are widespread' and adds that 'there is nothing special about the Federal Reserve in this respect' (Woolley 1984: 11). So, it seems that in terms of both the search for short-term political benefits and the avoidance of short-term political costs, central bank independence may indeed be a rational political act.

Second, Goodman provides two further reasons as to why governments may wish to grant their central banks a greater degree of independence. He argues that economic choices are determined by societal coalitions which reflect particular policy preferences (Goodman 1991: 331–2). For example, financial firms will 'tend to share an independent bank's bias towards monetary restriction . . .' whereas, all other things being equal, workers and manufacturers should be 'suspicious of attempts to institutionalize monetary restriction in the form of central bank independence' (Goodman 1992: 333). In normal circumstances, the policy preferences of societal coalitions will remain stable; however, when there are external economic shocks these preferences may change. So, for example, during periods of rapid inflation manufacturers may become 'more worried by the increase in their real tax burden and the erosion of their financial holdings' (ibid) and so may come to support a greater degree of central bank independence. In this context, governments may have an incentive to respond to the changing preferences of the various actors and increase the degree of independence. Goodman also argues that policy choices are determined by 'the expectations of political leaders regarding tenure in office' (ibid). In particular, he argues that 'political leaders who expect to be in office for only a short period of time . . . may be willing to bind even their own hands in order to bind the hands of their successors' (ibid). For Goodman, therefore, the advent of certain economic or political circumstances may cause central bank independence to be a rational political act.

Greater central bank independence may also be brought about by a mixture of policy learning, policy convergence and the strength of epistemic communities. It is apparent that governments learn both from each other and from their own past mistakes. In this context, it is perhaps not coincidental that two countries which reacted comparatively well to the oil price shocks of the 1970s and early 1980s and which had relatively independent central banks, namely Germany and Switzerland, should have provided a model for other countries thereafter. In addition, the growing internationalisation of financial markets and exchange rate politics over the last thirty years has meant that governments everywhere have increasingly faced the same pressures and demands. Against this background, and in the context of the economic rationale for central bank independence discussed above, certain policies have increasingly seemed to suit not just individual countries but all countries generally. The process of economic and monetary union among the member states of the European Union is perhaps the best example of this process at work. Finally, policies become popular when they are backed by powerful epistemic communities, or networks of professionals with policy-relevant knowledge (Haas 1992: 3). Given the influence of economic arguments in favour of central bank independence since the 1970s, the cohesion of the central banking community, as expressed notably at the monthly meetings of senior central bankers in Basle (Deane and Pringle 1994: 10–12), and the proximity of central bankers to their respective governments, it might be argued that in some countries an epistemic community in favour of greater central bank independence developed (Dyson 1994: 250–2). In this context, the issue of greater independence came to be discussed seriously and, in many cases, to be implemented by political leaders.

Clearly, the political obstacles to central bank independence in many countries remain. For some countries, central bank independence might be considered to be somehow contrary to the logic of traditional constitutional thought (see for example the review by Busch (1994)). For others, the necessary economic and political context may not yet have emerged. However, as with the economic rationale for central bank independence, the political rationale has been present across an increasingly large number of countries over the last couple of decades, and has been partly responsible for the growing number of countries with relatively independent central banks.

A quantitative approach to core executive/central bank relations

For one observer, the concept of central bank independence 'implies a separation of central bank decision making from the regular decision making of the political system' (Hetzel 1990: 165): the greater the degree of separation, the greater the degree of independence. This book focuses on the degree of core executive/central bank separation in two countries, Britain and France; the next four chapters analyse in considerable detail the nature of the core executive/central bank relationship in these countries since the creation of their central banks in 1694 and 1800, respectively. Before embarking upon such an analysis, however, it is necessary to establish the means by which it will be possible to compare the degree of core executive/central bank separation, both across the two countries and across time within each country. In this section, a quantitative approach to the study of core executive/central bank relations will be outlined. Building on the work of Cukierman *et al.* (1992), it will be shown that it is possible to assign a numerical value to the degree of central bank independence in any country at any time. In the next section, a qualitative approach to the study of core executive/central bank relations will be outlined. Here, the contemporary relationship between the two institutions in various countries is described.

In recent years, various scholars have identified many different indicators of central bank independence, but there is still no common agreement as to which indicators are the most appropriate. For example, there is disagreement as to the appropriateness of individual indicators. Goodman asserted that there was widespread agreement that whether or not central banks controlled their own budgets was an important indicator of independence (Goodman 1992: 9), yet neither Fair (1979) nor Banaian *et al.* (1983) nor

Masciandro and Tabellini (1988) included this indicator in their assessments. There is also disagreement as to the number of appropriate indicators. Burdekin *et al.* (1992: 235) focused on three key indicators, whereas Cukierman *et al.* (1992: 358–9) considered sixteen. Finally, there is disagreement as to the appropriate classification of these indicators. Parkin (1987: 320–1) distinguished between financial and policy indicators of independence, Debelle and Fischer (1994) identified goal and instrument indicators, Masciandro and Spinelli (1994: 437–40) differentiated political from functional indicators and Plihon (1994: 5–8) separated functional from organic indicators.

Persistent disagreements of this sort led Woolley (1994: 63) to conclude that, as yet, there is 'no ability to say that some institutional features are necessary or sufficient for behavioral independence', and Bénassy and Pisani-Ferry (1994: 83) to state that: 'la mesure de l'indépendance d'une banque centrale est loin d'être une science exacte! (measuring central bank independence is far from being an exact science!)'. In fact, these disagreements simply demonstrate that the choice of indicators is the result of an essentially subjective process. As Eijffinger and Schaling (1993: 51) note: 'there is no non-arbitrary way of choosing criteria'. Different people, for different reasons, prefer to include certain indicators and leave out others. Nevertheless, criteria still have to be established which allow comparisons to be made both across time and across countries. For the purposes of this study, therefore, it is proposed to classify the indicators of central bank independence under two particular headings: political independence and economic independence (see Appendix 1).

'Political independence' may be defined as the central bank's ability to make policy decisions without interference from the core executive. The indicators of political independence include those elements which touch upon, first, the relationship between the core executive and the central bank's governor (or equivalent post), the sub-governors (where appropriate) and the members of the board of governors and, second, the core executive's intervention in the internal decision-making process of the central bank. In terms of the former set of indicators, political independence concerns appointments to the central bank (all other things being equal, where the central bank makes its own appointments there is independence, but where the chief executive makes the appointments there is dependence); how nominations for appointments are made (similarly); the length of the term of office (the longer the term the more appointments are insulated from political changes and so the greater the independence); whether appointees need professional qualifications (the more qualifications that are needed the greater the independence); whether they may be summarily dismissed from office (the greater the security of tenure the greater the independence); whether they may hold other posts simultaneously (the more multiple office-holding is forbidden the greater the independence); plus, in the case of the sub-governors and the board of governors, whether appointments are staggered (staggered appointments mean that there is less responsiveness to political change and so an increase in the degree of independence); and, in the case of the board of governors alone, whether there are core executive representatives on the board (the smaller the number of core executive representatives the greater the independence). In terms of the bank's internal decision-making process, political independence concerns whether or not the board takes decisions collectively (the more collective the process the greater the independence); whether its members have to take instructions from the core executive (the more members are free to decide themselves the greater the independence); whether core executive representatives have a veto (if not, the greater the independence); whether the bank must report to the legislature (if not, the greater the independence); whether the government fixes the board members' salaries (again, if not, the greater the independence); and, finally, whether the bank's capital is privately owned (once again, if not, the greater the independence). On the basis of these indicators, it may be postulated that if the level of core executive interference is consistently low, then the degree of central bank political independence will be high.

'Economic independence' may be defined as the central bank's ability to use the full range of monetary policy instruments without restrictions from the core executive (Alesina and Summers 1993: 153). The indicators of economic independence include the presence of an overriding mission (again, all other things being equal, the more explicit the mission the greater the independence); the bank's ability to control interest rate moves, exchange rate parities and monetary policy generally (the greater the ability the greater the independence); the ability to refuse to lend monies to the government and to intervene in the budgetary process (again, the greater the ability the greater the independence); and the responsibility for the regulating of the wider banking sector (the greater the responsibility the greater the independence). Once again, on the basis of these indicators, it may be postulated that if the central bank has a large number of monetary policy instruments at its disposal and if it may use those instruments without the imposition of restrictions by the core executive, then the degree of economic independence will be high.

This twofold classification provides the necessary and sufficient criteria by which to judge the degree of central bank independence from the core executive. A completely independent central bank would be one which is free of core executive intervention across the whole set of political indicators; it would have the full range of monetary policy instruments at its disposal, and it would be able to use all of these instruments without any core executive restriction. By contrast, a completely dependent central bank would be one which is subject to unbounded core executive intervention across the set of political indicators; and it would either have no monetary policy instruments at its disposal, or it would be subject to absolute core executive restrictions on all of those that it was able to use. However, two further remarks need to be made. First, a completely independent central bank and a completely dependent central bank represent ideal types. In practice, the degree of independence is bound to lie somewhere in between these two extremes. As Goodman (1992: 8) states: 'independence is best conceived as a continuous, not a dichotomous variable . . .', and so each bank will be found somewhere on the continuum of independence between the two end points. Needless to say, the exact point which the bank occupies will vary according to the extent of core executive intervention, the number of monetary instruments at the bank's disposal and the level of core executive restrictions on the bank's use of those instruments. Second, political and economic indicators of independence are not purely formal; they are not simply to be found in legal statutes and standing orders. Instead, they reflect the practice of core executive/central bank relations. In this sense, they reflect the behavioural relationship between the central bank and the core executive rather than just the statutory relationship (Woolley 1994: 62–3). So, in the chapters which follow, the comparative measurements of central bank independence will be derived both from formal statutes and, where appropriate, from core executive/central bank behaviour as well.

On the basis of the above indicators, it should be possible to compare the independence of central banks. In order to do so, however, it is necessary to construct a methodology which will indicate the place that any particular bank is occupying on the continuum of independence at any particular time. Many of the scholars who have identified indicators of independence have also attempted to compare the degree of central bank independence on the basis of their preferred set of indicators. Once again, though, there is no common agreement as to which is the best way of comparing independence. Some scholars have adopted an approach which allows them to distinguish between different types of central bank independence; others have been able to construct rankings of independence, while yet others have reached precise measurements of independence.

Parkin adopted an approach which allowed him to distinguish between different types of central bank independence. He identified six types of central bank independence on the basis of, on the one hand, whether the bank or the core executive had the final authority for the conduct of monetary policy and who appointed the bank's board and, on the other, whether the bank had the single mission of ensuring price stability or whether it had multiple missions or no mission at all (Parkin 1978: 176). On the basis of this typology, he placed the Bundesbank and the Swiss central bank in one cell, the US Federal Reserve in another, the Dutch central bank in another and the Australian, Belgian, British, Canadian, French, Italian, Japanese and Swedish central banks in a fourth cell. Two cells were empty. Subsequently, Parkin built on this approach and constructed a more complex sixteen-cell classification (Parkin 1987: 320). As before, this resulted in the Bundesbank and the Swiss central bank being classified together and the Federal Reserve being placed in a cell of its own. However, this time, the French and Swedish central banks were located together in one cell; the Belgian, Canadian, Dutch and Italian banks were classed together in another cell; and the Australian, British and Japanese central banks each occupied separate cells on their own. By adopting this methodology, therefore, Parkin was able to draw rough distinctions between different types of relationships between core executives and central banks.

Other writers have adopted an approach which has allowed them to construct indices of independence. For example, on the basis of three indicators (statutory policy independence, the proportion of government appointees on the board and the bank's legislated objectives), Burdekin *et al.* (1992) developed a three-point scale of independence. On this scale, the Bundesbank and the Swiss central bank scored 3/3 and were ranked most independent; the Federal Reserve and the Austrian central bank scored 2/3 and were ranked next; while ten other central banks (as above plus the unreformed New Zealand central bank) scored 1/3 and were ranked last. In a similar vein, Masciandro and Spinelli (1994: 437–8) identified two indices of independence, the first consisting of eight indicators of political independence (with each indicator scoring one point) and the second consisting of seven indicators of functional independence (with one indicator being worth two points and the rest a single point). For political independence, scores ranged from zero for the unreformed New Zealand central bank to seven for the Finnish central bank, while for economic independence they ranged from one for the Italian central bank to seven for the Bundesbank, the Federal Reserve and the Canadian, Norwegian and Swiss central banks. These two indices were then combined into a sixty-four-cell table, which demonstrated that the Bundesbank was the most independent overall and that the Portuguese and unreformed New Zealand central banks were the least independent. Again, by adopting this approach, distinctions may be drawn between different types of central bank independence in a manner similar to the one adopted by Parkin above.

By far the most sophisticated approach to date is the one devised by Cukierman *et al.* (1992). They have tried to measure the degree of central bank independence, identifying sixteen indicators of independence. Each of these indicators was coded on a scale from 1.00 for complete independence to 0.00 for complete dependence. For example, the first indicator dealt with the term of office of the central bank governor. This indicator was coded 1.00 if the term was over eight years, 0.75 if was from six to eight years, 0.50 if it was five years, 0.25 if it was four years and 0.00 if it was below four years. Similar codings were devised for the other fifteen indicators, and these sixteen individual indicators were then aggregated into eight sets of indicators. Each of these sets was then given a weighted value, ranging from 0.20 for the set of four indicators concerning the governor to 0.05 for the set containing the single indicator concerning the borrowers to whom the bank may lend. On the basis of the codings of individual indicators and the weighted values of the sets of indicators, figures for the degree of central bank independence in twenty-one industrial countries were calculated. These figures ranged from a high of 0.69 for the Bundesbank to a low of 0.17 for the Belgian central bank. Clearly, these figures give a false sense of precision in that they are built up from the subjective codings of essentially contestable indicators rather than objectively measurable and identifiable criteria. Nevertheless, this methodology has two particular advantages. First, it indicates that the extremes of complete independence (an overall score of 1.00) and complete dependence (an overall score of 0.00) are unlikely to be reached. This finding corresponds to the intuition that all central banks are likely to be found at some point on the continuum of independence rather than at either end of the two extremes. That is to say, the most independent central banks will always face some core executive control, while the most dependent central banks will always enjoy some degree of freedom. Second, it also indicates that there are likely to be small differences in the degree of independence even between seemingly proximate central banks. This finding corresponds to the further intuition that similar central banks are unlikely to operate identically. For example, even if the Bundesbank and the Swiss central bank are in many ways alike, they do not operate in precisely the same manner. So, this approach encourages comparison, but not over-generalisation.

For both of these reasons, the methodology devised by Cukierman *et al.* will serve as the general basis of comparison in the chapters which follow. However, it will be adapted and refined to suit the purposes of the current study (see Appendix 1). First, this study identifies a larger number of indicators; it considers thirty indicators of political independence, compared with five equivalent indicators in the Cukierman *et al.* study. For example, this study includes seven indicators which refer to the governor of the central bank, whereas the latter includes only four such indicators. Moreover, this study considers six indicators which refer to the bank's internal decision-making process, eight which refer to the sub-governors and nine which refer to the board of governors. The Cukierman *et al.* study includes only one indicator of the bank's decision-making process and gives no consideration to either sub-governors or the board of governors. As for economic independence, this study considers only seven indicators, whereas the Cukierman *et al.* study includes eleven equivalent indicators. However, of these eleven indicators, eight concern limitations on central bank lending to the government. In this study, these eight indicators are subsumed under one heading, while other key indicators that are omitted from the Cukierman *et al.* study will be considered here to provide a fuller picture of economic independence. In all, the revised methodology includes a more comprehensive set of political and economic independence indicators which are more appropriate to the case studies to be undertaken in the chapters which follow.

The second refinement is that the sets and sub-sets of independence indicators will be coded differently. The sets of political and economic independence indicators will each be weighted 0.50. What is more, within the set of political independence indicators, the sub-set of indicators concerning the governor will be weighted 0.30, as will the equivalent sub-set concerning the decision-making process within the central bank, while the sub-sets concerning both the sub-governors and the board of governors will each be weighted 0.20. Within the set of economic independence indicators, each indicator will be weighted equally and the mean calculated to provide an overall figure for economic independence.

This revised version of Cukierman *et al.*'s methodology provides a means by which to measure and compare the degree of central bank independence from the core executive. Moreover, it does so in a way which not only combines the advantages of the original study, but which also improves upon it by increasing the consideration given to political independence indicators and by broadening the number of economic independence indicators under consideration. The result is a methodology which can be applied to compare the independence of two or more central banks at a single point in time, or the independence of a single central bank across time.

A qualitative approach to core executive/central bank relations

This section outlines a qualitative approach to core executive/central bank relations. It does so by briefly describing the contemporary relationship between the core executive and the central bank in three countries. It examines the German case where the central bank is relatively independent, the US case where the central bank is slightly less independent, and the Brazilian case where the central bank is less independent still. In this way, it illustrates some of the various degrees of core executive/central bank separation that will be encountered in the chapters which follow.

The German Bundesbank was established in 1957 and is widely considered to be one of the most independent central banks in the world. In his typology of central banks, Parkin considers the Bundesbank to be one of only two banks which have final responsibility for monetary policy making and to which appointments are made 'by a diffuse process in which the government is not the sole dictator' (Parkin 1978: 177). In their study, Grilli *et al.* (1991) rank the Bundesbank as one of the two most independent banks in terms of political indicators, as one of the four most independent banks in terms of economic indicators, and as the most independent bank in terms of both indicators together. Finally, in their index of legal central bank independence, Cukierman *et al.* (1992) consider the Bundesbank to be the most independent of all central banks, scoring 0.69 on a scale from 0.00 for minimal independence to 1.00 for maximum independence.

The Bundesbank's high degree of independence is guaranteed by a number of legal and behavioural factors. With regard to economic indicators of independence, the Bundesbank's position is regulated by paragraphs 3 and 12 of the 1957 Bundesbank Act. Paragraph 3 states that the bank 'shall regulate the amount of money in circulation and of credit supplied to the economy . . . with the aim of safeguarding the currency' and paragraph 12 states that, whereas the bank 'is required to support the general economic policy of the Federal Government', it is also 'independent of instructions of the Federal Government'. Equally, even though the bank is not responsible either for fixing the exchange rate regime or for regulating the commercial bank sector, it does have a range of economic policy instruments at its disposal and restrictions have always been placed on its obligations to finance government borrowing. With regard to political indicators of independence, there is some involvement in the bank's operations but still a considerable degree of separation between the two institutions. For example, although the government appoints the governor, the members of the bank's administrative Directorate and the other members of the bank's main decision-making body, the Central Bank Council, the latter appointments are only made after a complicated process of consultation with members of the Council, the upper house of the federal legislature, the Bundesrat, and representatives of the Land governments. Moreover, appointments are staggered, the term of office is eight years, appointments are renewable and there is security of tenure. In addition, even though core executive representatives can attend Central Bank Council meetings, they do not have the right to vote. Instead, Council decisions are taken collegially with each member's vote being of equal value. Furthermore, the government does not have the right to veto Council decisions. It can only request that a decision be deferred for up to two weeks. To date, the government has never made such a request.

By virtue of these features, then, it is apparent that the Bundesbank exhibits a considerable degree of independence. This independence is both a reflection of the 'social consensus in favour of a policy geared towards price stability' (Gleske 1995: 23) in German political culture and a contributing factor to the reinforcement of such a consensus. It is also apparent, however, that the degree to which the Bundesbank is separated from the core executive is not absolute. There is a constant interaction, both formal and informal, between representatives of the two institutions. There are continuous attempts by one to influence the thinking of the other. The result is a situation in which clashes between the two institutions are commonplace. Indeed, Marsh states that there were a dozen serious disagreements concerning interest and exchange rate policy in the first twenty-five years of the Bundesbank's history, and that either directly or indirectly three Chancellors owed their downfall to the bank's policy decisions (Marsh 1992: 170). The result, however, is also a situation in which the independence of the bank is an established and highly valued aspect of the economic and political process. As Sturm notes: 'no matter how important and hard conflicts between the Bundesbank and the government of the day have been, the responsibility of the bank for monetary policies has always been respected by the politicians' (Sturm 1989: 5).

The US Federal Reserve System (or Fed) was established in 1914. For one writer, even though it is 'relatively independent from the administration and the Congress', its 'independent status is not as secure as that of the Bundesbank' (Henning 1994: 101). In this sense, it occupies an intermediate position on the continuum of independence. So, Parkin classes the Fed as the only example of a central bank where the bank board is responsible for making monetary policy but where the board is directly appointed by the government (Parkin 1978: 177). Grilli *et al.* (1991: 368–9) indicate that the Fed has a relatively high degree of both political and economic independence, meeting 5/8 and 7/7 necessary requirements respectively. Cukierman *et al.* (1992: 363) calculate that the Fed is the fifth most independent central bank in countries with an industrial economy, scoring 0.48 on a scale from 0.00 for minimal independence to 1.00 for maximum independence.

The similarities and differences between the Bundesbank and the Fed can be seen in terms of both the economic and the political indicators of independence. With regard to economic indicators, whereas the Bundesbank's overriding aim is to safeguard the currency, the Fed's responsibilities are more diverse. Section 2A of the 1977 amendment to the 1913 Federal Reserve Act states that the Fed 'shall maintain long run growth of the monetary and credit aggregates commensurate with the country's long run potential to increase production, so as to promote the goals of maximum employment, stable prices, and moderate long-term interest rates'. The fact that these goals are not necessarily consistent with each other means that the Fed does not have the same authority as the Bundesbank to insist on the adoption of a particular policy line. Nevertheless, like the Bundesbank, the Fed has responsibility for a range of monetary policy instruments, it is not obliged to finance government debt and, unlike the Bundesbank, it does have responsibility for regulating the commercial banking sector. With regard to political indicators, the appointment procedures and internal decision-making processes of both the Bundesbank and the Fed are ostensibly quite similar. For example, the President appoints the members of the Board of Governors of the Federal Reserve System (the equivalent of the Bundesbank's Directorate), including the chair and vice-chair, subject to Senate ratification. By extension, therefore, the President also appoints a majority of the members of the bank's main decision-making body, the Federal Open Market Committee (the equivalent of the Bundesbank's Central Bank Council). However, appointments to the Board of Governors are staggered; they are made for a non-renewable fourteen-year term and there is security of tenure, although the chair and vice-chair are only appointed for a renewable four-year term. Equally, the Open Market Committee's decisions are reached by a simple majority, each person has one vote and, in contrast to the German situation, there is no core executive representative on the Committee.

Despite the similarities between the Bundesbank and the Fed and contrary to some of the popular perceptions of the latter's behaviour (such as Greider (1987)), the Fed has tended to be somewhat more responsive to political demands than the Bundesbank. Empirical research has suggested that Fed policy has appeared 'to respond to the desires of the incumbent president' (Beck 1982: 443), and that there is statistically significant evidence to show that presidential influence shapes the decision-making process of the Board of Governors (Krause 1994: 140). In part, this is because Presidents have been able to shape the composition of the Fed rather more than the formal regulations suggest. The temptations of private sector rewards mean that the average term of office for members of the Board of Governors is just over five years, rather than the fourteen-year term that the law allows (Krause 1994: 127). It is also because Fed policy and government policy have tended to be less closely aligned in the US than in Germany. If Presidents have opposed Fed policy, then they have tended to use the fiscal powers at their disposal to manage the economy in a way that suits their own needs rather than those of the central bank (Beck 1982: 422). Finally, it is because the salient aspects of German and US political cultures differ from each other. As Deane and Pringle state: 'Germans almost unreservedly want what the Bundesbank does, price stability, whereas America's hugely diversified society is more torn if the choice is (misguidedly) seen as between loss of jobs or inflation' (Deane and Pringle Dean 1994: 215).

Having said that, what is common to both the US and German situations is that the core executive/central bank relationship is marked by a continual process of interaction. The Fed's policy expertise, its information network and the support of its financial constituency (Woolley 1984: 129) mean that it cannot be ignored by the president. Whether this process of interaction takes the form of explicit bargaining between the Fed and the president, as was the case during President Johnson's administration, or is merely a dialogue of the deaf is a function of the political and economic circumstances of the day. In general, though, for both institutional and, particularly, behavioural reasons the Fed may be considered to be slightly less independent than the Bundesbank.

The Brazilian central bank was founded in 1965. It is one of the least independent central banks in the world. Even though neither Parkin nor Grilli *et al.* include it in their studies, Cukierman *et al.* (1992: 362) calculate that it ranks number 44 of 51 central banks in countries with a developing economy, scoring 0.21 on a scale from 0.00 for minimal independence to 1.00 for maximum independence.

The contrast between the Brazilian and both the German and US cases is acute. In terms of economic indicators of independence, the Brazilian central bank is in a very weak position. For example, it has no overriding mission statement. It participates in the formulation of monetary policy only in an advisory capacity. It plays no role in the formulation of the state budget (although this is also the case for the Fed). It is true that there are limits to the amount that the government can borrow, but the government controls the terms of the amount borrowed. In terms of political indicators of independence, the Brazilian central bank is also in a very weak position. For example, the government controls the appointment of the governor and all the directors of the bank. Moreover, although there is no term limit to appointments (so potentially allowing appointees to be independent of the political process once in office), there is also no security of tenure and appointees can be dismissed from office at any time. There are also no rules preventing appointees from holding other offices, so creating the potential for conflicts of interest within the bank.

In short, the Brazilian central bank is subordinate to the country's core executive. One manifestation of this situation can be found in the fact that from 1980–89 central bank governors remained in office for an average of less than eighteen months. The reason for the bank's subordinate position is partly to be found in its relatively recent formation date. Maxfield argues that the bank 'is still struggling to build an institutional identity and centralize monetary control' (Maxfield 1994: 562). It is also partly to be found in the traditional strength of the economic and political interests that have opposed plans for greater independence (Maxfield 1994: 583). The economic and political rationales for greater central bank independence have not been present in the Brazilian system.

Conclusion

The next four chapters examine the relationship between the core executive and the central bank in Britain and France. In each case, the relationship is examined from the time at which the bank was founded to the present day. In so doing, the aim is to explore the politics of the core executive/central bank relationship both across time and cross-nationally. Moreover, in each case the relationship is examined both semi-quantitatively (based on the calculations set out in Appendix 2 and Appendix 3) and qualitatively. In this way, the aim is to build up as full and complete a picture of core executive/central bank relations as possible. Overall, these chapters analyse the politics of monetary policy in some detail so as to highlight the changing nature of core executive control in these two countries over time in this highly political and electorally significant area of public policy making.

3 The core executive and the Bank of England (1694–1987)

From autonomy to dependence

The Bank of England began life at the end of the eighteenth century, in the aftermath of the English Revolution, as a privately-owned bank which enjoyed a unique relationship with the core executive. Over the next two centuries, as it developed the modern techniques of central banking, it continued, under certain formal and informal constraints imposed by different governments, to exhibit substantial levels of economic and political independence. During the twentieth century, the central relationship between the core executive and the Bank has changed on several occasions. During the interwar years, successive governments engaged in a struggle with the Bank over monetary policy and by the 1930s, although the Bank continued to be relatively politically independent, practical authority for monetary policy lay in the hands of the core executive. In 1946 the Labour government led by Clement Attlee nationalised the Bank. For nearly 50 years, on the basis of the 1946 Act, the core executive decided monetary policy for itself and controlled appointments to the Bank. After September 1992 and Britain's departure from the European Exchange Rate Mechanism (ERM), the Conservative government led by John Major embarked on a series of reforms to the monetary decision-making process which, although leaving the formal structures of core executive authority and control untouched, allowed the Bank of England potentially to exercise greater influence over policy. In 1997, when a new Labour government took office, it quickly decided to give operational independence to the Bank so that the Bank will henceforth set monetary policy according to an inflation target set by the incumbent government.

In the following two chapters, the development of this historical relationship between the British core executive and the Bank of England will be reconstructed in detail. This chapter analyses the relationship between 1694 and 1987, and is divided into four parts. The first part provides an overview of developments between the creation of the Bank in 1694 and the outbreak of the First World War in 1914. The second part considers in some detail the period from 1915–39 and the struggle of successive British governments to exercise some control over monetary policy, as economic management in general became increasingly difficult. The third part examines the nationalisation of the Bank in 1946 and the manner in which governments, during the Bretton Woods era, largely controlled the Bank to their own political and economic ends. The fourth part explains how, once monetary policy became a significant political issue from the 1970s, political actors in the core executive, and in particular the Chancellor and the Prime Minister, eventually assumed supreme political control over both the substance of policy and the Bank itself. Finally, some conclusions are drawn as the basis for the discussion of the next chapter, which takes up the development of the relationship from 1988.

1694–1914

In 1689 England entered the Nine Years War with France, precipitating a crisis in the finances of the state. Five years later, the newly sovereign Parliament established the Bank of England with a charter to provide the means of raising and systematically managing funds to sustain the war effort (for discussion of the creation of the Bank of England within the context of the Revolution of 1688, see North and Weingast (1980)). For the next 120 years of its existence, the Bank operated against a background of almost incessant war[1] during which it developed a Janus-faced operation. In the public sphere, it was banker to the state and servicer of the war-induced spiralling national debt. By issuing a Bank charter, which required renewal on a periodic basis, Parliament established some control over the Bank's operations in this realm. Despite their reliance on the Bank as a money-raising machine, ministers were quite prepared to use the charter as a bargaining counter to keep at least a minimal grip on the terms of credit which they received.

Outside the war-dominated public realm the Bank was virtually a free agent, operating as a private joint-stock commercial organisation, trading and seeking profit on its own capital resources. Although Parliament had a clear interest in the creation and maintenance of a reliable bank of issue and used its authority to give the Bank a near monopoly of note issue in 1709, it was quite prepared to let the Bank manage its own commercial and monetary affairs and issue paper money on its own terms (see Bowen 1995).

Critically, the Bank's freedom included the power to select its own personnel, creating a high level of political independence. Initially, a Governor, Deputy Governor and Directors were chosen each year between March and April by proprietors holding not less than £500 stock. During the eighteenth century the Bank created the Committee of the Treasury, consisting of the Governor, Deputy Governor and the most senior of the Directors, which assumed the responsibility for drawing up the lists of proposals for the elections of Governors and Director. To qualify for the office of Governor, a candidate had to hold £4,000 stock of the corporation. While elections formally took place on an annual basis, it became normal practice for a person to serve two years as Deputy Governor followed immediately by two years as Governor. These appointment procedures continued remarkably uninterrupted until the First World War (Hennessy 1995). All told, at the time of its formation and for over 200 years thereafter, the Bank scored 0.59 on a scale from 0.00 for complete dependence to 1.00 for complete independence (see Appendix 2). This figure corresponds to a relatively independent central bank.

The first watershed in the relationship between the core executive and the Bank came in the late years, and immediate aftermath, of the Napoleonic Wars. In 1797 the Bank had suspended cash payments following a fall in gold reserves caused by the level of government borrowing demanded to fight the war against revolutionary France. This represented the first break in convertibility since sterling had been fixed at a gold price in 1717. As the war entered its penultimate stages, ministers became increasingly anxious to exercise greater control for themselves over the Bank's monetary and commercial affairs. In 1810, the Bullion Committee of the House of Commons recommended that when peace was made there should be a quick return to full cash payments and the effective gold standard. For the Bank, this was an unacceptable encroachment by Parliament into their private sphere of action, and it took two years of procrastination after Waterloo before the Bank made any kind of cash payment at all. Deeply dismayed with the Bank's inaction, the Tory Cabinet, inspired by William Huskisson and George Cannon, seized the legal initiative in 1819 and won a vote in Parliament forcing the full resumption of cash payments. In the same year the Bank Advances Bill defined and limited future Bank advances to the government and subjected them to parliamentary scrutiny (Hilton 1980: chapter 2). As Robert Peel declared, 'the moment has arrived, when the nature of the relations existing between the government and the Bank should be changed' (quoted in Hilton 1980: 53).

The Tory government's desire to control the terms of the Bank's monetary operations came from a sense of grievance both against the commercial gains the Bank had made out of non-convertible paper money and those manufacturing, commercial and financial interests that had generally profited from the wartime monetary instability and easy credit. This grievance was born out of their judgment not only that the financial consequences of the war had threatened the economic and political interests of the governing class – of which they were of course a part – but also a strong, if convenient, ideological belief that the economy should be an arena of natural justice in which only the supposedly virtuous should succeed (Hilton 1988). The return to the gold standard, ministers anticipated, would at least partially redistribute wealth away from those they dismissed as morally recalcitrant speculators, and whom they held responsible for the boom/bust cycle in which the economy appeared to be trapped. If this meant temporary deflation, given the discrepancy between the prevailing value of paper and the rate at which it would be fixed against gold, then, they believed, this would kill off only the speculators and debtors who had been prepared to ruin the economy during the war for their own illicit gains and deserved nemesis (Hilton 1980: 56–61).

At the same time, despite the fact that they had wrestled some monetary control back from the Bank, ministers saw in the renewed gold standard an automatic pilot which would allow the Bank to manage monetary affairs within the terms they themselves had laid down. If sound money was upheld, they judged, the economy would regulate itself, as Ricardo imagined was its natural wont, and there would be no need to trouble themselves with any kind of direct economic management. In the words of Huskisson, the Bank of England would be 'the great steam engine of the state, to keep the channel of circulation always pressing full', and the gold standard would be 'the regulator and index of the Engine, by which the extent of its operations and the sufficiency of the supply would be determined and ascertained' (Hilton 1980: 65). Consequently, when the economy plunged into a depression in 1819–22, Lord Liverpool's government saw no reason to revert to any kind of interventionist policies, despite fierce criticism from manufacturing interests, the Whig leadership and the Malthusians. Ultimately, the only concession ministers offered during the crisis was towards freer trade, effectively expanding the arena over which they did not wish to involve themselves and in which natural justice could be enforced (Hilton 1988: 205–7).

In 1825–6 Liverpool's government won its final victory over the terms of the Bank's monetary operations, on which its general attitude towards economic policy rested. As an economic boom turned to bust and liquidity dried up, ministers urged the Bank to pursue a more inflationary monetary policy. The Bank agreed but, with its gold reserves under serious threat, it requested the right to suspend convertibility if necessary. When the government refused, the Bank was forced hurriedly to procure gold for itself and the crisis was defused (Hilton 1980: chapter 7). Nonetheless the government was left acutely aware of the threat which had been posed to Britain's diplomatic and military strength by the liquidity shortage, and in part blamed the Bank's expansion of paper for the original boom. Over the next two decades, successive ministers considered various methods to reduce their dependence on debt (and hence the Bank) for war funds, fearing that any renewed threat to convertibility would produce economic and social dislocation and moral chaos (Hilton 1980: chapter 8). When, as a prelude to the repeal of the Corn Laws, the Peel government introduced income tax in 1842, ministers had finally found a means, in Parnell's words, of 'establish[ing] the practicability of carrying on new wars without adding to the debt' (quoted in Hilton 1988: 267).[2] In the same restrictive vein, two years later Peel further tightened the terms of the Bank's overall monetary operations.[3] By the 1844 Bank Act, the government separated the Bank's note issue from its banking operations, fixed a ratio between notes and gold and fixed at £14 million the amount of notes that might be issued against securities (Hilton 1988: 224). To prove that it was operating within these legal principles, the Bank was forced to publish weekly Bank Returns (for discussion of the Bank's use of monetary policy in the decade after the 1844 Act, see Hughes (1960)). Ultimately, the net effect of the Act was less deflationary than Peel had hoped, but this was only because in order to evade its full consequences, economic agents started to use cheques and deposits much more freely than Peel had believed possible (Hilton 1988: 224).

During the three decades after the Napoleonic Wars, the disposition of politicians towards the economy in general and the Bank in particular was marked by a profound conservatism. Both in 1819 and 1844, ministers sought to impose significant deflation on the economy to force the Bank to limit its potential to increase credit, and hence inflation. For all Britain's industrial expansion during this period, successive governments did not feel particularly comfortable either with economic growth or the less entrenched politics and society which was emerging in its wake (see Hilton 1988). By enshrining a deflationary bias in both the monetary structure and in public expectations, politicians freed themselves from responsibility for managing the domestic economy. They could, therefore, concentrate what energy they were disposed to exert on economic matters on the problems of law and order, induced by industrialisation, and guaranteeing the financial wherewithal for war (Hilton 1980: 65–6, 79–87).

If, however, the core executive now had an effective purchase on monetary control, then within the terms they prescribed to the Bank, it was more than prepared to allow the Bank virtually complete autonomy. By the 1870s, as other states began to fix their currencies against gold, the Bank's monetary operations, and in particular its judicious use of the Bank Rate[4], were assuming huge international significance. For the Bank, monetary policy was now primarily a matter of managing Britain's economic relations with the rest of the world. In no sense did the Bank see itself as making decisions which would impact on the domestic economy in terms of either production or trade. Rather it aimed to ensure that fluctuations in the balance of payments did not jeopardise Britain's gold reserves.[5] With, by contemporary standards, small changes to the Bank Rate, the Bank was able to influence the flow and outflow of gold and capital into London (for a full discussion of how the Bank managed the Gold Standard, see Sayers (1976: chapter 3)). Until the First World War, successive governments saw no reason to interest themselves in the Bank Rate. Speaking in 1929, Otto Niemeyer, a senior Treasury official, recalled, 'in pre-war days a change in the Bank Rate was no more regarded as the business of the Treasury than the colour which the Bank painted the front door' (quoted in Roberts and Kynaston 1995: 25). Neither was such autonomy confined to monetary policy. Despite the rather malign impact of financial structures on Britain's industrial development in the last decades of the nineteenth century (see Ingham 1984), successive governments did not concern themselves with the Bank's attitude towards the banking system and the supply of cash towards banks. Left to implement its own judgment, the Bank pursued a notably *laissez-faire* attitude towards banks suffering from cash problems, encouraging a national banking system which by the end of the century had become disengaged from industrial production (see Kennedy 1987). Perhaps unsurprisingly, the Bank's practical day-to-day independence was reflected in the physical isolation of the Bank from Westminster and Whitehall. As the formal executive centre of the Bank, the Court of Directors fixed and announced the Bank Rate at a weekly meeting. Within the Court, only the Governor of the Bank maintained any kind of personal contact with the Treasury (Sayers 1976).

The willingness of the core executive to allow the Bank such freedom, after the desperate effort to control the institution in the first half of the century, needs to be understood in several contexts. Crucially, the kind of monetary policy which the Bank pursued was firmly underpinned by the prevailing international economic setting, defined by Britain's industrial strength and financial hegemony. The free movement of capital and gold and Britain's generally favourable position on current account meant that interest rates never remained at high levels for significant periods of time (Moggridge 1972: 13). Indeed, even if interest rates had been persistently higher, then existing economic theory, however wildly interpreted by politicians, would not have led them to think about the domestic economy in this monetary context. Interest rates, according to the neoclassical economists, did not affect output or employment. In the last few decades of the nineteenth century, in so far as politicians believed anything about monetary policy, they often associated unemployment with low interest rates (Harris 1972: 6).

Meanwhile, the conjunction of Britain's economic success and the limited franchise allowed ministers to remain relatively detached from economic policy. Although economic growth no longer seemed to threaten politicians' conception of a sound economy, both the Liberal and Conservative governments, led by Gladstone and Salisbury respectively, built statecraft around foreign policy and religious and territorial matters. In the last decades of the nineteenth century, Britain's industrial production began to decline relative to that of Germany and the United States, but Salisbury worked extremely hard to keep any debate about general economic management out of political and electoral discourse, concentrating his political energy on the concurrent challenge to Britain's imperial position (see Marsh 1978). Significantly, even when unemployment did enter the mainstream public debate, it was very much as a matter of practical social administration (for a discussion of the terms of the political debate about unemployment, see Harris (1972)).

During the first decade of the twentieth century the respective Liberal and Conservative leaderships did think more about economic policy, in the face of the Labour Party's growing ability to mobilise economic discontent and dissatisfaction within their own parties with the old statecraft. Nonetheless, what ultimately distinguished the Edwardian era was the extent to which the most powerful party politicians wished to preserve the nineteenth-century approach. The Liberal government, elected in 1906 in a loose electoral pact with Labour, pursued elementary welfare and tax reform while remaining fundamentally committed to free trade and eschewing any interest in industrial modernisation. Of course the Conservative Party, under the influence of Joseph Chamberlain, did become preoccupied as a matter of electoral strategy and because of internal power struggles with Britain's external economic relations and just who was benefiting from international liberalism (see Sykes 1979). But even when the Conservative Party, self-destructively, turned to protectionism and imperial economic unification to try to give themselves a purchase on the working class vote, the gold standard and the Bank's conduct of monetary policy remained non-issues.[6] While protectionism conceived in its original guise was a means of combining an appeal to nationalism and social reform, the Conservative leadership saw practical monetary policy and finance as inconsequential for their own purposes (for discussion of how tariff reform developed from a strategy for imperial and domestic reform to a means to raise revenue to defend the propertied classes from higher direct taxation, see Sykes (1979)). In sum, in no sense were the high levels of independence from the core executive that the Bank enjoyed part of political debate.

1915–45

The first effort by the core executive to exercise control over the Bank beyond the terms of the compromise that had emerged in the nineteenth century came during the First World War. The massive levels of expenditure which the government required to finance the war effort inevitably produced a huge increase in the national debt. In the first months of the war the Liberal government and the Bank worked in relative harmony, quickly agreeing to a *de facto* suspension of the gold standard and a pegged exchange rate. But the effective end of gold convertibility and the return to deficit financing inevitably strained the relationship.[7] For its part, the Bank now lacked an uncontested rationale for the conduct of its monetary operations. Meanwhile, the core executive could no longer afford not to involve itself in the detail of debt management, because it was as essential to the war effort as military strategy. Neither could the core executive believe that it had no interests at stake in the general terms of credit set by the Bank, since it needed to borrow so much capital itself.

In these circumstances, ministers gradually began to exercise more control over the Bank. To defend the Bank's position in relation to sterling, in 1915 the Governor, Lord Cunliffe, persuaded the Chancellor, Reginald McKenna, to allow the Bank to continue to manage the exchange rate through a consortium of bankers which he chaired, known as the London Exchange Committee. However, officials in the Treasury, particularly after Bonar Law became Chancellor in 1916, could not accept the limitations that the Bank was imposing through the Committee on their financial room for manoeuvre. In July 1917, Cunliffe formally complained to Bonar Law that Robert Chalmers and Maynard Keynes at the Treasury were reducing the Committee to a 'cypher' by withholding information and assets and imperiously demanded their resignation (Skidelsky 1992a: 341). Finding Bonar Law unreceptive, Cunliffe proceeded to withhold the government's access to the Bank's gold in Canada just as the war and the war finances were at a critical stage. For the Chancellor, the Bank had stepped far beyond its legitimate prerogatives, and by semi-publicly articulating his anger he effectively forced Cunliffe's resignation (for a detailed account of this episode which is critical of the Bank, see Beaverbrook (1966); for a discussion of the general problems of financing the war which is sympathetic to the Bank, see Sayers (1976: chapter 5)). Certainly in terms of the indicators of political independence, this event was a significant watershed. While formal authority to appoint and dismiss the Governor still lay with the Committee of Treasury in the Bank, the core executive had demonstrated for the first time that it could in certain circumstances exercise indirect, but potentially potent, influence over these questions.

At the same time, during the late stages of the war the core executive began to venture, albeit hesitatingly, into the area of detailed monetary policy. As the core executive became ever more preoccupied with war finance, it felt far more the direct effects of high interest rates, conceived to protect the gold reserves, than it had during peacetime. In 1918 the Chancellor vainly pressed the Bank to lower rates in order to encourage the sale of war bonds. Nonetheless, if ministers could not as yet put sufficient moral pressure on the Bank to encompass their concerns when it took decisions, the size of the national debt and the government's consequent issue of Treasury bills that provided unlimited cash meant that ministers now had an indirect means of determining short-term interest rates and were prepared to do so with the barest consultation with the Bank (Sayers 1976: 100).

In retrospect, the war brought an end to a century in which the core executive had been content to allow the Bank to run the exchange rate and monetary management on an automatic pilot within a broad economic and political conception of sound money. The essential dilemma for politicians during the interwar years was that they could no longer quite believe that, left to its own devices, the Bank would deliver the economic results which they considered necessary for their own purposes, but they still craved the freedom to withdraw from such an esoteric policy area that they had enjoyed before 1914. In three fundamental senses, the context in which politicians were operating in economic policy was now different.

First, the war took a huge toll on the British economy, speeding up the process of relative economic decline which had begun in the last decades of the previous century. This decline was particularly acute in the heavy industrial sectors of the economy which were dependent on exports. While unemployment had fluctuated considerably before 1914, during the 1920s unemployment never fell below 10 per cent of the labour force, rising to 19 per cent in 1921 (Skidelsky 1967: 1). Unsurprisingly, unemployment was a prominent issue at each of the general elections held in the 1920s.

Second, the expansion of the franchise in 1918, taking the electorate from 8 million before the war to 21 million, meant that politicians were now operating in a different kind of representative democracy. In conjunction with the fall-out of the war, this transformed the dynamics of party competition. The new electorate would choose between two Liberal parties, a strengthened Labour Party and a divided Conservative Party. In these circumstances, politicians needed to conceptualise a framework of action about which they could make very little claim to reasonable knowledge of likely causality. In Cowling's words, 'in these circumstances, since they were playing in the dark, politicians either made up their tunes as they went along, or replayed the tunes they had learnt before the lights went out in 1914' (Cowling 1971: 4).

Third, the war had forced upon the politicians an at least partial awareness of the reality that the detail of monetary policy was not neutral in its impact on the domestic economy. Not only had they now experienced the constraints imposed by the level of interest rates on their own ability to borrow money, but they were beginning to learn to think that monetary policy had effects on domestic production, including house construction, a policy area of growing significance. Even by the end of the 1920s politicians certainly neither knew nor understood very much about monetary policy. In 1923, Maynard Keynes published his *Tract on Monetary Reform* claiming that if the level of credit was managed then the fluctuations of the business cycle could be evened out. Whilst at this stage politicians clearly did not trust Keynes, despite the transparent attractiveness of the theory in view of the level of unemployment, by the end of the decade Keynes had sown profound seeds of doubt in the minds of the most thoughtful as to whether monetary policy really worked in the relatively benign way the Bank kept insisting that it did.[8]

The central practical question at the beginning of this new world was what to do about sterling. At the outset, ministers demonstrated that they did not want to think very hard, or very critically, for themselves about this matter, despite the partial control over monetary matters that the core executive had wrestled from the Bank during the war. In 1918 the Coalition government appointed a Committee on Currency and Foreign Exchanges (the Cunliffe Committee) with the explicit aim of considering how to return sterling to gold at the prewar parity ($4.86). The Bank, in subsequent evidence, certainly did not question the premise on which the Committee was created and emphatically expressed its wish to return to gold in the period between the Armistice and the signing of a peace treaty. However, it cannot be said that the Bank imposed on ministers the subsequent decision to restore the old parity when possible. (A desire to blame the Bank for both the 1919 and 1925 decisions, as if they were nothing to do with the relevant ministers, can be found in Pollard (1982) and Ingham (1984)). After Austen Chamberlain had announced the decision to the House of Commons in December 1919, successive governments endorsed the policy. When Labour entered office for the first time in 1924, Ramsay MacDonald and Philip Snowden firmly expressed their support for the Cunliffe Report. At the same time, when the Conservative government, resuming office in 1924, took the opportunity of a rise in sterling towards $4.86 to return to gold in May 1925, on the evidence of the archival records, they quite clearly did so as the result of Churchill's own judgment (see Howson (1975), Moggridge (1972); for an intelligent defence of the decision, see Sayers (1970)). Indeed, after Churchill opened up discussions prior to the return and invited criticism from Keynes, it was a Treasury official, Otto Niemeyer, not the Governor of the Bank, who was the decisive influence on the Chancellor (Sayers 1970: 124). Ultimately, despite Keynes's robust plea for caution, the politicians themselves could not conceive of any alternative to restoring the architecture of the old world.

What is nonetheless true is that from 1919 to 1925, a succession of ministers viewed the prospect of the return to gold with an anxiety and angst which was almost entirely absent at the Bank. In 1919, the Coalition government was not prepared to prioritise gold over all other economic objectives, as the Bank wished. Thus, understanding perfectly well that, given a free hand, the Bank would use the Bank Rate to push sterling upwards and that this would be deflationary, Austen Chamberlain insisted that discretion over monetary policy now belonged to him. From 1919 to the spring of 1920, Lloyd George's government pursued a policy of 'cheap money' against consistent pressure from the new Governor, Montagu Norman, for a higher Bank Rate (Howson 1975: 14). In September 1919, when sterling was 15 per cent below its old parity, Norman wrote a letter to Chamberlain fuming that 'if the Bank had been free to exercise their proper functions they would long ago have taken steps to raise the value of money in the Country in order to protect the Exchanges' (Howson 1975: 16). What he failed to see was that ministers could no longer consider it their 'proper function' to allow the Bank to take decisions which could cause them immense electoral and political damage. Lloyd George's government was simply desperate for the economy to grow. From the beginning of 1919, the Labour Party increased their share of the vote significantly in every by-election. As disturbingly for ministers, within a month of their election victory, many sectors of the economy were immersed in industrial disputes. After violent scenes in Glasgow in June 1919, one Cabinet minister mused out loud about 'a Bolshevik uprising' (Morgan 1979: 48). The government's strategy, in the face of what Lloyd George himself saw as a threat to the state, was to sustain the boom as long as possible, introduce social reform and mediate with the trade unions at Downing Street to control wage bargaining (see Morgan 1979). Unsurprisingly, in these circumstances ministers wished to rely on their own political judgment about monetary policy, however untutored they were in the subject.

Only when the postwar boom in Britain produced rapidly spiralling prices, just as a financial and monetary crisis was developing on the continent, did the government allow the Bank to raise rates. After Chamberlain successfully resisted Norman's request for a rise in Bank Rate to 8 per cent in July 1920, ministers effectively restored to the Bank the discretion to run monetary policy as it saw fit. Despite the fact that the dear money policy which the Bank pursued, aimed at both domestic deflation and securing an appreciation in sterling, induced a depression and soaring unemployment, successive Chancellors from 1921 to 1925, both Coalition and Conservative, did not even question the Bank's authority to determine the Bank Rate (Roberts and Kynaston 1995: 27).

In part, the core executive relinquished the political control they had barely just won because, once the budget was back in surplus, they were in a weaker structural position to determine short-term interest rates. But more importantly, it would seem that the politicians lost faith in their ability to exercise their own judgment about economic policy. In accepting that the boom must be controlled and by handing monetary policy back to the Bank, the Coalition government fatally undermined its own statecraft. Unable to pursue social reform which it could no longer afford, to shape the European balance of power without economic recovery, or build any kind of partnership with the trade unions after the bitter defeat of a long miners' strike by the threat of starvation, from mid-1920 the Coalition government lacked any kind of coherent policy programme and began to disintegrate (Morgan 1979: 259–60). After the Conservatives returned to office, they showed themselves no more willing to assert themselves in economic policy. For example, on 12 June 1923, Stanley Baldwin told the House of Commons 'that there is no greater necessity for this country . . . than cheaper money' (Skidelsky 1992b: 147). But when, less than a month later, the Bank put the Bank Rate up by one per cent to correct a fall in sterling, no minister challenged the Bank. Politicians of all parties were far more comfortable looking to foreign policy solutions to the problem of unemployment than the domestic remedies which Keynes was beginning to offer (Cowling 1971: 300). In 1922–3 the Baldwin government assumed that the only economic option available to them was to stop France creating economic havoc in Germany and Central Europe. Once, after the French occupation of the Rühr, Baldwin wanted the Conservatives to adopt a different position than the other parties towards unemployment, he turned to protectionism, despite the fact that in a decade of trying before the war, the party had failed to find a way of building a winning electoral coalition around this policy (see Cowling 1971).

The internal discussions which preceded the eventual return to the gold standard in May 1925 certainly reflected acute differences in the attitude of ministers and the Bank, despite their ultimate agreement on an appropriate course of action. While the Bank, backed by the Treasury, stressed the long-term benefits of the gold standard, ministers could not afford this luxury, even presuming the Bank was right, given that the economic short-term and the long-term now conflicted in the way that was not true prior to 1914.[9] In Moggridge's words, 'time and time again in Niemeyer's briefs, the emphasis is on the long term; time and time again this emphasis is used to circumvent short-term problems raised by Churchill' (Moggridge 1972: 235). Churchill's worries about the short-term focused in particular on unemployment. He saw the problem as a grave danger not only to his own government's tenure in office, but to the social cohesion necessary to underpin representative democracy. Yet at the same time, he felt utterly impotent to act on a different economic basis, lacking either the confidence to produce a practical alternative or arguments to refute the case of the Bank and the Treasury that British prices and wages could be adjusted to make the policy work without serious deflation (see Moggridge 1972). In as damning critique as a Chancellor ever penned about the attitudes of the Bank, Churchill, in a memo to Niemeyer, laid bare his despair:

> The Treasury have never, it seems to me, faced the profound significance of what Mr Keynes calls the paradox of 'unemployment amidst dearth'. The Governor shows himself perfectly happy in the spectacle of Britain possessing the finest credit in the world simultaneously with a million and a quarter unemployed. The community lacks goods, and a million and a quarter people lack work. It is certainly one of the highest functions of national finance and credit to bridge the gulf between the two. This is the only country in the world where this condition exists. The Treasury and the Bank of England policy has been the only policy consistently pursued. It is a terrible responsibility for those who have shaped it, unless they can be sure that there is no connection between the unique British phenomenon of chronic unemployment and the long resolute consistency of a particular financial policy. I do not know whether France with her financial embarrassments can be said to be worse off than England with her unemployment. At any rate while that unemployment exists, no-one is entitled to plume himself on the financial or credit policy which we have pursued.
>
> It may be of course that you will argue that the unemployed would have been much greater but for the financial policy pursued; that there is not sufficient demand for commodities either internally or externally to require the services of this million and a quarter people; that there is nothing for them but to hang like a millstone round the neck of industry and on the public revenue until they become permanently demoralised. You may be right, but if so, it is one of the most sombre conclusions ever reached. On the other hand I do not pretend to see even 'through a glass darkly' how the financial and credit policy of the country could be handled so as to bridge the gap between a dearth of goods and a surplus of labour; and well I realise the danger of experiment to that end. The seas of history are full of famous wrecks. Still if I could see a way, I would rather follow it than any other.
>
> (quoted in Moggridge 1972: 75).

The profound ambivalence that Churchill felt at what he had done was reflected in the struggle which ensued between ministers and the Bank over the conduct of monetary policy from 1925 to 1931. The Bank may have wished to believe that the return to the gold standard restored to them an automatic pilot to operate according to the old rules. However, having left the Bank largely to its own devices after 1921 when a discretionary monetary policy was being pursued, under the supposedly rule-based gold standard successive governments sought to limit the Bank's autonomy. During the remainder of Churchill's chancellorship the Bank raised interest rates three times. On each occasion, Churchill tried to veto the increase and threatened to make public his disquiet with a policy directed at foreign confidence (Howson 1975: 35–7; Moggridge 1972: 162). As a result, Churchill commissioned two reports on Bank–Treasury relations and the authority to set monetary policy. Both reports came back with the answer that such authority belonged to the Bank (Moggridge 1972: 160). The reality, however, was more complex. Norman himself was essentially unsympathetic to Churchill's instinct that the return to gold and an externally-oriented monetary policy was to blame for Britain's economic problems in the late 1920s, believing that the country simply had to get used to changing patterns of international demand. But, while Churchill could not stop the Governor once the latter had made up his mind to act, Norman certainly felt constrained by ministerial views and was only prepared to raise rates when a transparent external rationale presented itself, and he had secured co-operation from other central banks (Howson 1975: 35–7; Moggridge 1972: 164). Indeed, by the time Labour took office in 1929 the new Chancellor, Philip Snowden, was able to exercise sufficient moral pressure on Norman in his Mansion House speech to delay a rise in interest rates by three months.

Yet, despite the limits they imposed on the Bank's ability to manoeuvre and their evident frustration with a tight monetary policy, politicians for the most part were not prepared to think seriously about any practical alternatives. With the collapse of the world economy and the rapid rise in unemployment in 1929, the general election of that year was dominated by the issue of joblessness. However, only the Liberal Party, advised by Keynes, challenged the orthodox assumptions which underpinned the Bank's policy without making any substantial electoral headway. Shortly after returning to office Snowden initiated the first public inquiry into the conduct of monetary policy. Again, however, the creation of the Macmillan committee represented an expression of the gulf in desire between politicians and the Bank rather than any effort on behalf of the former to decide policy strategically for themselves. Norman told the Committee that 'I have never been able to see myself why for the last few years it should have been impossible for industry starting from within to have readjusted its own position' (House of Commons 1931b: 3382). For the politicians, the answer was painfully obvious. As the miners strike and the General Strike showed, economic expectations and actions could not be divorced from their political and social context. The problem for politicians was that most of them had no idea how to translate that belief into an alternative mode of economic management.[10] During the crisis of the summer of 1931, which culminated in the fall of the Labour government and the eventual abandonment of the gold standard, the strategic initiative remained firmly with the Bank. The Governor put immense pressure on the Labour Cabinet to cut public expenditure to balance the budget, and within the terms of the gold standard policy there was precious room for ministers to resist, however wretchedly aware they were of the likely consequences (for a discussion, see Williamson (1992); for a discussion of the crisis from the perspective of the Bank, see Sayers (1976: chapter 17)). When the Bank itself realised that the policy was beyond redemption, its officials effectively took the decision to exit gold, leaving one now ex-Labour minister to remark 'nobody told us you could do that' (Williamson 1992: 416).

Once the gold standard was disbanded the core executive grasped the nettle rather more firmly, actively seeking outside advice (Williamson 1992: 499) and insisting that both exchange rate and monetary policy were now its prerogative. The National Government, unlike the Bank, clearly had no desire to find a way back to the past, and adopted a managed sterling float, protected by a tight fiscal policy and foreign exchange market intervention and a cheap monetary policy to stimulate growth.[11] Still intact remained the idea that the external constraint mattered, but, in line with Keynes' thinking, successive chancellors now directed monetary policy at the domestic economy. By the mid-1930s, just a few years after Norman had told the Macmillan committee that the Bank Rate affected only 'short money' leaving the 'whole mass of credit' little changed, the Bank had accepted the basic relationship Keynes had suggested between monetary policy and domestic output and prices (House of Commons 1931b: 3382). In terms of institutional authority, the Bank's influence waned further. In 1932 the Chancellor created the Exchange Rate Equalisation Account, which made the Bank the Treasury's agent in the foreign exchange market. Although the Bank retained autonomy in day-to-day operations, authority over sterling policy lay unequivocally with the core executive. To cement its control, from 1932 the Treasury insisted on new consultative committees, particularly in relation to exchange rate management, in which the Treasury and the Bank were both represented.

In essence, after 1931 the core executive largely determined monetary policy and exercised a *de facto* veto over the Bank's decisions. These changes are reflected in the calculations of the Bank's independence. After 1931, the Bank scored 0.46 on a scale from 0.00 for complete dependence to 1.00 for complete independence (see Appendix 2). Reflecting this situation, the

Governor's personal relationships with the core executive, on which the Bank had traditionally to press its concerns, now yielded little influence. Well aware of the loss of his authority, Norman declared in 1937, 'I am an instrument of the Treasury' (Fforde 1992: 15).

1946–71

During the period of postwar reconstruction the core executive sought, and was able, to consolidate its control over monetary policy. The result was a significant decline in both the economic and political independence of the Bank. In 1946 the Attlee government nationalised the Bank, with ownership passing from shareholders to the Treasury against government stock. In the words of Kenneth Morgan, 'the main purpose of the nationalisation . . . was as a reassuring therapy for Labour members, a symbol that the Bank could no longer sabotage a Labour government as it was felt to have done in 1931' (Morgan 1984: 100). In accordance with the 1946 Act, the Bank was now to act as the Treasury's agent except in the 'affairs of the Bank', when it was to be an autonomous entity. These 'affairs of the Bank' included supervision of the banking system, which continued on an entirely informal and non-statutory basis. In setting interest rates, Section 4 (1) of the Act stipulated that the government has the power to issue directions to the Bank 'as, after consultation with the Governor of the Bank, they think necessary in the public interest' (House of Commons 1959: 761). Only on the matter of issuing directives to the clearing banks did the core executive fail to gain the authority which it sought (Howson 1993: 117). Meanwhile nationalisation marked a profound change in terms of the indicators of political independence. At the symbolic centre of the Bank was the Court, consisting of the Governor, a Deputy Governor and sixteen Directors, all of whom were appointed by the core executive. The Governor and Deputy Governor were appointed for fixed five-year terms and the Directors for four years. No officeholder could be dismissed, and all terms of office were renewable. In contrast to the past, no particular qualifications, or expertise, for office were required. Within the Bank itself, authority was concentrated in the Governorship (Roberts and Kynaston 1995; Hennessy 1995). On a scale from 0.00 for complete dependence to 1.00 for complete independence, the Bank now scored only 0.20 (see Appendix 2). This figure corresponds to a central bank which is strictly controlled by the core executive and reflects the changing balance between the two institutions after the 1946 reform.

Just as importantly in the postwar period, the politicians within the core executive were able to create an economic statecraft in which what they desired economically could be reasonably reconciled with the management of a relatively easy set of policy instruments. This statecraft was motivated above all by a commitment, in the words of the 1944 White Paper, 'to the maintenance of a high and stable level of employment' and the expansion of the welfare state. Other objectives might, and most certainly did in practice, obtrude but both major parties appeared to believe that given the experience of the interwar years these were the economic yardsticks by which the electorate would hold them to account. The implications for the conduct of monetary policy were immense. Most obviously, in committing themselves to the maintenance of high levels of employment, politicians were implicitly repudiating the monetary policy which they had allowed the Bank to pursue in the 1920s. Similarly, by accepting the basic tenets of Keynesian demand management, albeit in a rather crude form, they were recognising that monetary policy alone – for example the 'cheap money' policy of the 1930s – was not sufficient to manage the economy to their desired ends. In specific terms, politicians believed that the physical administrative controls, imposed during the war and which continued into peacetime, allowed them to control inflation without recourse to monetary policy and all its awkwardness for this purpose. At the same time, the expansion of the floating debt to finance the war and the government's own emergence as a peacetime habitual net borrower meant that debt management was now a major problem of policy.[12] Once the Bank Rate was raised the cost of servicing the national debt was increased, creating a structural fiscal bias towards low interest rates. Viewed in this context, as the 1959 Radcliffe Report remarked, '[it was] therefore no longer appropriate to charge the monetary authorities with unambiguous tasks that [could] be sharply differentiated from other governmental action' (House of Commons 1959: 52).

If British politicians were now trying to bring a far broader range of domestic considerations into monetary policy, then they helped themselves by – in alliance with other governments, notably the United States – creating an international monetary and financial structure which underpinned that ambition (Ruggie 1982). As Keynes explained in justifying his insistence during the Bretton Woods negotiations that capital controls should be a permanent part of the postwar world:

> Freedom of capital movements is an essential part of the old laissez-faire system and assumes that it is right and desirable to have a equalisation of interest rates in all parts of the world. It assumes, that is to say, that if the rate of interest which promotes full employment in Great Britain is lower than the appropriate rate in Australia, there is no reason why this should not be allowed to lead to a situation in which the whole of British savings are invested in Australia, subject only to different estimations of risk, until the equilibrium rate in Australia has been brought down to the British rate. In my view the whole management

> of the domestic economy depends upon being free to have the appropriate rate of interest without reference to the rates prevailing elsewhere in the world. Capital control is corollary to this.
>
> (Moggridge 1980: 149)

With the use of capital controls, governments could now pursue monetary policy with far less regard for the external constraint, notwithstanding their commitment to maintaining a fixed currency parity under Bretton Woods.

In practice, it was clear from the earliest days of the Attlee government that its ministers thought about monetary policy exclusively in terms of their own non-monetary domestic purposes. From as early as 1945–7 the new Chancellor, Hugh Dalton, explicitly downgraded any external constraint on his freedom of action, believing that this was sufficiently taken care of not only by exchange and import controls but the loans from the United States and Canada. Even when the convertibility crisis of 1947 forced a painful reappraisal of Britain's external economic relations, Dalton tightened fiscal, not monetary, policy in order to strengthen sterling's position. As he later explained it, Dalton's rationale for monetary policy was far removed from anything that Norman could have countenanced:

> To save public expenditure on interest, to improve the distribution of income, to encourage investment and to be sure of full employment. The third of these reasons was not, in this period, of much importance . . . [since investment was directly controlled]. But I had some further reasons. I wished to help the local authorities to keep down the cost of housing programmes, and thus to keep down rents. . . . And I wished to prepare the way for the series of nationalisation Bills which, during this Parliament, we intended to pass. The higher the national credit, the lower the rate of interest, the less annual compensation charge corresponding to a given capital value.
>
> (Dalton 1959: 235; see also Dalton 1962)

During the entire Labour government successive chancellors made no change to the Bank Rate, leaving it at two per cent. Meanwhile, during his tenure of office, Dalton systematically tried to force long-term interest rates down, at a time of some inflationary pressure, so as to nationalise the railways on the terms that he desired. Whilst the Bank warned Dalton from the start that this policy would not work, as it indeed did not, the Bank was forced through 1946 and 1947 to try to issue government bonds with 2.5 per cent yields (see Howson 1993).

For its part, the Bank showed considerable unease in this new world. In the long discussions which preceded the creation of the Bretton Woods agreement, the Treasury, dominated by Keynes, effectively excluded the Bank from British strategic planning. In substantive terms, the Bank's desire to build a postwar economic strategy around the defence of the sterling area and imperial economic interests, without American aid, was far removed from Keynes' project of a multilateral world in which Britain would be both sustained and effectively policed by the United States (for discussion of the Bank's position, see Fforde (1992)). Once the new policy framework was in place, the Bank found it difficult at times to accept its subordinate position. After it was forced to pursue a long-term government bond policy to which it was opposed, the Bank became more forthright in 1949 about the general direction of monetary policy. In 1949 the new Governor, Cameron Cobbold, lobbied Treasury ministers ferociously, but unsuccessfully, for an increase in the Bank Rate and the reassignment of monetary policy to the external constraint, as well as for public expenditure cuts (Howson 1993: chapter 6).

When the Conservative government first entered office in 1951 the Bank hoped that it might be given back some greater practical autonomy, as the new ministers were apparently less anxious than their predecessors to decide monetary policy according to their broad range of political objectives.[13] The Conservatives had campaigned in the general election on the issue of decontrol of the economy which, as the party manifesto stated, would inevitably entail more active use of the Bank Rate (Fforde 1992: 398). Without nationalisation as a pressing domestic concern, and no doubt with one eye on the interests of the City, the new Chancellor, 'Rab' Butler, was largely sympathetic to the Bank's argument that there was still a significant external constraint on Britain's economic room for manoeuvre. Consequently, in 1951 and 1952 Butler sanctioned a series of rises in the Bank Rate to bolster foreign confidence in sterling and reverse the outward flow of reserves. At the same time, ministers were sufficiently worried about the inflationary pressure in the economy, induced by the Korean War, to begin to worry about the consequences of excessive credit creation. In seeking to control credit, they divided the labour between the core executive and the Bank. They allowed the Bank, without formal directives, to exercise qualitative and quantitative controls over bank advances and use gilt-edged funding to limit bank liquidity. Meanwhile, the Board of Trade began to execute special statutory control over consumer instalment credit (Fforde 1992: 407).

Notwithstanding these policy changes, however, the Conservative government showed no real inclination to disinvest itself of responsibility for monetary policy. Butler certainly was more prepared to listen to the Bank's advice than his Labour predecessors, but he very much wanted to present the new policy as his own, despite his undoubted discomfort with the dilemmas of economic judgment (Brittan 1971: 135). In his memoirs he recalled:

> In November I made a token increase in Bank Rate from 2 to 2 1/2 per cent, and in March braved the opprobrium of my political opponents by going to 4 per cent. This sharp rise was announced in the Budget – an unusual course which left the country, and the foreigner, in no doubt that I was prepared to make a thoroughgoing use of monetary as well as fiscal policy in controlling the economy.
>
> (Butler 1973: 158)

By the summer of 1953 Butler was at odds with the Governor over the Bank Rate, and Butler's will triumphed (Fforde 1992: 621). Interestingly enough, on this occasion it was Cobbold who wanted lower interest rates. Despite his expansionist confidence – 'the truth is that we must not be frightened at a little more ease and happiness, or feel that what is pleasant must necessarily be evil' (quoted in Brittan 1971: 115) – Butler appeared to believe that monetary policy could be used to maintain foreign confidence in sterling without deflationary consequences and that fiscal policy was the main macro-determinant of growth (see Brittan 1971).

Butler and his colleagues certainly felt less confident in their own judgment on the direct question of foreign exchange management and were inclined to turn to technical expertise. Confronted with a major decision about sterling, Churchill, as evidently plagued by doubt as to who to trust as in 1925, remarked, 'I don't know much about these technical financial matters myself, but I can't help feeling that when Cherwell and Salter [two advisers who had been long-standing opponents in many contexts] agree there must be something in what they say' (quoted in Brittan 1971: 119). In a similar vein, he wrote to Oliver Lytellton in the midst of a sterling crisis:

> I have seen a Treasury minute and already I know that the financial position is almost irretrievable: the country has lost its way. In the worst of the war I could always see how to do it. Today's problems are elusive and intangible, and it would be a bold man who could look forward to certain success.
>
> (quoted in Brittan 1971: 120).

In the space created by ministerial uncertainty, the Bank, in alliance with the Overseas Finance Section of the Treasury, seized the opportunity to try to shape the strategic agenda in regard to sterling and external economic relations more in accordance with their own judgment. As early as 1950, when the Labour government had committed sterling to the European

Payments Union, the Bank started to worry about the seeming contradiction in sterling's position as an international but non-convertible currency. During 1951 the Bank developed a plan, labelled Operation Robot, to make sterling convertible to non-sterling area residents at a floating rate of exchange while freezing certain sterling balances (see Milward 1992: chapter 7; Fforde 1992: chapters 6–7).

To free sterling in this fashion would have meant a complete reorientation of the framework of postwar British economic policy and would have fundamentally compromised the Bretton Woods system, which underpinned the general postwar political commitment to high employment, growth and the welfare state (see Milward 1992: chapter 7). Yet, on an issue of such magnitude, just five years after it had been nationalised the Bank felt sufficiently unconstrained to conduct secret negotiations with France without the knowledge of the Foreign Secretary, whose department was consummately concerned with the issues that Robot raised (Fforde 1992: 461). Although the Bank did find an ally in the Chancellor,[14] after Butler was twice defeated on the matter in the Cabinet in 1952 the Bank did not let the question rest. Again in tandem with the Treasury Overseas Finance Section, the Bank developed another proposal, the Collective Approach, in which a nucleus of states' currencies, those which British officials deemed internationally important, were made convertible at a fixed or (in the case of sterling) floating rate. When the United States put paid to this idea, between 1953 and 1955 the Bank used its technical expertise to have some convertibility controls lifted through administrative action. By 1955, three years before sterling was officially made convertible, the Bank had effectively achieved convertibility on non-resident sterling at, or very near, the official rate. As a result, problems developed in the balance of payments, sterling weakened, the foreign exchange reserves fell and the government was forced to initiate a significant 'stop' phase in the postwar British economic cycle (see Milward 1992: chapter 7).

If the Bank's presumption had reaped certain rewards for itself, ultimately the renewed importance attached to the external constraint from 1955 did not lead to any restoration of power to the Bank in monetary policy or exchange rate management. Despite left-wing mythology (see, for example, Pollard 1982), detailed empirical investigation has shown that the Bank exercised virtually no influence in the core executive on strategic decisions in the decade and a half from 1955. On the decision not to devalue in 1964 (Brittan 1971: 188; Bruce-Gardyne and Lawson 1970: 143–5), to devalue in 1967 (Brittan 1971: 231), the applications for EEC membership (Bruce-Gardyne and Lawson 1970: 170) and the decision to float sterling in 1972,[15] the Bank was either marginalised in discussions or uninfluential. While successive ministers certainly did not like having to expend as much energy as became necessary juggling their domestic objectives against the external constraint, they were not prepared to abrogate judgment to the Bank. In deciding for themselves during this period, ministers operated with two crucial dilemmas in mind. First, they struggled to reconcile their desire for higher growth with their belief that for largely foreign policy reasons – the maintenance of the Special Relationship and Great Power status – Britain must, as long as practically possible, defend the sterling parity. Second, they wanted to respond to any inflationary pressure in the economy without, if at all possible, resorting to formal wage restraint. For ministers from both parties, incomes policies involved just the kind of nuts-and-bolts economic intervention to which they had a deep aversion. Neither party, for different reasons, wanted to confront the trade unions, and the British constitutional settlement made it difficult to create the economic institutions on which successful wage restraint in other Western European states was ultimately dependent (Bulpitt 1986).

In this context, ministers again became unwilling to use the Bank Rate either to defend sterling or as an anti-inflationary weapon. Even Peter Thorneycroft, the most deflationary of chancellors during this period, emphasised in the crisis package which he introduced in 1957 that he did not want much attention to focus on his two per cent increase in Bank Rate (Brittan 1971: 130). In October 1964 Harold Wilson and James Callaghan did, after considerable prevarication, raise the Bank Rate when the balance of payments and sterling were under severe pressure; but thereafter, until sterling was devalued in November 1967, the Labour government did not increase the Bank Rate, despite the frequent pressure on sterling. When Callaghan introduced his crisis package in July 1966 to try to save the parity, including a curb on public expenditure, tightened hire purchase controls and a prices and wages freeze, monetary policy was conspicuous only by its absence (Brittan 1971: 194–5).

Meanwhile, to the chagrin of the Bank, the core executive became anxious to exercise as much direct control as possible, through qualitative means, on credit expansion. In 1955 the Bank promised Butler it would squeeze credit to make safe an expansionary budget. Within weeks of the Conservatives' re-election in May it was clear that the Bank had been almost completely ineffective in putting pressure on the banks to limit credit. With wages rising and sterling under pressure Butler was forced to introduce an emergency budget in July, containing strict hire purchase controls, cuts in investment for the nationalised industries and a rise in coal and steel prices. Most significantly, Butler issued a statement calling directly on the banks to reduce their advances, thus invading territory previously deemed the 'affairs of the Bank' (Roberts and Kynaston 1995: 48). One year later the Chancellor unprecedentedly summoned the representatives of the clearing banks and the main bank associations to demand that the contraction of credit 'be resolutely pursued' (House of Commons 1959: 422).

In 1957 the core executive forced the Bank to accept new arrangements for the control of credit. Fearing that the government would introduce legislation to give the Treasury authority to exercise direct controls over banks, Cobbold proposed the Special Deposits scheme in which the Bank could call for deposits from the banks with approval from the government. While ministers eventually accepted the proposal, they remained sufficiently angry at what they saw as the Bank's failure to achieve their monetary objectives to create the Radcliffe Committee to investigate the whole workings of the monetary system. The report, when it was delivered in 1959, deliberately downplayed the idea that the Bank had any special authority in monetary policy, calling for 'a constant co-operation, strategic and tactical, between the central bank on the one hand and those responsible for alternative or supplementary measures, essentially the Treasury and the Board of Trade, on the other' (House of Commons 1959: 67). However, given the difference in objectives, such co-operation was far from easy. In 1965, for example, the Treasury turned the Bank's general requests to the banks to restrain lending into precise arithmetical ceilings on the level of bank advances, leaving the Governor to fume in a series of speeches that ceilings were putting an excessive strain on relations between the monetary authorities and the banks and distorted the workings of the banking system (Moran 1986: 48).

At the heart of these monetary differences lay a substantial difference of opinion over how to control inflation. Ministers were anxious to control credit as directly as possible, largely because they did not want to take other action to contain the underlying inflationary pressure in the economy which was contributing to sterling's perpetual weakness. By trying to force the Bank to keep credit tight, ministers hoped for more room for manoeuvre where public expenditure and wage restraint were concerned. For its part, the Bank wanted to protect the autonomy it believed that the 1946 Act gave it over bank credit and could not understand why both Conservative and Labour governments would not either fiscally deflate further or took so long to introduce an incomes policy (Fforde 1992: 644).

The institutional processes through which monetary policy was made during this period entrenched core executive dominance over the Bank. After the partial bureaucratisation of monetary policy during the 1930s, the Governor was now again the almost exclusive voice of the Bank within the Treasury (Cairncross 1995: 78). As one Treasury official wrote in his diary during the Radcliffe Committee:

> The thing that I find most irritating about all our proceedings with Radcliffe is that the central fact is not being brought out and I do not

> suppose it can be brought out which is that the Bank hardly collaborates with the Treasury at all in internal policy matters – the Chancellor talks to the Governor in private and the Bank neither gives their assessment of the situation, nor of the part they expect monetary policy to play in it.
>
> (quoted in Roberts and Kynaston 1995: 40)

During the 1960s Bank–Treasury collaboration did increase and the Bank started to develop more general contacts within the core executive again, but still the Governor's position remained pivotal if the Bank wanted to exercise any real influence.[16] Given the unlikelihood that ministers and the Bank were going to agree, the continuing informality undoubtedly made it easy for Chancellors to dismiss the Governor's advice on a routines basis. At the same time the Labour government, led by Harold Wilson, showed that it was prepared to exercise as much political control as possible within the terms of the 1946 Act over appointments to the Bank. After a series of rows between the government and the Governor, Lord Cromer, during the first two years of the administration, in July 1966 Wilson decided not to renew Cromer's appointment, replacing him with the Deputy Governor, Leslie O'Brien.

1971–87

Since 1955, monetary policy – at least the Bank Rate – had been effectively downplayed as a policy instrument, leaving the core executive in firm control of both the instrument and the Bank itself. From the end of the 1960s it was becoming evident both inside and outside the core executive that monetary policy was in some disarray. With the Bretton Woods system struggling to bear the strain of American economic policies and the emergence of the Eurodollar markets in which capital could escape domestic control, both the international setting, which underpinned the prevailing economic statecraft, and some of the tools by which that statecraft was implemented were being undermined. In 1969 the Chancellor, Roy Jenkins, created a committee composed of both Bank and Treasury officials to discuss monetary policy. During the discussions of this committee the Bank seized the opportunity to press its longstanding desire to shift the burden of monetary policy away from administrative quantitative controls to the Bank Rate. In the autumn of 1970 the Bank convinced the Heath government to accept a new package of monetary control, Competition and Credit Control (CCC), which disbanded lending ceilings and concentrated monetary policy on the use of qualitative controls and the Bank Rate (Moran 1986).

Yet, despite the threat posed by the changing international economic setting to their economic statecraft, Heath and his Chancellor, Anthony

Barber, persisted with the hope that monetary policy could remain a low-key policy tool over which they retained control. At the same time as CCC came into effect in September 1971, the government reduced interest rates and over the course of the next year made no call for special deposits. Indeed, to make matters worse, the Chancellor made loans tax deductible for almost all purposes. The result of continuing cheap money in a turbulent monetary world was a credit-inspired boom, drawing the wrath of the increasingly influential monetarist economists and commentators (Smith 1987: chapter 3). By 1973 the economy was plunged into a secondary banking crisis, causing severe financial problems, particularly in the property sector, and requiring a rescue operation from the Bank (Smith 1987; Reid 1982). Initially the Bank did not press ministers for a tighter monetary policy. Fortuitously, Heath and Barber found themselves with a Governor who, unlike his predecessor, was sympathetic to ministerial concerns (Moran 1986: 66). Only in 1972 did the Bank become sufficiently worried to push Barber for higher interest rates.[17] Although the Bank secured agreement from the Chancellor to a series of interest rate hikes, Heath was determined to put a ceiling on the use of monetary policy. Heath clearly feared not only what he judged to be the deflationary consequences of high interest rates, but also their impact on mortgage holders, a constituency no Conservative government could want to alienate. Consequently, in April 1973 the government gave building societies grants to keep their interest rates below 10 per cent (Moran 1986: 69). Heath was not indifferent to the political consequences of inflation, but he was determined that rising prices should be controlled by means which would have minimal impact on output and employment. In practical terms, this meant a firm limit on the tightness of monetary policy combined with a statutory incomes policy, an expansionary fiscal policy and a floating exchange rate.[18]

By the mid-1970s, any hope that this could prove a stable policy mix had been destroyed. As the Heath government so painfully discovered, winning either co-operation from the trade unions or political support for an incomes policy was extremely difficult in the prevailing economic and political conditions in Britain. More crucially, the world economy had been transformed by the oil price shock, the advent of floating exchange rates and the partial re-liberalisation of capital markets (see Helleiner 1994). Politicians were now caught in a profound dilemma. If excessive monetary expansion was indeed a cause of inflation, as was increasingly difficult reasonably to deny, inflation could not be controlled without at least in part limiting growth and employment. But, given that unemployment was already rising and putting strain on a welfare state premised on full employment, a restrictive monetary policy could only push the economy into territory which seemed like electoral suicide. At the same time, even if ministers were inclined for domestic electoral reasons to ignore anti-inflationary interests, the operation of the foreign exchange and financial markets created a strong incentive for them to prioritise the control of inflation. In sum, there were good reasons for politicians to give monetary policy a central role in whatever new economic statecraft they now fashioned for themselves.

Contrary to what might have been expected, however, this did not mean that ministers in the 1970s or the 1980s were over any length of time prepared to cede genuine power from the core executive to the Bank. From the time when ministers began to manipulate interest rates regularly again until the Lawson chancellorship from 1983–9, a pattern emerged for monetary policy decision-making in which the Bank proposed policy changes and the Chancellor and Prime Minister made a decision on that advice. As one former official described the balance of power, 'the initiative was nearly always with the Bank' (non-attributable interview). During these two decades the Governor and the Chancellor met for informal weekly meetings, usually in the presence of the Treasury Permanent Secretary, to discuss whatever monetary matters seemed pressing. No decisions were made at these meetings, and no minutes were taken. When the Bank did want to press for a change in interest rates, the Bank arranged meetings, through Treasury officials, between the Chancellor and Governor specifically to discuss the matter. Although again no formal minutes were taken, Treasury officials did record any decisions and their rationale. In the words of one official:

> The old system was meetings took place. Nobody knew about them. They were called when the ordinary informal discussions and the telephone were not sufficient to deal with a problem and, therefore, we needed to get together for a heart-to-heart around a table, as and when. You might have two in a week. You might have two in two months.
>
> (non-attributable interview)

At an official level, regular formal meetings did take place with senior Treasury and bank officials meeting once a month to review monetary developments (non-attributable interviews). With its continuing emphasis on informality and the absence of written rules, this structure of decision making in many ways amounted to a means of coping with perpetual crisis management. Ministers were still ultimately responsible for the level of interest rates, but the opaqueness of the process allowed them to try to blame the Bank when things went wrong.[19]

In substantive terms the 1976 sterling and IMF crisis made the Labour Cabinet quite self-consciously aware thereafter of the limits imposed on economic management by the external constraint in the post-Bretton Woods world. At the same time, by re-establishing monetary policy as an important tool of economic policy, ministers put themselves in a position where they could increase their substantive dependence on the Bank to manage that constraint if they so wished. Certainly Denis Healey was prepared to listen to the advice of the Bank Governor, Gordon Richardson. Most notably, Healey was persuaded by Richardson during the second half of 1976 to adopt and publish targets for monetary growth (Fay 1987: 79) and also agreed to a succession of interest rate changes proposed by the Governor (non-attributable interviews). Even so, Healey and Callaghan were not prepared to subordinate all economic objectives to a monetary or exchange rate discipline in which the Bank was presented with an automatic pilot to manage. They persisted in using a range of policy instruments, including a statutory incomes policy and fiscal restraint, to try to control inflation, well aware of the general consequences of allowing monetary policy to bear the entire burden of this task. Moreover, in 1978 they decided not to join the Exchange Rate Mechanism (ERM) of the European Monetary System in which decisions about interest rates would have been made according to informal rules determined by the exchange rate. While Healey, in particular, saw the attractions of some level of exchange rate stability, neither he nor Callaghan could see how to convince the Labour Party that membership would not place monetary policy on a permanent deflationary footing ill-suited to British economic interests (Ludlow 1982). If Healey respected the technical competence of the Bank over monetary matters and was inclined to listen to Richardson, he still wanted to preserve a strategic sphere in which he and Callaghan would exercise their own judgment according to the broad range of political constraints in which they operated.

For its part, the first Thatcher government initially wanted to build a new economic statecraft around reduced income tax, trade union reform and a non-discretionary monetary policy in which interest rates would be adjusted according to fixed rules. If monetary policy could reduce inflation by itself without recourse to an incomes policy, then the new ministers hoped they could find the space in which to recreate their competence as a governing party after the shattering experience of the collapse of the Heath government (Bulpitt 1986). In this context the Chancellor, Geoffrey Howe, set out targets for the growth of the broad monetary indicator, Sterling M3 (£M3), in the Medium Term Financial Strategy (MTFS) of March 1980. The Bank's role was to monitor the performance of £M3 so that the Chancellor could then make decisions about monetary and fiscal policy based on this information.

In terms of implementation the Bank's operations were put at the centre of the new statecraft but this in itself did not give the Bank practical influence within the core executive. Indeed, the first Thatcher government asserted a far greater need to judge monetary and exchange rate policy for itself than had its predecessor. For example, less than six months after entering office Howe completely disbanded exchange controls, a decision of monumental significance for the entire global political economy (Helleiner 1994). While the Bank had pressed for the gradual elimination of controls during the second half of the 1970s, it was now surprised at the speed with which Howe and Thatcher acted (Fay 1987). Just as confidently, ministers quickly decided to act as if the exchange rate imposed no constraint on the pursuit of their new statecraft, an attitude which, at least within the walls of the Bank, Richardson was quick to condemn (Keegan 1984). In regard to direct monetary policy, the government distinguished itself by the number of ministers actively involved in the decision-making process. Not only the Chancellor but the Prime Minister and the unprecedentedly influential Financial Secretary, Nigel Lawson, immersed themselves in the detail of monetary aggregates. Much to Richardson's chagrin, Lawson frequently challenged the Bank's advice about market operations, and the government began to decide for itself on some technical monetary issues (Keegan 1984; Lawson 1992).

The problems with the MTFS were, for the first Thatcher government, twofold. First, it proved extremely hard either to control £M3, or even for the Bank to provide accurate information about its behaviour (Keegan 1984; Smith 1987). In part, the government itself made the Bank's job more difficult when it dismantled exchange controls in October 1979, effectively abolishing the utility of the corset which had been introduced in the 1970s to set limits on the growth of banks' interest-bearing liabilities (Keegan 1984: 149–50). With the figures showing £M3 spiralling out of control, Howe continued to tighten monetary policy for seventeen months after the Conservatives entered office, despite the onset of a deep recession. Second, both the domestic statecraft as an entity and the deployment of monetary policy in particular failed to take account of the external constraint at a time when the government had already reduced its room for manoeuvre by the abolition of exchange controls. In the face of high interest rates, sterling appreciated massively, destroying the competitiveness of large sectors of British manufacturing industry with hugely detrimental consequences for levels of output and employment. Unable to believe that the Conservative party was re-electable in the circumstances, by the end of 1980 Thatcher and Howe were searching for a new means of stimulating growth and employment without compromising their desire to reduce inflation. Their solution, a looser monetary policy to engineer a depreciation in sterling combined with a tightened fiscal stance, placed the external constraint firmly at the heart of policy for the remainder of the first Conservative term in office (Smith 1987).

The government's abandonment of monetarism did not lead to any contrition on behalf of ministers or any less willingness to trust their own judgment. For her part, Thatcher wanted a scapegoat for the failure to achieve the £M3 target and lashed out at Richardson, whom she knew had never been convinced by the monetarist dogma of the MTFS. When Richardson's existing term of office expired, she refused to renew his position. In his place she appointed Robin Leigh-Pemberton, a man without any experience of central banking and someone she clearly believed the Chancellor and the Treasury could easily dominate (for discussion of core executive–Bank relations during the early 1980s, see Keegan (1984: 146–56, 198–9); Fay (1987: 114–27)).

In June 1983 Lawson moved to the chancellorship and, apparently unbruised by the failure of the MTFS, brought to the job an overriding confidence in his own judgment not only about the big strategic issues but the day-to-day operation of policy (Fay 1987: 79). In the ensuing years he neither waited for the Bank to take the initiative about monetary policy nor bowed to the Bank's technical advice about the exact timing of interest rate changes and government bond issues. On occasions Lawson would even, against all previous protocol, telephone directly the Bank's foreign exchange market operators to give instructions (Stephens 1996: 83–4). In all senses, Lawson believed he could decide for himself. As he told the House of Commons Treasury and Civil Service Select Committee, 'we take the decisions but they do the work' (Smith 1992: 103–4).

In 1984, Lawson's and Thatcher's respective opinions of the Bank plummeted further after the collapse amid fraud of the Johnson Mathey Bank (JMB). In 1979 the Labour government had passed legislation to create a statutory framework for the Bank's supervision responsibilities. In this instance the Prime Minister and Chancellor concluded that the Bank had failed to supervise properly. Nonetheless, the Governor and Deputy Governor agreed to rescue, and inject funds into, JMB. Significantly, they did so without informing Lawson of their actions until it was too late for him to reverse their decision. When, as a result, Lawson unintentionally misled the House of Commons about the use of public money, Thatcher was so furious with the Bank that she canvassed the possibility of taking bank supervision away from the Bank altogether (Fay 1987: chapters 9–10; Lawson 1992: 402–9).

In terms of replacing the MTFS within the government's original statecraft, Conservative ministers still very much wanted to act for themselves. Their problem was that, increasingly, they could no longer agree with each other. What the Prime Minister and successive chancellors seemed to want was a measure of, at least short-term, exchange rate stability to act as some counter-inflationary framework without high interest rates or the loss of their freedom of action in fiscal policy. From this rationale, Howe in 1981–82 and Lawson from 1985–89 pressed the Prime Minister to join the rule-based ERM, studiously ignoring the fact that from 1983 at least, sterling's membership of the system would have limited their own fiscal options (Thompson 1996). By contrast, Thatcher, although sharing her chancellors' desire to find a monetary control for inflation, apparently could not abide the idea of any institutionalised acceptance of the external constraint, or any appearance that the Bundesbank was deciding monetary policy for British ministers. In vetoing membership for the best part of a decade, Thatcher assumed the entire authority to decide for herself, denying not only her chancellors but the Treasury, successive foreign secretaries and Leigh-Pemberton, who all supported membership in the mid-1980s (for discussion of the long internal debate about ERM membership, see Thompson (1996)).

Outside the ERM and scarred by their own disagreement, Lawson and Thatcher ended up running a discretionary monetary policy very much on their own terms and with complete disregard for the Bank. Despite a salutary lesson in January 1985 from the foreign exchange markets about the dangers of unilateral monetary and fiscal expansion when sterling tumbled towards parity with the dollar, Lawson and Thatcher persistently took risks against the external constraint as and when they judged it suited their short-term electoral interests. Most notably, they engineered the unsustainable monetary and fiscal boom of 1986–9 (see Smith 1992). In 1987 Lawson, with Thatcher's consent (Thompson 1996: 87–9), decided to use monetary policy to shadow sterling against the deutschmark without even bothering to notify the Bank of his decision (Thompson 1996: 89–90). Given that sterling was appreciating, this meant not only a series of interest rate cuts but huge levels of intervention in the foreign exchange markets on a daily basis for which the Bank was responsible. For their part, officials at the Bank were left fuming not only at Lawson's institutional audacity, but the fecklessness of a policy which assumed that international investors would keep on buying sterling to prop up a widening balance of payments deficit in the face of mounting inflation. The continuing ritual of Chancellor–Governor meetings notwithstanding, relations between the core executive and the Bank were in complete disarray (non-attributable interviews).

Viewed in a historical context, the attitude of ministers towards their own ability to judge monetary policy and exchange rate strategy during the first and second Thatcher governments seem far removed from the experience of the early interwar years. During both periods, ministers were operating against an external constraint which by necessity elevated monetary policy into a central tool of economic management and a domestic climate which made the level of interest rates into a highly salient issue of electoral discourse. But while in the 1920s ministers were ultimately prepared to let the Bank decide for them, however much they did not like the substance of policy which the Bank delivered, Thatcher and Lawson were so supremely confident in their own judgment that even the Bank's advisory services became all but redundant. If during the interwar years the struggle about authority over policy took place between the core executive and the Bank, then by the mid-1980s the battleground had shifted to within the core executive itself and the conflicting wills of the Prime Minister and the Chancellor.

In the run-up to the 1987 general election, all that mattered from the point of view of Conservative ministers was that between them Lawson and Thatcher had guided economic policy to their successful electoral advantage. Yet it was precisely their ability to act in this way which contained the seeds of future problems. In profound contrast to the nineteenth century, it was now the politicians, not the Bank, who were feared as an inflation-creating machine. In a decade and a half of experience in an international setting in which monetary policy was important, the foreign exchange and financial markets had become routinely suspicious about the willingness of politicians to judge monetary policy according to short-term electoral considerations. In this context, by 1987–8, Thatcher and Lawson were living on borrowed time. Not only were they very clearly deciding, or cobbling together, policy for themselves – unlike, for example, the German government – but they were not accepting any formal constraints on their freedom of action – unlike, for example, the French government inside the ERM (see Chapter 6). The result was a British interest rate premium over most of the other European Community states (see Thompson 1996). Ministers now had achieved supreme control within the core executive over the Bank, but to carry on using their own judgments in the manner in which they were presently doing would become increasingly dangerous.

4 The core executive and the Bank of England (1988–97)

The primacy of domestic politics

From the late 1980s, a debate about the value of central bank independence gathered momentum throughout the OECD area. While Britain was certainly not immune from the outflow of academic and media analysis of the subject, from the beginning the debate was always likely to leave British politicians in a particularly uncomfortable position. In the first instance, the idea of giving the Bank of England greater autonomy may have seemed an attractive position both in terms of the substance and process of British monetary policy. Given the volatility of British interest rates during the previous two decades and the interest rate premium over those states participating in the Exchange Rate Mechanism (ERM) demanded by the foreign exchange markets for most of the 1980s, any new arrangement which injected counter-inflationary credibility into British policy could only in itself be welcome. At the same time, the escalating public war of words between Margaret Thatcher and Nigel Lawson over monetary and exchange rate policy did not encourage confidence that decisions about interest rates were being taken for either economically sound or long-term reasons. Surely, it was tempting to conclude, subjecting the Bank so completely to the conflicting wills of the Prime Minister and the Chancellor within the core executive had only brought monetary policy into a state of disarray.

Yet, whatever the immediate attractiveness of the idea, any British government that wanted to give the Bank autonomy would inevitably face a series of minefields to navigate through, over and above those confronting most of their EC colleagues on the matter. Economically, and hence in electoral terms, short-term interest rates tended to have greater significance in Britain than elsewhere. As the Treasury and Civil Service Select Committee later commented:

> The United Kingdom is . . . almost certainly unique amongst the major developed economies in the political importance attaching to the level of short-term interest rates, because housing is financed mainly by vari-

> able rate mortgages linked to short-term rates and because of the high degree of dependence on short-term interest rates amongst small businesses. . . . In other countries the impact of movements in short-term interest rates on the individual voter is much less where fixed rate mortgages absorb a smaller proportion of average family income.
>
> (House of Commons 1993a)[1]

At the same time, if an autonomous Bank of England could be presented as a solution to Britain's post-1960s inflationary problem, then it begged the question of whether such an anti-inflationary instrument could be successfully imposed on an economy in a state in which inflationary pressures appeared embedded into the very structures of the economy. With a decentralised approach to wage bargaining and a housing market driven by asset owners betting on higher prices in the future, above-average inflation had become an all too predictable outcome of even modest levels of economic growth (on the persistence of wage-driven inflation through the 1980s, despite trade union reform, see Johnson (1992: chapter 7)).

Faced, unlike their German counterparts, with an electorate in which considerable sections had an expressed interest in rising prices, British governments seemingly found it difficult to believe that they could win elections without injecting some inflation into the economy. Indeed, the Thatcher government's own experience was testament to this predicament. During the first administration economic ministers found it difficult to build any kind of coherent anti-inflationary statecraft, despite their intentions on entering office (Bulpitt 1986). When inflation finally did decline from 1982, this was due as much to the good fortune of falling world commodity prices as to the government's own efforts. After 1983, Thatcher and Lawson found it difficult to accept that inflation control should be a priority at all whenever the economy was not growing quickly enough for their liking. Unlike, for example, French politicians, who after 1983 had pursued the anti-inflationary *franc fort* strategy, for the British government accepting a binding anti-inflationary discipline would represent a radical departure.

In this context, unless British politicians accepted the neoclassical and monetarist assumption that inflation is purely a monetary phenomenon, then an autonomous Bank of England was likely to become a burden. Without the backdrop of the restrictive approach to wage bargaining deployed in Germany, an independent Bank would face a considerable incentive to use monetary policy to try to squeeze inflationary wage increases. Whereas successive British governments had allowed exchange rate depreciation to offset wage inflation, an independent Bank would, by virtue of its remit, need to be less accommodating, particularly given Britain's history of sterling weakness and inflation. Consequently, despite the fact that the theoretical argument about central banks postulated that independence led to higher long-term growth and employment, if there was any such institutional arrangement in Britain critics would be able to present a seemingly plausible argument that the net result of an independent Bank would be higher interest rates.

These potential economic problems were confounded by the British constitutional settlement. Of course, in terms of the real exercise of power the doctrine of parliamentary sovereignty was largely a meaningless façade (Mount 1992). At the same time, the introduction of qualified majority voting in the Council of Ministers in the Single European Act had already struck a theoretical blow against the notion that in the final instance the British Parliament holds power. Clearly, however, to take authority away from elected politicians on a highly salient political issue and give it to unelected Bank officials, who, if the Bundesbank model were to be followed, would not be held accountable to Parliament, would be an altogether different proposition (Busch 1994). Accustomed in office to be able to claim the reward for popular policy outcomes and to expect to pay the price for the reverse, whatever the reality about causality and agency, British politicians were always likely to find it difficult to divest power from themselves. If they were likely to be blamed or praised for the outcome in any case, then there was good reason to continue to judge monetary policy for themselves, even if the economic benefit was less equivocal.

The remainder of this chapter is divided into five parts. The first part explains how the core executive retained a very firm control over the Bank of England between 1988 and 1990, despite some support from within the Conservative government for giving independence to the Bank. The second part examines how the issue resurfaced during the two years of Britain's membership of the ERM. The third part traces the process through which the Major government, after sterling's exit from the ERM, tried to impose more self-discipline on itself over monetary policy without really giving any greater autonomy to the Bank. The fourth part describes how from 1993 the government created new policy structures that in the first instance appeared to reduce its control over the Bank, but in practice effectively concentrated authority over monetary policy in a single site within the core executive, namely, with the Chancellor. The final part briefly considers the decision in May 1997 of the incoming Labour government to give effective operational independence to the Bank and draws some conclusions.

1988–90

Somewhat paradoxically, it was Nigel Lawson who first proposed taking power away from the core executive in monetary policy, just as he had achieved supreme control over the Bank of England in the area. In September 1988, Lawson asked a somewhat astonished group of senior Treasury officials to draw up a proposal for an independent but accountable Bank. At no stage during the subsequent preparation of the Treasury paper was the Bank told of Lawson's interest in the subject (Lawson 1992: 867–8). Indeed, it was only when Lawson publicly revealed the proposal in his resignation speech a year later that the Bank came to know what had transpired. Lawson's initiative at this time needs to be understood against the background of the tortured set of relationships that had developed since 1985 between the Prime Minister, Chancellor and Governor. With general relations between the Bank and Chancellor already at a low ebb, at the end of 1987 Lawson and Leigh-Pemberton had a fierce argument over whether the Chancellor had the authority to tell the Governor to intervene in the foreign exchange markets in deutschmarks, contrary to the European Monetary System agreement to which Britain was a signatory (Lawson 1992: 787–9). Meanwhile, Lawson and Thatcher had reached the point where they could no longer even discuss with each other the question of ERM membership. In March 1988 they engaged in a very public row over Thatcher's insistence that the policy of shadowing the deutschmark should be abandoned. In a notorious put-down to her Chancellor in the House of Commons, Thatcher declaimed, 'there is no way in which one can buck the market' (Smith 1992: 137). Thereafter, Lawson and Leigh-Pemberton were forced back into an alliance to try to persuade a reluctant Thatcher of the need to raise interest rates (House of Commons 1993c: 197, 202).

The net result, as Lawson knew well enough, was a substantial policy muddle. Britain was outside the ERM, at Thatcher's insistence, but in 1987–8 the government had shadowed the deutschmark. In March 1988 Thatcher had put an end to shadowing, prohibiting reserve intervention but initially allowed Lawson to continue to cut interest rates to curb the upward pressure on sterling. In David Smith's words, 'the markets were therefore faced with the bizarre situation of a Chancellor trying to talk the currency down, while the Prime Minister appeared to be relishing its rise' (Smith 1992: 138). Once inflation accelerated in June and interest rates were clearly heading upwards, Lawson faced, in his own mind anyway, a hard struggle ahead to persuade Thatcher of the need to use monetary policy as a counter-inflationary discipline. In his memoirs he recalled:

> Low interest rates had an unfailing appeal for Margaret. Despite her reputation as a die-hard opponent of inflation, and her dislike of it was undoubtedly genuine, she was as almost always in practice anxious to reduce interest rates, and thus, the mortgage rate.
>
> (Lawson 1992: 478)

In these circumstances, for a somewhat penitent Chancellor who wished to reattach monetary policy to inflation control, an independent Bank must have seemed a far better bet than the vagaries of Thatcher's judgment.

At the heart of Lawson's expressed critique of existing arrangements was the problem of credibility. As he later told the Treasury and Civil Service Select Committee, 'It was not because I was suddenly struck with the feeling that central bankers were supermen and that politicians were inferior mortals: it was simply that I felt that as an institutional arrangement it would work better' (House of Commons 1993c: 196). Inside the ERM the situation might have been different, but so long as Thatcher remained in office Lawson knew this was almost out of the question:

> The purpose of the proposal was to entrench the use of monetary policy to fight inflation and secure price stability. . . . Part of the background to it was the repeated rejection by Margaret of ERM membership. An independent Bank was to some extent an alternative way of entrenching the commitment to stable prices and, as I put it in my paper, 'making it a permanent feature of UK economic policy, while at the same time assisting us in the completion of our present task'.
>
> An independent Bank would not, of course, have had the merit of replacing discretion by rules. But it would at least, in the words of my paper, 'be seen to be locking a permanent anti-inflationary force into the system, as a counter-weight to the strong inflationary pressures which are always lurking'. In particular it would do something to 'depoliticise interest rate changes'.
>
> (Lawson 1992: 868)

In this context an independent Bank was for Lawson an alternative monetary means to control inflation in the wake of the abandonment of the monetary targets and his failure to secure ERM membership (for a discussion of the reoccurrence of this theme in the search for policy answers during the Thatcher governments, see Thompson (1996: 31–2, 50–1, 219–22)).

On 28 November 1988, Lawson sent Thatcher a memo outlining his proposal, with the recommendation that a White Paper be published with the 1989 budget so that legislation could be introduced at the beginning of the following parliamentary session. The Bank, Lawson suggested, should be given responsibility for monetary policy, which meant setting short-term interest rates and monetary targets, and it would have 'a statutory duty to preserve the value of the currency'. Ministers would retain responsibility for the exchange rate regime, and the Treasury would assume responsibility for government borrowing but would not be permitted to do this in a way that added to money or liquidity. To ensure a measure of accountability, the Governor of the Bank would be answerable to a parliamentary select committee set up specifically for the purpose. The Court of the Bank would be appointed by the government for an eight-year term, subject, except for the Governor, to approval by the select committee (Lawson 1992: 1059–61).

When Lawson and Thatcher met to discuss the matter shortly afterwards, the Prime Minister was unreceptive. In her view the issue could only be considered when inflation was coming down, because in the present circumstances it would look like the government was admitting that it could not itself bring inflation down. In her own words:

> My reaction was dismissive. Here we were wrestling with the consequences of his diversion from our tried and tested strategy which had worked so well in the first Parliament; and now we were expected to turn our policy upside down again.
>
> (Thatcher 1993: 706)

Lawson sensed, however, that her objections ran far beyond contingent circumstances. Not only was she 'not going to give up the levers of power which control of interest rates, as she saw it, represented', but she simply could not abide any new ideas which came from her Chancellor after their ERM feud (Lawson 1992: 871).

According to the accounts given by both protagonists, Thatcher did not engage with the argument about credibility that Lawson had presented. Even if her Chancellor could argue, as he had done with the ERM, that for a given exchange rate it would be possible to have lower interest rates if the Bank were independent, what concerned Thatcher was the appearance of policy. While Lawson wanted to stress the problem of market credibility, Thatcher was preoccupied with the perception of policy responsibility by the electorate, over and above any particular monetary outcome. After their meeting Lawson decided to let the matter rest temporarily, seeing no point in trying to resurrect the matter at Cabinet level (Lawson 1992: 872). One year later, after he had resigned office in frustration at Thatcher's use of her personal economic adviser, Alan Walters, to undermine his authority, Lawson revealed Thatcher's rejection of his proposal to the House of Commons. His successor, John Major, decidedly subordinate to the Prime Minister, showed no interest in taking up the issue in his year in the chancellorship.

In the wake of Lawson's failure, the core executive, and the Prime Minister in particular, kept a firm practical control over the Bank.[2] Although Major obviously did not possess the self-confidence in economic judgment that Lawson had displayed, Thatcher used the latter's departure to strengthen her own control over monetary policy. As sterling slid substantially in the last months of 1989 and the start of 1990, Thatcher insisted, contrary to the advice of both the Bank and the Treasury, that interest rates would not be raised above their existing 15 per cent level. Whatever the rise in inflation, which was finally to peak above 10 per cent, she was not prepared either to hurt mortgage holders or to increase the risk of recession. In October 1990, with the economy now in recession anyway, she finally decided that sterling should join the ERM after the most minimal consultation with the Bank. In the words of one Bank official:

> I am not quite sure what was going on in 1990. I don't think there was a great deal of actual debate about ERM membership or the basis of ERM membership, though it is quite clear that the markets in 1990 were getting hold of the idea that the ERM was something we were clearly about to join. . . . There were no set pieces that I could recall involving the official machine. Obviously, in all the institutions with an interest in the subject, including our own, we were doing our best to assemble our ideas. . . . But we were not, as it were, concerting on a game plan such as would have produced this pretty blatant talking up of expectations of membership and thereby of the exchange rate at the other end of town. We got to know it was happening. But it was not something that I was ever involved in discussing – whether it should be done, how it should be done, or whatever.
>
> (non-attributable interview)

Afterwards, a furious Leigh-Pemberton denounced Thatcher for coupling the announcement of ERM entry with a cut in interest rates without his knowledge (Thompson 1996: 172–5).

1990–2

After Thatcher's departure from office, the question of an independent Bank of England resurfaced within the government in 1991–2. When it did, the context in which this happened was profoundly different than the circumstances in which Lawson had made his proposal to Thatcher. Now inside the ERM, British economic policy was firmly tied to a European anti-inflationary discipline built around using interest rates to maintain the value of sterling against the deutschmark. At the same time, in negotiating an 'opt-in' to the single currency at Maastricht, Major ensured that a British government would need to make the Bank of England independent to be able to exercise that option. The legal position in regard to this issue was complex. According to Article 108 of the Treaty of European Union, 'each

Member State shall ensure, at the latest date of the establishment of the ESCB [European System of Central Banks] that its national legislation, including the statutes of its national central bank, is compatible with this Treaty and the Statute of the ESCB'. Article 109e(5) goes on to state that during Stage 2 each Member State shall start the process leading to the independence of its central bank 'in accordance with Article 108'. However, while Britain was formally committed to participation in Stage 2, the protocol on the British 'opt-in' to Stage 3 states that Article 108 does not apply to Britain. If there was therefore no hurry for the British government to make the Bank independent, not even to think about it in the medium term was tantamount to ruling out British participation in a single currency.

For its part, the Bank itself was in a somewhat stronger position than in the late 1980s. After Lawson had revealed his independence proposal in November 1989, the Bank had begun a series of internal discussions on the subject. As one Bank official recalled:

> We began to think about what our response to this ought to be. Fundamentally we were in favour of it. We did not have to think very hard about that. But we did have to think about what kind of institutional structure, if there were to be independence, that domestically we would like to have.
>
> (non-attributable interview)

By 1991 the Bank was making it publicly clear that it wished to be given independence within a monetary framework set by Parliament (*Financial Times*, 16 May 1991). More significantly, the Bank was no longer marginalised from the core executive within the monetary decision-making process. In part this was a simple function of the removal from the scene of a Prime Minister who believed that she could decide for herself; but at the same time, sterling's membership of the ERM made it harder for any Prime Minister or Chancellor to ignore the Bank's advice. In the words of one Bank official:

> If there are operational constraints on carrying out policy then the person who carries out has that much more input. . . . If they're saying we'd like the exchange rate to be three cents higher then it becomes a technical question of whether you can really do that. And at that point it's not just a question of what should it be but what it can be.
>
> (non-attributable interview)

Against this background, the Chancellor, Norman Lamont, and the Treasury worked well with the Bank during the ERM period. Lamont wanted to meet the Governor on a regular basis. Initially the idea emerged of holding a monthly meeting, but as sterling's position within the ERM deteriorated, the two men met on an 'as needs' basis, culminating in daily discussion. With such little room for manoeuvre, there was extremely little scope for disagreement (non-attributable interviews).

In substantive policy terms, the two years of ERM membership were far removed from the economic and electoral climate in which Lawson had proposed making the Bank independent. By the end of 1991 the economy had been stuck in recession for over a year with no end in prospect, and the government was facing a general election within six months. While initially ERM membership had provided interest rate cuts that, given the level of inflation in 1990–1, would probably not have been possible outside the system, British short-term rates were now only marginally above German levels. This left further interest rate cuts dependent on the Bundesbank loosening German monetary policy when it seemed determined to do the opposite, given the inflationary pressure in the German economy induced by reunification. For the British government this was a huge problem. Not only were high interest rates always unpopular, but after the credit expansion of the 1980s the number of people deeply affected by them was greater than ever. Most crucially for the government, there were over a million households trapped in negative equity in terms of their property and mortgage (for discussion of the effect of the recession on the housing market and its political consequences, see Smith (1992: chapter 2)).

Unsurprisingly, the main preoccupation of the government in late 1991 and 1992 was to try to find a way of reducing interest rates. In the year leading up to sterling's exit from the ERM in September 1992, Major and Lamont tried on various occasions to secure a general realignment of ERM currencies, including the French franc, against the deutschmark, which would probably have allowed for lower German interest rates, and to bully the Bundesbank into a looser policy (Stephens 1996: chapters 8–10). Unsuccessful on both counts, the Prime Minister and Chancellor were left looking impotent to affect the economy. In May 1991, after Leigh-Pemberton had warned against 'premature cuts in interest rates' (*Financial Times*, 16 May 1991) that could not be justified in terms of sterling, one Conservative backbench MP angrily asked Lamont in the House of Commons, 'Are you running the economy or the Governor of the Bank of England?' (*Financial Times*, 17 May 1991). Of course it was still true that authority lay with the Chancellor but, given the decisions that the government had already made to improve the credibility of monetary policy, he was in no position to use it.

It was in this broad context that Lamont took up the baton which Lawson had left behind. On taking up the chancellorship in November 1990 Lamont had shown no interest in, nor any particular view on, the subject of Bank independence (non-attributable interview). During the first months of 1991, however, Lamont concluded that an independent Bank would both strengthen sterling's position within the ERM and be necessary to ensure market credibility if, for any reason, the government was ultimately unable or unwilling to sustain Britain's membership of the system (non-attributable interview). He was particularly interested in considering how the model of the New Zealand central bank, given operational independence in 1990, could be applied to Britain (House of Commons 1992: 142). In the second half of 1991 Lamont started to correspond with the Prime Minister, setting out his case for an independent but accountable Bank in the interests of price stability. Like his predecessor, Major showed little interest, telling Lamont that his proposal could not be reconciled with the system of democratic accountability in Britain. The only context, he conceded, in which he would be prepared to seriously think about the subject was the single currency. As in 1988, the Bank was left unaware of events; indeed, Lamont specifically told the Bank to refrain from pressing their own agenda on the subject with the Prime Minister (non-attributable interview).

What was ultimately striking about this issue during these two years was how the British debate, limited as it was, was removed from that taking place in other EC states. Prior to sterling's ejection from the ERM the Major government appeared determined to preserve the 'opt-in' as opposed to the 'opt-out' of the single currency. In December 1991 the Prime Minister told the House of Commons:

> Let there be no doubt: Britain is among those which will meet the strict convergence conditions. We took the lead in setting them and will continue to be involved at every stage leading up to the decision whether to launch a single currency.
>
> (House of Commons 1992: 142)

But, unlike the other EC heads of governments without independent central banks, Major thought that he could leave thinking about the issue into an indefinite future. Meanwhile, his Chancellor, whatever his later protestations of lifelong Euroscepticism, endorsed the Treaty of European Union only to suggest simultaneously that Britain adopt a model of independence for the Bank incompatible with its statutes. While the Treaty prescribed that governments should make their central banks independent in the manner of the Bundesbank, the New Zealand model, which Lamont desired to emulate, created a contract between the government and the central bank that obliged the latter to achieve a fixed inflation target, but which the former could override in exceptional circumstances. Paradoxically, the

British government wanted to keep open the possibility of participating in a monetary union in which unelected bank officials from across the EC would decide monetary policy, when even its most forthright supporter of an independent Bank of England wished British politicians to retain some ultimate control over monetary policy.

1992–3

When the British government decided to take sterling out of the ERM on 16 September 1992 (Black Wednesday), after the DM2.95 central parity had been destroyed in a furious wave of sterling selling, it effectively isolated itself from the rest of the EC in monetary terms. Although Italy joined Britain outside the system, and other ERM states devalued in the currency crisis of September 1992, only in Britain did ERM membership, and with it the practical prospect of joining a single currency on the Maastricht timetable, become a virtually taboo policy option. From this time on the British Conservative government would debate the question of the appropriate relationships between core executives and central banks purely in domestic British terms.

What the Conservative government lost above all on Black Wednesday was its credibility. Despite having raised interest rates by 5 per cent in a single day in a recession and spent billions of pounds of foreign exchange reserves, the government's economic policy, to which the Prime Minister and Chancellor had committed large amounts of their personal integrity, was in ruins. As a result, just six months after the Conservatives' fourth general election victory, the electorate dramatically turned against the government. Since the 1970s the Conservatives had held a comfortable lead over Labour in terms of voters' perceptions of who could best handle the economy. Immediately after Black Wednesday the parties switched places (*The Economist*, 18 June 1994). For their part, the Conservative backbenches were no longer prepared simply to trust the government on European policy matters, making the necessary ratification of the Treaty of European Union a massively difficult prospect. Meanwhile, the financial markets saw a government that had miscalculated the terms and timing of its entry to the ERM, misjudged the *de facto* rules of the system in trying to bully the Bundesbank and, over a longer period of time, presided over a disastrous boom/bust policy in which short-term considerations had appeared to dominate monetary discussions.

In the initial weeks after the crisis, no one in the government appeared to have any firm grip on how credibility could be restored. Given the attitude of much of the Cabinet and an acrimonious exchange of words between Lamont and the Bundesbank, a quick return to the ERM at a new parity was out of the question. After a series of somewhat contradictory pronouncements from the Prime Minister and the Chancellor, Lamont finally laid out a new economic strategy on 8 October 1992 in his speech to the Conservative Party conference and a letter to John Watts, the chairman of the Treasury and Civil Service Committee. The government, Lamont announced, was setting itself an inflation target. During the remainder of the Parliament the government would endeavour to contain the annual rate of inflation, for retail prices excluding mortgage interest rate payments (RPIX), in a range of 1–4 per cent. By the end of the Parliament inflation would be in the lower range between 1 and 2.5 per cent. In terms of monetary policy, Lamont continued, the government would make decisions on a discretionary basis, looking at a range of indicators including monetary aggregates, asset prices and the exchange rate. If the government failed to achieve its inflation target, then, Lamont promised, 'it will have a duty to explain how this had arisen, how quickly it intended to get back within the range, and the means by which it could achieve this' *(Financial Times*, 9 October 1992).

In his Mansion House speech on 29 October, Lamont added a new role for the Bank to the anti-inflation strategy. From now on, the Chancellor announced, the Bank would be responsible for monitoring the government's progress in pursuing the inflation target through a new Inflation Report. (Initially the Inflation Report was published in the Bank's Quarterly Bulletin, but from 1994 it became a separate publication). The aim of the report would be to assess 'thoroughly and openly' the prospects for inflation over the succeeding eighteen to twenty-four months. The report would be shown to the Treasury prior to publication, but, unlike previous economic assessments published by the Bank, the Treasury would have no authority to edit. At the same time, to create greater transparency in the actual decision-making process, Lamont declared that the Treasury would publish in advance the dates of monthly meetings between himself and the Governor. After the meeting the Treasury would publish the monthly report, which formed the basis of the discussions of the meeting and set out in detail the basis of any changes that were made to interest rates. In the same vein, the Chancellor continued, he would set up a panel of seven independent economic forecasters to meet at regular intervals and publish an assessment of the overall performance of the economy (*Financial Times*, 30 October 1992).

At the heart of this new strategy lay a determination to build credibility and a measure of openness into economic policy generally and monetary affairs in particular. Ministers and officials wanted to draw a line under not only the experience leading up to Black Wednesday but the confusion that had developed in monetary policy during the last years of the Thatcher government. In the words of one official, 'above all we wanted to respond to the things that had not gone well prior to the ERM' (non-attributable interview). In practice this meant several things. In operating a discretionary monetary regime again, there should be no return to the kind of conflicts that had bedevilled the Thatcher/Lawson/Leigh-Pemberton triangular relationship. For the same reason, ministers wanted to dispel the perception that they took decisions on a short-term basis. If interest rate adjustments usually make a significant difference over a two-year period, then ministers needed to show that they recognised this fact in taking their decisions (Burns 1995: 8). By adopting a relatively tough medium-term inflation target and offering public explanations for their actions, they could hope to convince the electorate and the markets that decisions, even if ultimately wrong, were being made for good, rather than bad, reasons.

In more substantive terms, the new strategy meant that the government was accepting a new yardstick by which it could be judged as some kind of safeguard against sterling going into free fall. For their own part, ministers were committing themselves to a greater degree of fiscal discipline, particularly necessary in view of the burgeoning public sector borrowing requirement (PSBR). Having already established a new system of public expenditure control in July 1992, Lamont announced expenditure cuts and a public sector pay freeze in the Autumn Statement. This was followed by an increase in both direct and indirect taxes in the 1993 budget, to be implemented the following year. Unless Lamont reduced the PSBR, interest rates clearly could not be cut significantly without the government losing yet more credibility. Yet just as crucially, in shaping its new strategy as it did, the government was recognising that it could not restore credibility simply by its own efforts. In a fundamental sense, its power was part of the problem and it needed to give at least some influence to an external body. The most obvious, if not only, option was the Bank. As one official wryly remarked, 'we could have called the IMF to run the inflation target' (non-attributable interview).

Nonetheless, if the Bank was being given the explicit authority to judge the government's economic performance, ministers were also hoping to make the Bank itself more accountable in the advice it gave. Undoubtedly, ministers were anxious to blame Treasury and Bank officials and their forecasts for part of the ERM debacle (Stephens 1996: 189–90). If the Bank's position on policy was to become more public, they perhaps hoped that next time things went wrong the blame might be cast more widely. Noticeably, in deciding on a successor to Leigh-Pemberton, whose term of office was to expire in June 1993, the government did not give the Bank a wholehearted vote of confidence. Although Eddie George, the Deputy Governor, was elevated to the top spot, he himself was replaced by a complete outsider in Rupert Pennant-Rea, the editor of *The Economist*. When, in April 1995, he resigned after allegations about his personal life, the government deliberately replaced him with another outsider, Howard Davies, the President of the Confederation of British Industry (*Financial Times*, 25 April 1995). After Pennant-Rea's appointment, a former Deputy Governor, Kit MacMahon, described the move as 'a breath-taking insult to the Bank. . . . Whatever his intrinsic merits may prove to be, he has *prima facie* no qualifications for the job' (House of Commons 1993e: 555).

Whatever the complexity of the government's motives, the Bank certainly saw the new arrangements as a positive opportunity. In the words of an official, the Bank was 'delighted with the inflation target', particularly after the ERM experience with a sterling discipline: 'We were not keen on exchange rate targeting. We were not keen on money supply targets. In fact we were not keen on intermediate targets at all' (non-attributable interview). Similarly, Leigh-Pemberton heralded the Bank's monitoring of the inflation target as 'a giant leap for the authorities' (*Financial Times*, 14 September 1996). Bolstered by these developments, from the autumn of 1992 the Bank began to display a new confidence to speak in public about the direction of economic policy (House of Commons 1993a: 21).

If the economic strategy that Lamont announced in October 1992 was supposed to represent a new departure in the substance and process of monetary policy, the ensuing months gave good cause to ask just how much had really changed from the pre-ERM days. For the Bank to be an active influence over the core executive in a discretionary decision-making process, it needed a stable and co-operative relationship between the Prime Minister and the Chancellor. But, in the nine months after Black Wednesday this particular relationship was deeply troubled. In the autumn of 1992 the government was in as deep a hole as had perhaps been faced by any postwar British administration. Already castigated for Black Wednesday and facing an uphill struggle to ratify the Maastricht Treaty, the government quickly hit a new low when Michael Heseltine announced, to widespread public outrage, that thirty British coal mines were to be closed, costing 30,000 miners their jobs. After a rebellion by Conservative backbenchers, the government was swiftly forced into a humiliating, if temporary, U-turn. For the Prime Minister, whose personal reputation had been battered since the April election victory, the overriding priorities during this period were to give the Conservative Party and the electorate some immediate cheer and to regain some control of events. This set him at odds with his Chancellor, who was sceptical about Maastricht ratification and wanted economic policy to be determined solely by the inflation target.

In this context, Major was adamant that he would be centrally involved in monetary policy and that decisions about interest rates would not simply be left to the Chancellor and the Bank. On 13 October Lamont told the

Treasury and Civil Service Select Committee that there could be no rapid reduction of interest rates because that would jeopardise the inflation target and put sterling at risk (*Financial Times*, 14 October 1996). Three days later, just after Heseltine's pit closure announcement, the Prime Minister imposed an interest rate cut of one per cent on his Chancellor (Stephens 1996: 275). In January 1993 Major insisted on another cut in interest rates against Lamont's wishes (Stephens 1996: 284). Neither was the Prime Minister content to listen to the advice of either the Chancellor or the Bank on the timing of changes, seemingly believing that the government was in too desperate straits to be concerned about what he saw as purely technical matters. To the Bank's profound disquiet, in early 1993 he decided to cut interest rates at a time which clashed with its efforts to hold an important auction of government gilt-edged stock (*Financial Times*, 24 November 1993). Clearly upset by Major's behaviour, Lamont would later proclaim in his resignation speech that the timing of interest rate changes 'should never be used to offset some unfavourable political event' (*Hansard*, 9 June 1993: 284).

Major's control over Lamont was further evident on the continuing question of independence for the Bank. Outside the ERM, Lamont was more convinced than ever that this was the best way to create long-term anti-inflationary credibility. In the last months of his chancellorship, without the Bank's knowledge, he drew up a formal proposal to give the Bank autonomy to present as a White Paper with the 1993 budget (Stephens 1996: 278–9; *Financial Times*, 10 June 1993).

Again Major rebuffed him, publicly stating in January 1993 when appointing Eddie George to the governorship that he was opposed to such a move and that it was the Bank's job *to help* the government to reduce inflation (*The Economist*, 28 August 1993). In May 1993, after a series of poor public performances by Lamont and a nearly 30 per cent swing against the Conservatives in a critical by-election, Major sacked his Chancellor. In a bitter resignation speech, Lamont placed the issue of an independent Bank back in the Westminster arena, revealing, as Lawson had done previously, his vain efforts to persuade the Prime Minister to act. Major responded swiftly, telling the Commons that there was a 'genuine case for independence' but:

> The very real concern that I have always faced is one that I believe is spread widely across the House: the need for accountability to Parliament for decisions on monetary policy matters. Were a way to be found to get the benefits of an independent central bank without a loss of parliamentary accountability, my views would be very close to those of my Right Hon. Friend.
>
> (*Hansard*, 9 June 1993: 281, 293)

Yet, though Lamont himself had been defeated, his revelation certainly raised the political temperature on the issue. Michael Howard, the influential right-wing Home Secretary, quickly went out of his way to stress that an independent and unaccountable central bank would be unacceptable to Conservative right, particularly if such a proposal would lead Britain towards participation in a single currency (*Financial Times*, 11 June 1993). Meanwhile, at the Bank Leigh-Pemberton used a farewell speech to call on politicians, academics and the City to devise a 'form of accountability that might enable [Britain] to have the advantages of a more autonomous central bank within the constitutional arrangements of [British] parliamentary democracy' (*Financial Times*, 16 June 1993).

1993–7

On arriving as Chancellor in June 1993, Kenneth Clarke quickly stated that he did not intend to rush into a debate on independence for the Bank (*Financial Times*, 16 June 1993). On 21 July he told the Treasury and Civil Service Committee:

> I am sitting on the fence and I have not reached a hard and fast opinion on what is usually called the independence of the Bank of England. I certainly do not think it is the duty of the Treasury to spend its time second-guessing the Bank on a lot of responsibilities. I do think it is necessary for the new Governor [Eddie George] and the new Chancellor to devise a relaxed relationship between the two.
>
> (House of Commons 1993d: 621)

But if Clarke wished to bide his time in deciding upon an appropriate relationship between ministers and the Bank, the *status quo* was under serious pressure. In 1993 Belgium and France made their respective central banks independent, and Spain and Portugal were preparing to follow suit. For the government to continue to do nothing would certainly push the government's EU policy further in the direction of the single currency 'opt-out', and leave Britain one of the few OECD states without an independent bank. At Westminster, during the second half of 1993, the Treasury and Civil Service Committee held hearings on the role of the Bank. Its report, published on 16 December, called for a more autonomous Bank along the lines of the New Zealand central bank. The Bank should, the report recommended, be given a primary statutory objective of maintaining price stability and the government should agree with the Bank's publicly-stated targets to achieve that objective. In 'exceptional' circumstances the government would be empowered for a six-month period, subject to parliamentary approval, to override the price stability objective. The Bank would be made accountable through an annual report, which would be debated in Parliament, and appearances in front of the Treasury and Civil Service Committee (House of Commons 1993a). The report additionally called for the Chancellor to publish the minutes of his monthly meetings with the Governor.[3]

The committee's hearings gave the Bank the opportunity to set out its own proposal for autonomy which it had developed since Lawson's resignation. In their evidence, both Eddie George and Rupert Pennant-Rea argued that greater autonomy would improve Britain's inflation performance (House of Commons 1993e: 584). In a similar vein to the committee's final recommendations, they argued that the Bank should be given a statutory and permanent objective to pursue price stability. The government, with the support of Parliament, would then stipulate to the Bank the specific inflation objective that it wished the Bank to deliver over a particular period of time. The Bank accepted, the two men admitted, that it would be necessary for constitutional reasons to allow the government the authority to revoke the strategic objective 'within commonsensical limits' (House of Commons 1993d: 587). In the words of the Deputy Governor to the committee:

> I do not see that it is appropriate or desirable for a central bank to be utterly independent of you, the elected politicians. I think it is right that we should be a servant carrying out the task which you have set us, and I think it is right for the Government to be able to specify what that task is. . . . In the last analysis I believe it is a matter for politicians to ask the Bank as an executive agency to carry out something that it thinks the Bank can do better than it can.
>
> (House of Commons 1993e: 588)

Even if Clarke was prepared to ignore the full momentum of these developments, to do nothing on the issue could only diminish the credibility the government so desperately needed to create. Lamont's resignation charge that Major's diktats over the timing of interest rates had undermined both 'the credibility of policy and the credibility of the Chancellor' pressed hard (*Hansard*, 9 June 1993: 284). Shortly before Eddie George took up the governorship, he hold the Treasury and Civil Service Committee:

> It is undoubtedly true that there are times when short-run tactics are adjusted to take account of events which are actually not a lot to do with monetary policy. In any single incidence in my experience, that can be damaging for a little while. The impact of that single incident gives rise to discussion about, 'This was done for political rather than monetary

> reasons'. Provided actually it was not an unreasonable thing to do in a strategic sense, that does not last for very long, but it has a corrosive influence over time.
>
> (House of Commons 1993b: 123)

To add to the Chancellor's vulnerability on monetary credibility, he could not reasonably claim that in terms of outcomes the strategy laid out by the government the previous autumn was working as hoped. The Bank's Inflation Report, published on 2 November, warned that inflation would rise over the months ahead with 'a slight possibility' that it would briefly exceed the top of the government's target range (*Financial Times*, 3 November 1996). While inflationary expectations, as manifested in the bond markets, had fallen since 1992, they were not low enough to suggest that the markets believed that the government would consistently hit its inflation target. On this score most of the ERM states, despite the currency crisis of July–August 1993 which had led to the suspension of the narrow bands of the system, were still doing better than Britain. To make matters worse, Clarke knew that the PSBR was still, despite Lamont's tax increases, too high not to worry about its future effects on market credibility and interest rates (Stephens 1996: 290).

In this context, the Chancellor began to think seriously about different practical options in the autumn of 1993. On his first day in the job he had received a letter from the Treasury Permanent Secretary, Terence Burns, suggesting some changes in regard to the Bank and monetary policy including giving the Bank the authority to decide the timing of interest rate changes and publishing the minutes of the monthly monetary meeting. In September 1993 Clarke began to act. First, he announced that the Treasury would no longer see the Bank's Inflation Report in advance of publication (Pennant-Rea 1995: 221). On 23 November, in announcing a 0.5 per cent cut in interest rates, he declared that the precise timing of this change had been decided by the Governor and that this practice would continue in the future (*Financial Times*, 24 November 1996).

Two weeks later, George told the Treasury and Civil Service Committee that the Bank would have up to a month to implement any change that the Chancellor requested (*Financial Times*, 9 December 1996). As the Bank understood it, the Chancellor was giving up a small measure of control:

> The fact that they cannot announce it at the most convenient time for them and we can announce it at the most inconvenient time for them is an example of them tying their hands, lashing themselves to the mast in a good conservative, with a small 'c', central banking way.
>
> (non-attributable interview)

In the same manner, in March 1994 the Chancellor gave the Bank greater freedom to operate in the government bond market. Henceforth, once the Treasury agreed annual guidelines on funding policy the Bank would be effectively free to choose the timing and nature of gilt issues (*Financial Times*, 18 March 1994).

While these changes were being made, the Chancellor was already planning his most radical shift in the monetary policy process. In autumn 1993 he decided that publication of the minutes of his monthly monetary meeting with the Governor could add credibility to British policy and started to experiment. As Terence Burns told a select committee:

> When we made the decision to publish the minutes of the monthly monetary meetings, we went into this with a lot of care and we had a trial period where we prepared the minutes of meetings. We then put them away and we brought them out six weeks later (which would have been the day when they would have been published) and we looked at them and said 'How do they look? Is this really a problem?' We then went through the final stage where the Chancellor wanted to be clear and confident himself, that if the day came when there was a disagreement between himself and the Governor, that could be handled. Once we had been through one of those situations we decided we could go live, so to speak.
>
> (House of Commons 1995: 363)

In late 1993 and early 1994 there were a series of delicate negotiations between the Treasury and the Bank as to the precise form the minutes should take. As one Bank official recalled:

> We began to experiment with what it would look like. We started off with the Treasury. I mean the minutes had existed before and they were bald and the Governor did not like them at all as a way of summarising his views. The key thing is not for us that they're summarising the Chancellor's decision – everybody knows that – they're telling you what the Bank's advice was. So the key thing was to have it made clear what we had advised. And so we started to get this gradually built into the drafts. Firstly, the background set of stuff. At the same time we said that we'd publish the monetary report which was our paper on the table for the monthly monetary meeting. . . . Eventually the monthly monetary report got absorbed into the opening paragraphs.
>
> (non-attributable interview)

After this preparation, on 13 April 1994 the Chancellor published the minutes of the two meetings that had taken place between himself and the Governor in February (*Financial Times*, 14 April 1994).[4]

The decision to publish the minutes was very much the initiative of Clarke and the Treasury and something to which the Prime Minister only reluctantly agreed (Stephens 1996: 292). For Major, there were several problems with the new process. Whatever reassurances he was offered by Clarke to the contrary, most Treasury officials believed that, henceforth, it would be very difficult for the Chancellor to overrule the Governor's advice (non-attributable interviews). As one Treasury official later admitted: 'I think we, and most commentators, over-estimated the extent to which power in decision-making had passed to the Governor' (non-attributable interview). But in April 1994, at the very least, the reaction of the markets to any future disagreement must have seemed uncertain. Even if Clarke was ultimately right, Major was still forced to sell what could appear a policy of handing over interest rate decisions to the Bank, to a Cabinet and party many of whom openly blamed the government's present electoral woes on what they saw as handing monetary policy over to Germany in 1990–2. To make matters worse, this apparent new economic stringency coincided with the introduction of the new tranche of tax increases delivered in the two 1993 budgets. Meanwhile, as the Treasury well understood, the new arrangements would alter the Prime Minister/Chancellor relationship within the core executive as much as the Chancellor/Governor relationship on monetary matters. If the tension in successive Prime Minister/Chancellor relationships had damaged British credibility, then Clarke had found a means of marginalising to some extent the Prime Minister's influence within the core executive.

For his part, Clarke appeared confident that the new arrangements would increase the credibility of policy without any sacrifice of his autonomy. Open government, as Clarke saw it, was a means of getting the benefits of independence without having to pay the price, at the same time as making the Bank accountable for its advice (non-attributable interview). The potential threat to his autonomy would come from the financial markets responding negatively to any disagreements that now arose between the Chancellor and the Governor, but Clarke was confident that the markets would respond rationally so long as such disagreements as occurred were simply reasonable differences of opinion. The only option ruled out, he hoped, would be decisions based on electoral panic without any substantial economic rationale. Certainly Clarke did not appear to regard his new policy as a second-best option because he knew that Major would not agree to an independent Bank (non-attributable interviews). Indeed, the evidence is that he shared Major's belief that British politicians could not escape the responsibility of judgment. As Terence Burns reflected on the general reluctance of British politicians to hand over control to the Bank:

> The main area of doubt has been on the subject of accountability. In a system where economic policy is still near the centre of the political debate it seems a big step to attempt to take monetary policy out of the political arena. If the government is going to get the blame or credit for the outcome there is still some reluctance to withdraw from the process itself.
>
> (Burns 1996, para. 21)

In terms of process, the publication of the minutes ushered in a more elaborate formal set of procedures for policy-making than had hitherto existed. One week before the Chancellor/Governor monthly monetary meeting, the Treasury chief economic adviser began to chair an internal Treasury meeting in which officials made a systematic evaluation of the latest economic indicators, and the department's Inflation Team presented their advice. Around the same time a similar meeting of officials took place at the Bank. After this meeting, the Deputy Governor sent a letter to the Permanent Secretary at the Treasury setting out the Bank's provisional views for the month. Two days before the monthly monetary meeting, a joint meeting of Treasury and Bank officials took place, chaired by the Permanent Secretary, at which the Bank's letter was tabled as one of the papers. The minutes of this meeting then became one of the papers for the monthly monetary meeting. After the meeting the Treasury briefed the Chancellor on the Bank's views and then communicated to the Bank how the Chancellor was thinking. For his part, the Chancellor saw the Prime Minister. On the morning of the monthly monetary meeting the Bank finalised its advice at a meeting of senior officials (Burns 1995: 8; non-attributable interviews).

The monthly meeting itself was attended by between 20–25 people, including the Chancellor, his private secretary and special advisers, junior Treasury ministers, seven or eight Treasury officials, including the Permanent Secretary and Second Permanent Secretary, and five or six Bank officials, including the Governor and Deputy Governor. The Governor began the meeting by making a formal presentation of his advice, which then appeared verbatim in the minutes. The Chancellor responded to the Governor's comments before opening the meeting to others. In this subsequent discussion the Chancellor and the Governor continued to dominate and other ministers and officials usually made no more than one intervention each. On most occasions the Chancellor concluded meetings by taking a decision on whether interest rates would be changed. If he did not finalise his judgment on this occasion, a further meeting was scheduled after he had reflected on the Governor's advice. The minutes of the meeting were taken by the Chancellor's private secretary and a junior official in the Treasury inflation team (non-attributable interviews). These minutes were published six weeks later. The minutes were divided into five sections. First, there appeared a report on the month's economic and monetary developments. This was followed by record of the Governor's opening statement, the Chancellor's response and a summary of other points made in the discussion. Finally, the minutes explained the Chancellor's reasons for whatever decision he had made.

During the first twelve months of these new arrangements the evidence suggested that the Chancellor had indeed ceded some practical control to the Bank. The minutes of the monthly monetary meeting held on 8 February 1994 revealed that Clarke had wanted to cut interest rates by 0.5 per cent, against the Governor's advice. After a further series of meetings, the two men compromised on a 0.25 per cent reduction. In May 1994 the Bank's Inflation Report warned that 'on the assumption of unchanged interest rates, the most likely outcome for RPIX is 3–3.5 per cent' (*The Bank Inflation Report*, May 1994: 3). At the next month's monetary meeting the Governor told Clarke that, although there was no reason to adjust policy yet, in the Bank's judgment the next move in interest rates should be upwards (Minutes of Monthly Monetary Meeting, 8 June 1994, para. 15). This left Clarke with a profound dilemma. As the August Inflation Report revealed, underlying inflation, touching 2.2 per cent in July 1994, was running at its lowest level for twenty-seven years and appeared to be still falling. Yet, on the Bank's projections, if the government was serious about its commitment to take medium-term decisions according to the inflation target, brakes needed to be applied to the economy. At the monthly monetary meeting on 7 September, George recommended to Clarke that a 0.5 per cent interest rate increase would now be judicious, citing the deterioration in the position of long-term government bonds as the most pressing cause for concern (Minutes of Monthly Monetary Meeting, 7 September 1994, para. 19). According to his Treasury officials, Clarke reacted initially with dismay (Stephens 1996: 294), but after two days' reflection he finally agreed to accept the Bank's advice (Minutes of Monthly Monetary Meeting, 7 September 1994, paras. 27–8). After this first pre-emptive strike against future inflationary pressure, the two men then agreed to two further increases in rates in December 1994 and February 1995.[5]

Before too long, however, Clarke chose to prove that he still believed himself his own master. In May 1995 the Conservative government was in deep trouble. Despite the economic recovery which had taken place in 1993, both in terms of growth and unemployment, the government was still facing the likely prospect of a severe electoral defeat. Since Black Wednesday the government had seen its parliamentary majority eroded by by-election defeats in nominally safe seats, lost a swathe of councillors in the 1994 and 1995 local elections and been humiliated in the 1994 European Parliament elections. Meanwhile, the Conservative party remained bitterly divided, particularly on the question of Europe. The previous autumn the government was forced to resort to a vote of confidence to secure the passage of the EU Finance Bill through the House of Commons. Even then, eight Conservative backbenchers defied the government and were promptly stripped of the party whip, technically depriving the Prime Minister of his parliamentary majority. Unsurprisingly in the circumstances, John Major's leadership of the party came under fierce pressure. Indeed, one month later, in June 1995, Major himself forced an ultimately successful leadership election in a desperate attempt to strengthen his position.

On 5 May, the day after the local election defeat, the Chancellor turned down the Bank's advice for a further rise in interest rates in the light of a fall in sterling of 4.7 per cent between the beginning of February and May. As the minutes recall, George stressed that the risk to the inflation outlook was quite large:

> The Governor concluded that the Bank's view on all this was quite clear. On the balance of risks he was bound to advise that interest rates be increased by 1/2 per cent now. If this did not happen, the authorities could be faced very quickly with a loss of credibility and a very difficult market situation. While it was never possible to be sure about the market reaction, that was not a risk he could advise the Chancellor to take.
>
> (Minutes of Monthly Monetary Meeting, 25 May 1995, para. 25)

But, rebuffing the advice of his Treasury officials as well (*Financial Times* 22 July 1995), Clarke insisted that the empirical evidence suggested that 'growth had been slowing down to a more sustainable rate' and that he was not simply going to oblige the financial markets (Minutes of Monthly Monetary Meeting, 5 May 1995, paras. 27, 32). Afterwards Clarke boasted cavalierly to the *Financial Times*:

> What if the latest Bank of England forecast turns out to be more accurate than any of their previous forecasts and inflation does come in at 3 per cent? I am still entitled to turn round and say that is not much short of a triumph if you look at previous recoveries.
>
> (*Financial Times*, 26 May 1995)

In a similar vein in June he told Conservative MPs that 'events' might mean that the government would not reach its inflation target and that he aimed, in setting interest rates, to keep inflation between 1–4 per cent 'most of the time' (*Financial Times*, 15 June 1995). Having reaffirmed his control over policy, Clarke continued to rebuff the Governor at the next three monthly monetary meetings.

What was perhaps most striking about Clarke's behaviour was that he chose to exert his authority over the matter of sterling. Through his struggle with the Governor during the summer of 1995, Clarke repeatedly stressed that 'he would continue to base his decisions on interest rates solely on the economic evidence on a month-by-month basis', and he 'would discount the views of the financial markets' (Minutes of Monthly Monetary Meeting, 7 June 1995, para. 24). Certainly in refusing to raise interest rates to defend sterling, he avoided an immediate confrontation with those within the Conservative Cabinet and party who wished to blame the ERM experience for all the government's woes. But, at the same time, he took the risk that the foreign exchange markets, by continuing to sell sterling, would tie his hands in the future. In the event the gamble was won. On the day of the meeting sterling fell to a record low against the deutschmark, as the markets immediately suspected that the Chancellor had overridden the Bank's advice, only to stabilise again within weeks on the back of a firm dollar. Well aware of the precariousness of Clarke's victory, the Governor later told the Treasury and Civil Service Committee:

> We were bailed out of that, frankly, by a change in sentiment on the dollar. . . . I think it turned out very fortunately for him. If risks are taken consistently on that side, then they won't necessarily always turn out as happily as they did in May.
>
> (*Financial Times*, 8 December 1995)

Nevertheless, the Chancellor had succeeded in pushing the Bank on to a defensive footing. Despite the Bank Inflation Report of August 1995 recording that the 'central projection for inflation two years ahead was similar to that in May', at the monthly monetary meeting the following month the Governor withdrew his request for an immediate rise in interest rates. In December Clarke secured George's agreement to a 0.25 per cent cut in rates. Although at a joint press conference announcing the cut the Governor conceded that he believed that the government was now on course to hit its inflation target (*Financial Times*, 14 December 1995), in the previous Inflation Report, published in November 1995, the Bank had concluded that such an outcome was 'by no means assured'. At the first monthly monetary meeting of 1996, George chose not to oppose Clarke's wish to cut interest rates further when on his own admission he would have preferred to delay for at least another month (Minutes of Monthly Monetary Meeting, 17 January 1996, para. 21). Whatever the role of fortune, two years into the new framework, it was evidently the Bank, not the Chancellor, on whom the burden of prudence had set.

Appearing to have secured his autonomy, in the middle of 1996 Clarke set himself up for another confrontation with the Governor. According to the Bank's May Inflation Report it was 'marginally more likely than not' that inflation would be above 2.5 per cent in two years' time if policy were not changed. But not only did Clarke not want to raise interest rates, with a general election now less than a year away, he wanted to continue to loosen policy. Consequently, at the monthly monetary meeting in June Clarke imposed another 0.25 per cent cut in interest rates, contrary to George's advice. Over the following months economic growth accelerated and inflation increased. By the end of October Clarke was forced to admit that the Bank's caution may well have been justified and he and George agreed to reverse the previous cut with the prospect of an even tighter policy to come. Yet, despite the Chancellor's retreat on this occasion, his future autonomy did not appear to have been damaged. To the Chancellor's good fortune once more, in the summer and autumn of 1996 sterling started to appreciate, therefore reverting any risk that policy would need to be tightened purely to repair credibility.

Indeed, in the six months preceding the general election in May 1997, Clarke resisted the Governor's attempts to secure a further increase in interest rates. Just one week after the October rise, the Bank warned in its Inflation Report that the Chancellor was still not on course to meet his inflation target (*Financial Times*, 7 May 1997). Then, at four successive monthly monetary meetings between 11 December 1996 and 5 March 1997, Clarke turned down George's request for a 0.25 per cent rise in interest rates. In the Bank's view, while the economy was not 'accelerating out of hand', it had been 'picking up steadily to a pace that could not be sustained for long consistent with the inflation target two years ahead' (Minutes of Monthly Monetary Meeting, 5 February 1997, para. 20). For his part, in January 1997 Clarke publicly attacked the Bank, telling journalists that 'the Bank of England took too much notice of predictions in the financial futures markets that interest rates would have to rise' and that 'it was usually wrong to assume that the markets had a feel for the real economy which the Treasury lacked' (*Financial Times*, 29 January 1997).

Once more the position of sterling was central to the power struggle. Substantively, the two men disagreed about the implications of sterling's steady appreciation through the second half of 1996 and the first months of 1997 towards the bottom of its old ERM parity range of DM2.78. George undoubtedly did not want to take the exchange rate into consideration in setting interest rates. In the words of the minutes, the Bank's view was that 'there was very little that could be done about [sterling's effective appreciation] through monetary policy' (Minutes of Monthly Monetary Meeting, 5, March 1997, para. 20). Clarke, however, insisted that sterling's rise was acting as anti-inflationary pressure to mitigate the effects of the growth in domestic demand (Minutes of Monthly Monetary Meeting, 5 February 1997, para. 28; Minutes of Monthly Monetary Meeting, 5 March 1997, para. 32). More critically, sterling's strength, which was in large part attributable to the fact that Britain's interest rates were high relative to other leading economies, provided cover for Clarke's refusal to act in the run-up to the general election. If Clarke's judgment was indeed motivated by electoral considerations, then the circumstances of the markets and the cyclical position of the British economy nonetheless continued to give him considerable autonomy.

1997

If Kenneth Clarke proved during his chancellorship that political control of monetary policy from within the core executive was still possible, the new Labour government, elected with a landslide majority in May 1997, quickly demonstrated that it was not interested in reaping the fruits of his efforts. On 6 May, just five days after becoming Chancellor, Gordon Brown announced that the Bank of England would be given the authority to decide monetary policy. Henceforth, Brown declared in a letter to the Governor of the Bank of England, 'the Bank will have operational responsibility for setting short-term interest rates to achieve an inflation target which the government will determine.' In 'extreme economic circumstances', he continued, if 'the national interest demands it, the government will have the power to give instructions to the Bank on interest rates for a limited time period'. Such power, however, 'could only be exercised through subordinate legislation approved by parliament' (*Financial Times*, 7 May 1997). At the same time, Brown explained, the government will continue to be responsible for determining the exchange rate regime, but the Treasury will assume from the Bank the responsibility for debt management.

Within the Bank itself, in these new arrangements, operational decisions on monetary policy will be made by a monetary policy committee comprising the Governor, two deputy governors (one responsible for monetary stability and one for financial stability) and six members. Decisions will be made at monthly meetings by a vote of the committee with each member having one vote. If there is no majority, the Governor will have the casting vote. The Treasury will have the right to be represented at meetings of the monetary committee but not to vote. The Governor and deputy governors will be appointed by the government for five-year renewable terms. Of the other six members of the monetary policy committee, two members will take management responsibility for monetary policy and market operations, respectively, and will be appointed by the Governor, after consultation with the Chancellor, for three-year renewable terms. The remaining four members of the committee will be appointed by the Chancellor, also for three-year renewable terms. At the same time the Chancellor committed the new government to reform of the traditional Court of the Bank. Henceforth the non-executive members of the Court, four of whom will be newly appointed by the Chancellor and drawn widely from industry, commerce and finance, will review the performance of the Bank as a whole, including the monetary policy committee. The Bank will be made externally accountable to the House of Commons through the Treasury and Civil Service Select Committee (*Financial Times*, 7 May 1997). Fourteen days after making this declaration of intent, the Chancellor announced that as a further part of the reform package the government would be taking responsibility for banking supervision away from the Bank and giving it to the Securities and Investments Board (*Financial Times*, 21 May 1997). The net result of the changes is that the Bank now scores 0.48 on a scale from 0.00 for complete dependence to 1.00 for complete independence. (See Appendix 2). In terms of both economic and political indicators, the reformed Bank is now significantly more independent than was previously the case.

In opting for operational independence for the Bank, the new Prime Minister and Chancellor took virtually everybody, including Labour MPs, by surprise. In the months preceding the 1997 general election, Brown, after discussions with Eddie George, promised that Labour would keep the monetary policy-making framework established by Kenneth Clarke except to create a monetary committee at the Bank that would be formally responsible, instead of the Governor, for giving advice to the Chancellor. Only after the new committee's performance could be assessed, Brown insisted, would giving operational independence to the Bank of England be considered by a Labour government (*Financial Times*, 27 February 1997). Labour's manifesto stated only that the party was committed to 'reform the Bank of England to ensure that decision-making on monetary policy is more effective, open, accountable and free from short-term political manipulation' (Labour Party 1997: 13). Yet, on the eve of the general election, Tony Blair and his Chancellor-in-waiting decided to place new legislation for the operation of monetary policy in the Queen's Speech. Five days later Brown informed the Bank of England of his intentions (*Financial Times*, 7 May 1997).

The clear rationale for the decision for the new Prime Minister and Chancellor was to increase domestic credibility in the pursuit of price stability. For Brown, the publicly stated imperative was to 'remove the suspicion that short-term party political considerations are influencing the setting of interest rates' (*Financial Times*, 7 May 1997). Undoubtedly, Clarke's refusal, against the Governor's advice, to raise interest rates in the run-up to the general election had done nothing to allay such suspicions in the markets. For all Clarke's short-term success and sterling's strength in the second half of 1996 and the first half of 1997, the long-term government bond market indicated that British monetary policy lacked credibility. Symbolically, after Brown's announcement, government bond prices made their biggest one-day gains for more than five years (*Financial Times*, 7 May 1997). In immediate practical terms Labour was forced to confront the economic consequences of the manner in which Clarke had exercised political control over monetary policy in the long run-up to the general election. In Brown's first monthly meeting with George on 6 May, the new Chancellor, unlike his predecessor, accepted the Bank's request for a 0.25 per cent rise in interest rates. In Brown's own words, 'my judgment is that we have inherited a situation in which, in the absence of corrective action, inflation will overshoot the government's inflation target next year' (*Financial Times*, 7 May 1997). Indeed, the internal forecasts of Treasury officials that welcomed him into office suggested that inflation would be rising towards 4 per cent by the end of 1998. In this context, by taking the decision to give the Bank autonomy so quickly, the new government could certainly hope to deflect the blame for what was likely to be a series of interest rate increases in the following months.

Nonetheless, within the European context, the British government in its new guise remained wed to an idiosyncratic approach to the questions of central bank independence from the core executive. Quite explicitly, the legislation proposed by Brown fell short of the stipulation in the Maastricht Treaty that member states must give full statutory independence to their central banks. By contrast, the British government will continue to determine for itself what price stability means in any particular setting and when that economic objective might conceivably be overridden. To qualify for monetary union in 1999, the Labour government would need to pass two pieces of legislation on the Bank before 1998. In fact, as Labour had in opposition shifted ever further in a Eurosceptic direction in general and the single currency issue in particular, it had no real incentive to Europeanise the issue when in office. In making his announcement, Brown reiterated the government's position, formulated in a somewhat *ad hoc* manner during the general election campaign, that it 'was very unlikely' that Britain would join monetary union in 1999 (*Financial Times*, 7 May 1997). Whatever the complexity of the new government's more long-term attitude towards monetary union, in May 1997, only domestic considerations effectively counted. Consequently, mindful of Britain's constitutional structure and the political expectations it produces, the government was not prepared to sacrifice final political control over monetary policy. Not only did the government want to use appointments to make the Bank, in Brown's words, more 'representative of the whole of the United Kingdom', but it kept for itself the right to reclaim power in exceptional circumstances (*Financial Times*, 7 May 1997).

By 1988 the British Prime Minister and Chancellor had established a firm grip over the Bank. The problem for the Conservative government was that by claiming so loudly the discretion to judge for itself, in terms of policy outcomes it reduced its room for manoeuvre. As Lawson understood in pushing for an independent Bank of England, control over the Bank and the ability to use that control effectively to a sustained purpose were far from the same thing. This was particularly true since the two principal actors within the core executive were so divided about exchange rate management and monetary policy. Once the foreign exchange markets turned against the government in 1989, the government could decide for itself only at the price of either higher interest rates, or higher inflation, or both. By entering the ERM in October 1990, the government was tacitly admitting that credibility could only be restored by the pursuit of a less discretionary monetary policy. Ministers continued to decide but on the basis of rules, not according to their own self-sustaining judgment. Nonetheless, in the final instance it was too late for ministers to escape hubris for their previous use of power. Having entered the ERM in panic-induced circumstances without due regard for the medium-term consequences, the Conservative government reaped only a small reward for its belated self-discipline. Not only did the government ultimately lose the credibility it acquired during the first year of membership, but it was made palpably impotent in the worst possible economic circumstances.

For the remainder of 1992 and the first half of 1993, the government tried to re-establish its practical autonomy from the ERM states in what were, on the surface at least, unpromising international circumstances. Yet, although the government was relatively successful in achieving some respite from the constraints of the foreign exchange markets, the question of who was deciding British monetary policy quickly became as troublesome as in the immediate years before ERM membership. For his part, Lamont, certainly no fan of the discipline of the ERM, judged that in any sustainable medium- to long-term monetary decision-making process the Bank would, to a lesser or greater extent, have to be given more autonomy and that politicians needed to commit themselves to price stability as a permanent objective. By contrast, Major was not particularly comfortable with either ceding any real power to the Bank, even over the timing of interest rate changes, or accepting *a priori* policy objectives independent of circumstances. In the summer of 1993, despite the inflation target and the Bank's Inflation Report, it was Major's view which appeared to have triumphed, risking all the perennial dangers of a prime minister-dominated monetary policy.

What was critical about Kenneth Clarke's reforms was that he consolidated the ability of the government to judge monetary policy for itself, in seemingly unpropitious international circumstances, by giving the Chancellor a means within the core executive itself to control the Prime Minister on the matter. Even in the face of the EU and OECD march towards independent central banks, Clarke effectively insisted, a British government could judge interest rate decisions for itself so long as it was seen to be taking price stability seriously and it stuck to a formal structure of decision making. What a government could not afford to do was to continue to allow the Prime Minister/Chancellor relationship to dominate the monetary process within the core executive. In this context, since 1994, Clarke was able to use his own policy judgment with less risks than bedevilled Lawson in the last years of his chancellorship, even if in significant part he was simply lucky because of the particulars of sterling's performance.

For the new Labour government, the issue was clearly not that they could not in the circumstances of May 1997 judge for themselves, nor that there was any significant danger in them continuing to do so into the immediately foreseeable future. Choosing to give operational independence to the Bank was simply a different response from that of the Conservative government to the different cost/benefit matrices of short- and long-term considerations in monetary matters. Obviously, at the beginning of a new Parliament with a huge majority and facing a decimated opposition, Labour ministers had a relative freedom from short-term pressures that their immediate predecessors never enjoyed. At the same time, given the likely upward trajectory of interest rates for the remainder of 1997 and into 1998, they could, by divesting themselves of autonomy, try to depoliticise the likely economic consequences of a tighter monetary policy. In these circumstances, therefore, they were in a position to risk trying to secure the benefits of long-term credibility while undoubtedly hoping that they had preserved for themselves, both through setting their own inflation target and the process of appointments, a means of continuing to exercise some control from within the core executive over the Bank.

5 The core executive and the Bank of France (1800–1981)

The old regime

The Bank of France was established at the very beginning of the nineteenth century. At that time the Bank's capital was privately owned and it was run by representatives of the 200 principal shareholders. In 1806, however, a law was passed which increased the core executive's involvement in the Bank's affairs with the creation of the posts of a state-appointed governor and two sub-governors. Thereafter, the general relationship between the Bank and the core executive is best encapsulated in Napoleon Bonaparte's famous statement: 'Je veux que la Banque soit assez dans les mains du gouvernement et n'y soit pas trop' (I want the Bank to be sufficiently in the hands of the government but not too much so). This situation changed fundamentally in 1936, when the core executive became the dominant partner, and the new relationship was then reinforced in 1945 when the Bank's capital was nationalised. In 1973 a further law confirmed this unequal balance of decision-making power. For nearly fifty years, then, from the end of the Second World War to the early 1990s, the Bank of France was owned by the state and controlled by the core executive. Writing about this period, John Goodman has noted that '... the fortunes of the Banque de France have waxed and waned, but at no point has French central-banking legislation or actual practice left any doubt of the central bank's subordinate position vis-à-vis the government' (Goodman 1992: 210). In 1993, however, a fundamental shift occurred in the relationship between the Bank and core executive. With the Bundesbank model clearly in mind, French political leaders granted the Bank of France a considerable degree of economic and political independence. Although still state-owned, the Bank now exhibits a great deal of autonomy and representatives of the core executive are obliged to persuade, cajole and win over members of the Bank in order to try to influence the monetary policy-making process.

In this chapter and the next, the relationship between the French core executive and the Bank of France will be explored. This chapter examines the links between the two in the period from 1800 to 1981. It consists of three parts. The first provides an overview of the relationship between the Bank and the core executive from the time of the Bank's establishment in 1800 to its fundamental reform in 1936. The second part considers the Popular Front's reform of 1936, the nationalisation of the Bank in 1945 and the links between the core executive and the Bank during the period of postwar reconstruction. The third part examines the reform of 1973 in some detail and identifies the relationship between the Bank and the core executive until 1981. The following chapter then considers the relationship from this point on. It examines the conflict between the Bank and the newly-elected socialist government from 1981–4, considers the moves towards independence which began in earnest with the arrival in power of the right-wing coalition in 1986, and finally, pays particular attention to the preparation, passage and implementation of the reform of 1993.

1800–1936

The Bank of France was established by official decree on 18 January 1800. At this early stage the Bank enjoyed only a relatively limited degree of economic independence from the core executive. It did not have the exclusive right to issue bank notes within the national territory; it competed within the same financial system as other private banks; and, even though it was not obliged to finance central government debt, there was provision for it to do so if the bank agreed. By contrast, the Bank enjoyed a considerable degree of political independence (Noël 1888: 98). Its capital was privately owned and its day-to-day operations were supervised by a three person Comité Central (Gentral Committee) which was appointed by the Bank's Conseil Général (General Council). The Conseil Général consisted of fifteen Regents and three non-voting *censeurs* (auditors) who ensured that the Bank's business was properly conducted. The Regents were elected by the Assemblée Générale des Actionnaires (General Assembly of Shareholders) which comprised the 200 principal shareholders in the Bank who represented some of the major banking interests in the state. The President of the Bank served for a one-year renewable term and presided over the Comité Central, the Conseil Général and the Assemblée Générale des Actionnaires. At the outset, then, in terms of the index of central bank independence the Bank of France scored 0.57 on a scale from 0.00 for complete dependence to 1.00 for complete independence (see Appendix 3). As with the Bank of England during the same period, this figure corresponds to a relatively independent central bank.

Even though at this stage the Bank of France was simply one bank amongst a number of others in the system, from the outset it could be distinguished from its rivals in one key respect. It had the support of the First

Consul, soon to be Emperor, Napoleon Bonaparte. Bonaparte was close to the group of bankers who proposed the creation of the Bank; he bought shares in the Bank when it was founded, and he encouraged his family, his government, his generals and members of his personal entourage, including his private secretary, to do the same. Bonaparte's support for the Bank was motivated by the desire to create a stable financial system following the monetary chaos that had occurred during the French Revolution. Indeed, he favoured the creation of a privately owned institution rather than a public one, so as to increase the confidence of investors in the system. He believed that if the level of confidence increased, then so too would the level of financial certainty which would in turn reduce the level of interest rates and allow the government to borrow money at a lower cost than might otherwise be the case (Desaunay 1956: 474). Indeed, Bonaparte is reported to have said: 'I have created the Bank in order to allow discount at 4 per cent' (cited in Goodhart 1991: 118).

Bonaparte's overriding aim was to create a system in which there was only a single private banking institution. This was because he feared that if there were several institutions, then a crisis of confidence in one would have repercussions across all the others (Redon and Besnard 1996: 7). Consequently in 1803, amid rumours that the government had deliberately undermined the financial credibility of rival banking institutions (Redon and Besnard 1996: 8), a law was passed which changed the Bank of France's position. Henceforth it was given the exclusive right of note issue in the Paris area. In the context of a highly centralised political and economic system, this reform meant that competition from the Bank's rivals was effectively abolished, and so the Bank of France assumed the role of the central bank. The 1803 reform also made some minor changes to the organisation of the Bank. Most notably, the composition of the Conseil de Régence was slightly amended to ensure that seven of its fifteen members represented the industrial and commercial classes. In addition, the President's term of office was extended to a two-year renewable term. For the most part, however, the Bank's independence was scarcely altered. At the time when it assumed the role as the country's central bank, representatives of the 200 principal shareholders were still free to make policy themselves.

This situation did not last for long. As early as 1803 the Bank had lent the government over 85 per cent of its reserves (Lévy 1911: 24). By the autumn of 1805, during Bonaparte's Austerlitz campaign, the Bank was faced with an increasing number of demands from private sector borrowers who demanded the restitution of publicly-issued bills. However, the Bank's liquid reserves were insufficient to meet all their demands and the Conseil Général voted to limit the amount of money that borrowers could be reimbursed. The effect was to undermine confidence in the system, to provoke a number of bankruptcies and to call into question the Bank's authority. Bonaparte reacted angrily. On 27 January 1806, the day after he returned from his victory at Austerlitz, he called together his economic advisers, sacked the Treasury Minister and gave the incoming minister the responsibility for reforming the Bank of France. By early April the law was ready and the Emperor made his position quite clear: 'Mais je dois être le maître dans tout ce dont je me mêle, et surtout dans ce qui regarde la Banque, qui est bien plus à l'empéreur qu'aux actionnaires, puisqu'elle bat monnaie' (I have to be the master of everything in which I get involved, particularly with regard to the Bank, which belongs more to the Emperor than to the shareholders, because it prints money) (quoted in Redon and Besnard 1996: 9). In short, Bonaparte had decided to introduce a degree of public control over the Bank.

The law which was passed on 22 April 1806, along with the subsequent decree which was issued on 16 January 1808 (the so-called 'statuts fondamentaux' (basic statutes)), reformed both the role of the Bank and its administrative organisation. By virtue of these reforms, the core executive was given greater powers to control the Bank. The Comité Central was abolished and in its place the head of state, on the proposal of the Finance Minister, appointed a governor and two sub-governors, all of whom served for an indefinite period. In addition, the composition of the Conseil Général was reformed. It now consisted of fifteen people elected by the Assemblée Générale, three of whom had to represent state financial institutions and only five of whom now had to represent commercial and industrial interests. All members of the Conseil Général served for a five-year renewable term. In addition, the Assemblée Générale also elected three non-voting *censeurs* representing commercial and industrial interests, who served for a three-year renewable term. Decisions of the Conseil Général were made subject to the governor's countersignature, and the governor also had the power to make certain internal appointments within the Bank. At the same time, however, the level of core executive control was attenuated somewhat by the fact that the governor was paid by the Bank and had to own 100 of the Bank's shares (sub-governors had to own 50 shares each). According to Jean Bouvier, this latter requirement meant that the governor was 'l'obligé absolu de la haute banque' (totally in debt to the Bank) (Bouvier 1973: 171) because the governor was usually forced to borrow from the Regents in order to buy the shares. Finally, the Bank's exclusive right of note issue was extended, its capital was increased and its shareholders benefited from a reform in the distribution of dividends. In terms of the index of central bank independence after the 1806 and 1808 reforms, the Bank of France scored 0.42, confirming that the Bank was slightly less independent than before (see Appendix 3).

The 'statuts fondamentaux' established the basic relationship between the Bank and the core executive which lasted until 1936. It is certainly the case that during this period there were calls for the degree of core executive control to be reformed. For example, in 1814, following Bonaparte's fall from power, the Bank lobbied heavily for greater political and economic independence. In particular, the Assemblée Générale des Actionnaires wanted to regain the right to appoint the governor and the sub-governors, and was supported in this aim by the Finance Minister but not, significantly, by parliament. A similar reform was also defeated five years later. By contrast, in 1848 Proudhon called for the Bank to be taken under public control and for it to be known as the Banque Nationale de France (French National Bank) (Noël 1888: 114). Similarly, in the 1890s the socialists criticised the Bank and Millerand warned of the 'danger qu'il y a à remettre le premier instrument de crédit aux main toutes-puissantes de quelques financiers internationaux' (danger of putting the main instrument of credit in the all-powerful hands of a few international financiers) (quoted in Bouvier 1973: 176). Even though the basic relationship between the Bank and the core executive remained the same during this period, there were some important operational changes. For example, in 1848, when the Bank's exclusive right of note issue was extended to cover the whole national territory and not just Paris, the Bank also agreed to advance the Treasury certain limited sums of money for a fixed period (Lévy 1911: 28) and continued to do so regularly thereafter. More generally, Redon and Besnard note that each time the Bank's exclusive right of note issue came up for renewal the state took the opportunity to insist on 'des concessions réciproques' (reciprocal concessions) (Redon and Besnard 1996: 18). So, for example, in 1857, against the background of accusations that the Bank was maintaining a high discount rate in order to maximise the profits of its shareholders, the state renewed the Bank's note privilege for a further forty years but also insisted that if the discount rate was raised above 6 per cent then a share of the resultant profits would be transferred to the state's social funds. In 1897 this figure was then reduced to 5 per cent.

In short, the 1806 and 1808 reforms established a relationship of mutual dependence between the Bank and the core executive. This relationship was based on a '[s]ubtile répartition des pouvoirs' (subtle power-sharing arrangement) (Bon-Garcin 1994: 5). Following these reforms, it is apparent that the Bank and the core executive were 'étroitement associée' (closely associated) (Plessis 1985: 3). For example, the Finance Minister and the Bank's governor met regularly, the Finance Minister was informed of the Bank's situation on a daily basis (Plessis 1985: 8–9) and interest rate decisions were discussed and approved by the Conseil Général but only 'après que le ministre des Finances ait été informé des intentions de la Banque et qu'il ait donné au moins tacitement son consentement' (after the Finance Minister had been informed of the Bank's intentions and had at least tacitly given his consent)

(Plessis 1985: 328). Similarly, there was a close imbrication of political and financial elites. Bank representatives frequently sat in the legislature and, occasionally, in government and there were also close social and personal ties between core executive and Bank representatives (Plessis 1985: 6–16).

As a result of the mutually dependent relationship between the Bank and the core executive, the relationship between the two institutions was for the most part cordial. Accordingly, in their study of the Bank, Redon and Besnard state that 'les conflits entre gouverneur et Conseil général sont quasiment inexistants jusqu'en 1914' (conflicts between the governor and the General Council were just about non-existent until 1914) (Redon and Besnard 1996: 10). Similarly, in his study of the correlation between changes in government and core executive appointments to the Bank, Aubin finds that during this period incoming governments rarely used their formal powers to shape the composition of the Bank (Aubin 1985). Indeed, Gambetta's decision to dismiss governor Denormandie in 1881 is perhaps the sole exception to the general rule. It is certainly the case that the Bank and the core executive sometimes had divergent interests. For example, Bouvier notes the occasions when the government, which wanted a lower interest rate so as to boost the economy, came into conflict with the Bank, which feared that any subsequent inflation would threaten its profits (Bouvier 1988: 76). Overall, however, the 1806 and 1808 reforms did not simply establish either a politically and economically dependent central bank or one which was able to manipulate core executive representatives at will. Instead, Bonaparte's famous dictum quoted at the beginning of this chapter accurately reflects the relationship between the Bank and the core executive during most of the nineteenth century and the early part of the twentieth century.

The turning point in the relationship between the Bank and the core executive came as a result of events which occurred in the interwar period. During the war the Bank had been instrumental in financing the government's war effort. By the end of the war, however, the franc was worth only one-fifth of its 1914 value. Consequently, deflationary policies were needed if the value of the franc was to be restored to its prewar level. However, such policies proved to be very difficult to maintain and resulted in the Bank and the core executive each perceiving that they had increasingly divergent interests. Hence conflict between the two institutions became almost inevitable. Faced with the need to finance the budget deficit, public institutions (the government and/or the parliament) were unwilling either to cut expenditure significantly or to raise taxes sharply. Faced with this situation the Bank, under the direction of the governor, Georges Robineau, squared the circle in the short term by reluctantly agreeing to exceed the amount of money that it could legally lend to the government and to publish balance sheets which would hide this fact (Simmons 1994: 153). However, as successive governments, notably those headed by left-wing Cartel des Gauches representatives from 1924–6, failed to address the underlying economic problems, so the financial position continued to worsen and the relationship with the Bank deteriorated. In 1925 the illicit practices became public and the government fell. The new government, however, continued to follow the same policies. As a result, in July 1926 Robineau's successor at the Bank, Émile Moreau, supported by the Conseil Général, announced that he was immediately cutting the Treasury's borrowing facility. In the face of another economic crisis, the Cartel des Gauches finally collapsed and the right returned to office. In his memoirs Moreau noted: 'L'attitude ferme de la Banque de France, en obligeant le gouvernement à dévolier publiquement la mauvaise situation de la Trésorerie et en l'empêchant, pour y remédier, de recourir à des subterfuges illégaux, a beaucoup contribué à ce résulat' (The Bank's firm stance, by obliging the government to reveal publicly the bad state of the Treasury and by preventing it, in order to remedy the situation, from resorting to illegal subterfuges, contributed greatly to the end result) (Moreau 1954: 38).

The experience of the Cartel des Gauches changed popular attitudes towards the Bank and hardened the opposition of the left and centre-left. It highlighted the fact that the organisation of the Conseil Général had not been altered for over a hundred years; it showed that the Conseil Général was dominated by the major industrial, commercial and banking concerns (the '200 families' as the members of the Assemblée Générale came to be known); it indicated that when there was a severe conflict of interest between the Bank and the government, then the core executive had few powers to influence the Bank's decision-making process; and it demonstrated that the Bank was willing to bring about the downfall of democratically elected governments. In the light of this experience and against the immediate background of further conflicts between the Bank and successive governments during the mid-1930s, the left resolved to reform the Bank. When it was elected to office in 1936, the communist, socialist and radical coalition, the so-called Popular Front government, dismissed the existing governor and set about reforming 'la grande dame de la rue de La Vrillière'.

1936–73

In the 1936 election, the Popular Front's manifesto was unequivocal:

> Pour soustraire le crédit et l'épargne à la domination de l'oligarchie économique, faire de la Banque de France, aujourd'hui banque privée, la banque de la France: suppression du conseil des régents; élargisse-

> ment du pouvoir du gouvernement sous le contrôle permanent d'un conseil composé de représentants du pouvoir législatif, de représentants du pouvoir exécutif et de représentants des grandes forces organisées du travail et de l'activité industrielle, commerciale et agricole; transformation du capital en obligations, des mesures étant prises pour garantir les intérêts des petits porteurs' (To remove credit and saving from the domination of the economic oligarchy and to make the Bank of France, currently a private bank, France's bank: abolition of the General Council; extension of the government's power by way of the permanent control of a council composed of legislative and executive branch representatives and representatives of the great organised forces of labour and industrial, commercial and agricultural activity; transformation of the capital into government bonds, measures taken to guarantee the interests of the small shareholders).
>
> (quoted in Prate 1987: 131)

Against this background, when it assumed power in May 1936, the Popular Front immediately signalled that a reform of the Bank of France was one of its legislative priorities.

On 6 June 1936, the newly-formed government announced that it was preparing 'une réforme des statuts de la Banque de France garantissant dans sa gestion la prédominance des intérêts nationaux' (a reform of the Bank of France's statutes guaranteeing the predominance of national interests in its work) (Prate 1987: 132). By wording the announcement in this way, the government left open the question of whether the Bank's capital should be nationalised. The Finance Minister then devolved responsibility for preparing the details of the bill onto an expert 'Para-ministerial Commission' which unanimously recommended that the Bank's capital should be nationalised (Dauphin-Meunier 1936: 199). In fact, however, as the government's initial announcement had indicated, there was little ministerial support for nationalisation within the coalition. The Radical party was opposed to any such measure, and the Socialist and Communist parties were reluctant to insist on this aspect of the reform for fear of jeopardising the government's overall economic programme by alienating the support of the centrist Radical party (Dauphin-Meunier 1936: 199). By 19 June, therefore, the matter had been resolved; it was decided that the Bank's capital would remain privately owned and that its governing structures would simply be reformed.

The law of 24 July 1936 did not significantly change the economic indicators of independence. However, it did fundamentally reform the political indicators. The law shifted the balance of political power between the Bank and the core executive and, in so doing, established the basic political division of responsibilities between the two institutions that lasted until 1993. Even though the Bank officially continued to set interest rates after 1936, the reform changed the relationship between the Bank and the core executive in a number of ways. First, it changed the composition of the Assemblée Générale des Actionnaires. Rather than being restricted to the 200 principal shareholders, the Assemblée Générale was opened up to all 40,947 shareholders, so ending the overwhelming influence of the '200 families'. Second, it changed the position of the governor. Although the governor's powers were not significantly altered, the governor was no longer obliged to hold shares in the Bank and his salary was now fixed by the state rather than by the Bank. Both measures were designed to reduce the governor's dependence on the Bank. Third, and most importantly, the law changed the size and composition of the Conseil Général. In addition to the governor and sub-governors, the Conseil Général now consisted of twenty councillors. Two of these were elected by the Assemblée Générale from among 'les manufacturiers, fabricants et commerçants' (factory owners, manufacturers and traders) and, notably, not from amongst representatives of the banking class; nine represented the 'intérêts collectifs de la nation' (the collective interests of the nation), three of whom were appointed by the Finance, Economy and Colonies Ministers respectively and six by state-owned organisations such as the Caisse des Dépôts et des Consignations; and nine represented 'les intérêts économiques et sociaux' (economic and social interests) such as the Chambers of Commerce, the Bank's staff and the communist CGT union confederation. In these ways, therefore, even though the powers of the Conseil Général were scarcely altered, the nature of the institution was fundamentally modified. Those appointed by the core executive now enjoyed a clear majority. In terms of the index of central bank independence, the Bank of France now scored 0.13 which was equivalent to a relatively dependent central bank (see Appendix 3).

Even before the reform was officially voted, its effects were apparent. For example, in June 1936 the Bank agreed to lend the government 24 billion francs so as to meet its immediate spending requirements. Furthermore, the level of additional advances that the Bank agreed to lend increased incrementally from a ceiling of 10 billion (milliards) francs in 1936 to 55 billion francs in 1939 (Prate 1987: 140). During this time the Bank did not lose sight of its preoccupation with currency stability. Indeed, in 1938 the governor wrote to the Minister of Finance to voice his concerns. Nevertheless, the contrast between the situation prior to and after the 1936 reform is striking. As Prate notes, somewhat sourly: 'sans doute les circonstances étaient-elles exceptionnelles, du fait des menaces extérieures. Mais on ne peut que constater au moins une coïncidence dans le temps entre l'affaiblissement de la Banque de France, la multiplication des avances au

Trésor et la dépréciation de la monnaie' (Undoubtedly the circumstances were exceptional, as a result of the foreign threat. But one cannot fail to notice the coincidence between the weakening of the Bank of France, the increasing number of advances to the Treasury and the depreciation of the currency) (Prate 1987: 141).

During the Second World War and the German occupation of France the Bank was subject to further reform. First, in November 1940 a law was passed which reformed the size and the composition of the Conseil Général. The number of councillors on the Conseil Général was reduced from 20 to 11, with the Finance Minister appointing four members, public sector financial interests and the Assemblée Général three each and the Bank's staff one. Equally, the number of *censeurs* was increased to four, with two as before being elected by the Assemblée Générale and two being appointed by the Finance Minister, including, most notably, the Directeur du Trésor. Second, in June 1941 the Commission de Contrôle des Banques (Banking Control Commission) was established, which assumed responsibility for regulating the banking sector. The Commission was headed by the governor of the Bank of France, but was largely under the control of the core executive as it consisted also of the Directeur du Trésor (the head of the Treasury) and the president of another state-controlled banking regulation committee who was appointed by the Finance Minister.

In the furore surrounding the Liberation, the Bank of France was again a focus of political attention. As early as December 1944 the Liberation government moved to modify the size and composition of the Conseil Général once more. This time the number of councillors was increased from 11 to 14: four councillors were chosen by each of the heads of four public sector financial institutions, the Caisse des Dépôts et des Consignations, the Crédit Foncier de France, the Crédit National and the Caisse Nationale de Crédit Agricole; seven, representing the industrial, commercial and agricultural sectors, were appointed by the Finance Minister; one was elected by the Bank's staff; and two were designated by the Assemblée Générale. Councillors were appointed for a renewable, four-year term on a staggered basis. Furthermore, and in contrast to the situation in 1936, a consensus emerged that the Bank's capital had to be nationalised. Indeed, three of the main political forces, the communists, the socialists and the Conseil National de la Résistance (National Council of the Resistance), all proposed reforms to this effect. In part, this consensus was the result of long-standing grievances against the Bank arising out the experience of the 1920s and 1930s. In part, it was also the result of the fear that if the Bank remained privately owned then, whatever the composition of the Conseil Général, it would still try to undermine the government's state-directed postwar economic reconstruction strategy. Certainly in the context of the extensive nationalisation programme which the government was committed to undertaking, it was soon apparent that this time the Bank of France stood little chance of being spared.

The bill to nationalise the Bank of France was prepared during the course of 1945 (see Koch 1983: 45–51). Responsibility for drafting the reform lay with Finance Ministry officials in the Direction du Trésor (the Treasury). However, successive versions of the reform were also sent to the governor of the Bank, Emmanuel Monick, for his comments. The governor tried to convince officials both that the state should take a controlling share in the Bank's capital rather than simply nationalising it outright, and that the governor and sub-governors should be appointed for a fixed-term five-year period so as to increase their independence. However, following political arbitrations by the Finance Minister, neither recommendation was accepted. As Prate observes generally: 'la Banque elle-même n'est pas en position de se faire entendre' (the Bank was not in a position to make itself heard) (Prate 1987: 168); and as Koch notes about the latter proposal more specifically: 'il est évident qu'une telle réforme ne se concilie pas aisément avec les idées des détracteurs de l'Institut d'émission' (it is clear that such a reform was not easy to square with the ideas of those who belittle the Bank) (Koch 1983: 47). In the end, the Bank had to be satisfied with little more than the fact that its exclusive right of note issue was extended indefinitely.

For Goodman the law of 2 December 1945 'represented a change greater in form than in substance' (Goodman 1992: 47), indicating that the 1936 reform was more significant in changing the relationship between the Bank and the core executive. Indeed, the calculations in Appendix 3 confirm this fact. In terms of the index of central bank independence the Bank of France scored 0.13 still (see Appendix 3). Certainly the centrepiece of the 1945 legislation, as set out in the first line of Article 1 of the law, was the nationalisation of the Bank's capital. Notwithstanding the importance of this aspect of the reform, other elements of the Bank's relationship with the core executive remained largely unchanged. For example, the law established the Conseil National du Crédit (CNC, National Credit Council) which was designed to act as a mini-parliament (Goodman 1992: 47) to discuss credit policy. The Bank was officially to participate in these discussions and to provide information for the other participants. However, the CNC scarcely lived up to the ambitions of its founders and credit policy was to all intents and purposes managed by the Direction du Trésor. Similarly, Article 3 of the law simply stated that the composition of the Conseil Général and the Bank's statutes would be modified by a further law to be passed before 28 February 1946. In fact, although the government did prepare a bill to this effect, no such law was voted. In May 1946 the bill was withdrawn because the minister responsible, André Philip, stated that the reform was being proposed 'pour éviter qu'elle [la Banque de France] ne soit tentée à l'avenir de continuer à mener une politique indépendante de celle du Gouvernement . . .' (so as to avoid the Bank being tempted in the future to conduct a policy independent of the government's) (quoted in Secrétariat d'État à la Présidence du Conseil et à l'Information 1946: 13). Even though the Bank had been nationalised the previous year, parliament still considered that the minister was overstepping the mark by presenting the reform in this way. As a result, the composition of the Conseil Général was still determined by the December 1944 decree with the exception that the two places previously reserved for representatives of the Assemblée Général des Actionnaires were abolished (along with the places for the *censeurs* that it elected) as the institution itself was now defunct.

The 1936–45 reforms created the formal, statutory context within which the relationship between the Bank and the core executive operated until 1973. The core executive was clearly the dominant partner in this relationship. For example, in the period from July to December 1947 the Bank (reluctantly) agreed to increase the level of temporary advances to the Treasury from 100 to 200 billion francs. Similarly, through 1953 the Bank again (equally reluctantly) agreed to increase the level of direct advances to 240 billion francs. For Prate, these examples 'illustrent bien les limites du système dans lequel la Banque ne dispose pas des pouvoirs nécessaires pour s'opposer aux demandes du Trésor' (illustrate well the limits of a system in which the Bank did not possess the powers necessary to refuse the Treasury's demands) (Prate 1987: 180). This is not to say that the Bank was a silent partner in the relationship; for example, Bouvier cites one former Bank official who argues that after 1945, '[a]ucune décision importante n'est prise de part et d'autre sans consultation préalable' (no important decision was taken on either side without prior consultation) (Bouvier 1987: 24). Similarly Koch, himself a former official at the Bank, cites the former Directeur du Trésor, François Bloch-Lainé, as saying that in his experience '[on aboutissait à] un système forcément un peu équivoque de partage des attributions entre les deux pouvoirs' (we arrived at a system which was necessarily a little equivocal whereby there was a distribution of responsibilities between the two institutions) (Koch 1983: 372). For Koch, successive governors tried to warn of the consequences of the government's economic and monetary policy but the Bank was not in a position to insist that its policy recommendations be pursued (ibid.).

Even though the Bank was clearly subordinate to the core executive after 1945, it did occasionally attempt to assert its authority. Particularly during the economically and politically troubled Fourth Republic (1946–58), the Bank tried to shape the government's economic policies. In the immediate postwar period the budget deficit stood at 14 per cent of GNP in 1946 and 6 and 7 per cent respectively in 1947 and 1948. Partly as a consequence of this and partly as a result of other factors, the level of inflation was also very high, with prices increasing by 80 per cent in 1946 and 60 per cent in the period from March–December 1947 (Koch 1983: 83). Faced with the need to finance reconstruction and being unwilling to raise taxes considerably, the government was bound, as at previous times, to resort more and more frequently to the Bank to cover its budget deficit. Keen to remedy this situation, the Bank began to consider raising the discount rate, which stood at 1.6 per cent after January 1945, to control credit, reduce inflation and shore up the value of the franc. Early in 1947 the Conseil Général decided on a first increase and then in November 1947 a second, bringing the rate to 2.5 per cent. In his role as *censeur* on the Conseil Général, the Directeur du Trésor, concerned about the rising cost of government borrowing, objected to the second increase but was unable to prevent it (Prate 1987: 172). However, as a result of pressure from the Finance Minister personally the rate was soon lowered to 2.25 per cent. Quickly, though, pressure to raise the discount rate resurfaced. On 4 September 1948 governor Monick convened an extraordinary meeting of the Conseil Général which, again despite 'les plus expresses réserves' (the most formal reservations) (Koch 1983: 147) of the Directeur du Trésor, agreed to a 1 per cent increase. Again the Minister intervened and again the rate was reduced slightly. Nevertheless, the Bank showed that it had the capacity to influence monetary policy at the margins.

By 1950 the combination of a new governor, Wilfred Baumgartner, and further pressure from the government resulted in further reductions in the discount rate. For Prate these reductions demonstrated the weakness of the Bank and the political and economic preoccupations of the government: 'la Banque de France . . . doit céder aux injonctions du Trésor, celui-ci étant animé par le seul souci de réduire les charges de la dette publique et indifférent aux conséquences inflationnistes du financement monétaire du déficit budgétaire' (The Bank had to give in to the Treasury's demands, the latter being motivated simply by the desire to reduce the cost of servicing the public debt and being indifferent to the inflationary consequences of financing the budget deficit by printing more money) (Prate 1987: 173). Soon, however, the Bank's preoccupation with monetary stability and the government's concern for economic growth again came into clear conflict. Early in 1952, Edgar Faure's newly formed government was in severe economic and political difficulty and in the night of 28–29 February it was brought down by parliament. The next day Faure (who was also the Finance Minister) wrote to Baumgartner requesting that the Bank grant further temporary advances to the Treasury to meet the state's immediate economic needs. That same day the governor convened the Conseil Général which refused in principle but did agree to some exceptional measures. In his formal reply to Faure, Baumgartner stated categorically that 'c'est le sentiment profond du Conseil Général que l'État comme les particuliers vivent au-dessus de leurs moyens' (it is the Conseil Général's firm belief that the state and its citizens are living above their means) (see *Le Monde*, 2 March 1952). Baumgartner's letter, which was made public, had a profound effect on political opinion. Indeed, the new Finance Minister, Antoine Pinay, followed a policy which was much closer to the wishes of the Bank than his predecessors and in so doing he gained the reputation of having come to the rescue of the franc. For Prate the fact that the Bank did actually bale out the government showed that it had few powers other than the 'droit de remontrance' (the right to reprimand) (Prate 1987: 181). Moreover, it appears that Faure and the President of the Republic, Vincent Auriol, may have published Baumgartner's letter in order deliberately to provoke a crisis which would highlight the country's perilous economic position (Elgey 1968: 28). Whatever the truth of the matter, this incident does demonstrate that the Bank was influential in shaping the economic and political context within which political decisions were taken. Indeed, the Directeur du Trésor at the time has personally confirmed the governor's influence: 'il pesait . . . du moins d'un poids suffisant pour jouer . . . un vrai rôle' (he was at least sufficiently important to play a real part) (Bloch-Lainé 1976: 98).

These examples show that during the turbulent years of the Fourth Republic the Bank was sometimes in a position to assert some authority. However, increasingly and especially during the early years of the more stable Fifth Republic (1958–), it was less well placed to do so. For example, according to Saint-Geours, the Bank had little involvement either in the preparation or the implementation of the 1958 Rueff economic programme (Saint-Geours 1979: 108). Although this version of events is contested by both Koch (1983: 281) and Prate, who, notably, emphasises Baumgartner's role in the 1958 devaluation (1987: 190–1), it is certainly the case that the Bank had only one representative on the eight-person committee which drafted the programme. Similarly, also according to Saint-Geours, the 1963 economic stabilisation plan was the brainchild of the Foreign Affairs Minister, Maurice Couve de Murville, and one of his advisers, Olivier Wormser, and was prepared by senior ministers and their advisers in a series of meetings chaired by President de Gaulle personally. On this occasion, Prate himself acknowledges that: 'rien n'indique que l'Institut d'émission ait joué un rôle moteur dans l'élaboration d'une politique de stabilité' (nothing indicates that the Bank played an active part in drawing up the economic stabilistation policy) (Prate 1987: 199). Finally, the decision not to devalue the franc in November 1968 was taken by de Gaulle himself. The then governor, Jacques Brunet, is said to have been in favour of a devaluation, and the fact that he left office less than six months later led to rumours that he was being punished for proposing such a policy (*Combat*, 4 April 1969). It should be noted, though, that the franc was in fact devalued in August 1969. Overall, Saint-Geours argues that from 1956 onwards 'la puissance du gouverneur de l'institut d'émission tend à diminuer' (the governor's power tended to diminish) (Saint-Geours 1979: 109). Indeed, by the late 1960s he argues that the Bank 's'astreint à un rôle presque exclusivement technique . . .' (forced itself to keep to an almost exclusively technical role) (Saint-Geours 1979: 110).

1973–86

By the early 1970s the environment within which the Bank operated was changing. In 1969 the Marjolin–Sadrin–Wormser Report recommended various reforms of the Bank's economic functions. By 1970 the government was increasingly relying on its obligatory credit restriction policy (l'encadrement du crédit) to control borrowing. Finally, the increasing internationalisation of financial markets and the collapse of the Bretton Woods agreement meant that the Bank's attentions were directed more and more to this area. Against this background, in 1971 the newly appointed governor of the Bank, Olivier Wormser, proposed to update the Bank's statutes so as to accommodate recent developments and to prepare for future ones. Accordingly, the Bank's services began to draft a bill to this effect. When it was complete it was sent to the Finance Ministry where officials in the Direction du Trésor drafted a 'contreprojet' (counterbill) (Coudé de Foresto 1972: 10). Following the final arbitrations of the Finance Minister, Valéry Giscard d'Estaing, and then a very limited number of parliamentary amendments, the reform finally became law in January 1973. This law established the formal relationship between the Bank and the core executive that lasted for the next twenty years.

Despite the public declarations of governor Wormser (Coudé de Foresto 1972: 13), it is apparent that in the preliminary stages of the bill's preparation the Bank and the Treasury had somewhat different conceptions of the trajectory that the future relationship between the two institutions should take. For example, the Bank's bill stated that the Bank would participate in the preparation of monetary policy, whereas the Treasury's bill stated that the Bank would participate only in its implementation (*Le Monde*, 22 March 1973). Similarly, the Bank's bill proposed that the Bank should be 'chargée de la gestion des réserves officielles de changes' (responsible for managing official currency reserves), whereas the Treasury's bill proposed that the Bank's role in this area should only be conducted 'sous la responsabilité de l'État et dans le cadre des instructions du ministre de l'économie et des finances . . .' (under the responsibility of the State and in the framework of the Finance Minister's instructions) (*Le Monde*, 22 March 1973). Finally, the Bank's bill recommended retaining the existing composition of the Conseil Général, whereas the Treasury's bill recommended reforming it so as to give the Finance Minister greater powers of appointment (Duprat 1976: 413, note 206). Overall, the impression in both France and abroad was that Giscard wanted 'n'accorder à la Banque qu'un rôle consultatif dans les questions de politique monétaire' (only to grant the Bank a consultative role in monetary policy matters) (quoted in Bouvier 1987: 29). In fact, however, following a meeting in March 1972 between Wormser and Giscard the bill which was finally agreed represented a compromise between the Bank's and the Treasury's positions. According to the bill which was agreed by the Council of Ministers, the Bank would participate in the preparation of monetary policy (Article 4) but it would still have to manage currency reserves in the framework of the Finance Minister's general instructions (Article 3), while the composition of the Conseil Général would be reformed (Article 14) but its functions would also be expanded (Article 15).

During the parliamentary stage of the process, the government's bill was subject only to relatively minor amendment. In the Senate the bill's rapporteur, Yvon Coudé de Foresto, focused on two particular aspects of the bill that the Finance Commission believed needed to be reformed; the Bank's legal status and the composition of the Conseil Général (Coudé de Foresto 1972: 3). First, the Commission wanted Article 1 of the bill to state that the Bank was 'une entreprise nationale en la forme d'une société anonyme' (a national company in the form of a limited company). In the Senate debate, however, Giscard made it quite clear that he personally had decided not to insert any such statement in the bill bccause he considered the Bank to be a unique organisation unlike any other state-owned company (Sénat, Débat, 2 November 1972: 1901). Consequently, Giscard used the government's majority to defeat the amendment. Second, the Commission wanted both to amend the proposed composition of the Conseil Général so as to maintain the representation of the public sector financial institutions, such as the Caisse des Dépôts et des Consignations, and to ensure that appointments were not to be made by simple ministerial decree (with the Prime Minister's countersignature) but by the Council of Ministers as a whole. This time, Giscard used the government's majority to veto the first amendment but he accepted the second. In the National Assembly, even fewer changes were both proposed and passed. Indeed, the bill's rapporteur, Guy Sabatier, proposed a total of only thirteen amendments affecting only ten articles. Again, the main focus of attention concerned the composition of the Conseil Général. Giscard accepted an amendment to increase the number of *censeurs* to two but then, rather confusingly, proposed to withdraw the amendment that he had already accepted in the Senate whereby appointments were to be made by the Council of Ministers. This proposal was accepted by the National Assembly, the amendment was reintroduced during the bill's second reading in the Senate and passed against the government's wishes. Rather than creating any more confusion or ill-will on this issue, during the bill's second reading in the National Assembly the government decided to accept the amendment. Following a third reading in the Senate, the bill was passed on 18 December 1972 and became law on 3 January 1973.

Prior to the 1973 law, the Bank was governed by a total of 192 articles contained in 35 laws, 6 ordinances, 16 conventions, 6 decree laws and 40 decrees (Sabatier 1972: 2). Indeed, Article 42 stated that the new law was replacing legislation which dated as far back as 1803. For governor Wormser, the Bank had long been operating 'sous l'empire de textes complexes, voire archaïques . . .' (under a regime of complicated, indeed, archaic texts) (Coudé de Foresto 1972: 13). Similarly, for one historian, the relationship between the Bank and the government was marked by 'l'incohérence qui engendre fatalement discordes et mécomptes' (an incoherence which unavoidably breeds discord and disappointment) (Elgey 1968: 121). So, the 1973 law was significant if for no other reason than that it represented the first wholesale revision of the Bank's statutes for at least forty years. This is not to say, however, that the final text was either comprehensive or unambiguous; during the course of the parliamentary debates, the government was accused more than once of not addressing certain issues such as the role of the Conseil National du Crédit, and of addressing others in a rather vague manner. In this context, it is noteworthy that a senior Bank official publicly insisted that the text needed to be general (quoted in Bouvier 1987: 30) and according to one former senior Treasury official the ambiguous wording of the text was a premeditated decision which was 'savamment négocié' (presciently negotiated) between Giscard and Wormser (Haberer 1990: 28, note 2). Still, by virtue of the fact that the 1973 law affected both the political and economic indicators of independence, then its contents are worthy of brief examination.

In terms of political independence, all four aspects were addressed (see Appendix 3). For example, Article 10 stated that the governor and the two sub-governors were to be appointed by presidential decree. In addition, Article 12 stated that they were not able to hold other positions. However, no mention was made that prior qualifications were needed for appointment; there was no official nomination mechanism, no fixed term of office, no indication as to whether the appointments were renewable, no staggering of appointments and no provision for dismissal. All of these elements are consistent with a relatively dependent central bank. The conditions concerning the Conseil Général and the Bank's decision-making process were slightly different. One member of the board was elected by the Bank's personnel and the rest were appointed by the Council of Ministers on the basis of proposals made by the Minister of Finance. Appointments were staggered, limited to six years, and appointees had to have some professional qualifications. Moreover, there was a collective decision-making process amongst members of the Conseil Général. Indeed, in the Senate debate Giscard emphasised this point vigorously: 'Aux États Unis, par exemple, c'est le conseil général du système de réserve fédéral qui délibère d'une façon approfondie sur la politique monétaire. Je voudrais que nous ayons un organisme de cette nature . . .' (In the US, for example, it is the Federal Reserve's equivalent of the General Council which considers monetary policy in a thorough way. I want us to have an institution of this sort) (Sénat, Débat, 2 November 1972: 1905). All of these factors are consistent with a relatively independent central bank. However, there was no security of tenure and there were government-appointed *censeurs* on the board who had an effective veto over decisions.

In terms of economic independence, Article 1 of the 1973 law gave the Bank for the first time a specific mission. It stated that: 'La Banque de France est l'institution qui, dans le cadre de la politique économique et financière de la nation, reçoit de l'État la mission générale de veiller sur la monnaie et le crédit' (The Bank is the institution which, in the framework of the nation's economic and financial policy, receives from the State the general mission to watch over the currency and credit). Similarly, Article 3 indicated that the Bank intervened in exchange rate policy but only in the framework of the general instructions laid down by the Minister of Finance, and Article 4 stated that the Bank participated in the preparation and implementation of monetary policy but that the government was responsible for deciding such policy. Also, various articles made provision for Bank lending to the Treasury, while no mention was made of any Bank involvement in the governmental budgetary process and no changes were made to the supervision of the wider banking system in which the Bank was already involved.

For Giscard, the 1973 law was designed to increase the autonomy of the Bank of France, most notably by making the Conseil Général a more deliberative institution (Assemblée nationale, Débat, 28 November 1972: 5681). Rather confusingly for Giscard's colleague, the Secretary of State for the Budget, Jean Taittinger, the law was designed not to increase its autonomy but to ensure its independence. In the context of the 1993 debate between Édouard Balladur and Edmond Alphandéry on the status of the Bank of France (see Chapter 6), this distinction between 'autonomy' and 'independence', however spurious, is quite interesting. For Taittinger, the concept of 'autonomy' implied that 'la politique monétaire du pays pourrait être pratiquement conçue, définie et exécutée par la Banque de France' (the country's monetary policy could be virtually thought up, defined and implemented by the Bank), whereas 'independence' (somewhat tautologically) meant that 'la politique monétaire appartient aux pouvoirs publics, mais que la Banque de France a un caractère d'indépendance qui lui permet d'exprimer sa volonté dans le cadre et le respect, bien entendu, qui la régissent . . .' (monetary policy belongs to the government, but that the independent nature of the Bank allows it to express its will in the context of and still respecting, of course, the texts which govern it) (Sénat, Débat, 14 December 1972: 3093).

In fact, the 1973 law did not fundamentally change the relationship between the Bank and the core executive. In terms of the index of central bank independence the Bank of France scored 0.18 (see Appendix 3). Overall, the contents of the 1973 law were still consistent with those of a relatively dependent central bank, both politically and economically. For Goodman, the effect of the law was to show that 'the Banque de France is clearly subordinated to the government in the conduct of monetary policy' (Goodman 1992: 50). For the Conseil Économique et Social, ' . . . l'intervention de l'État (en pratique la Direction du Trésor du ministère de l'économie et des finances) est partout présente' (the intervention of the State (in practice the Treasury) is present everywhere) (Conseil Économique et Social 1993: 12). For Bouvier, 'Une chose est sûre: l'État n'a rien cédé de ses droits, bien au contraire' (One thing is certain: the State gave away none of its powers, quite the contrary) (Bouvier 1987: 32). Indeed, governor Wormser was one of the first to appreciate that the core executive was still the dominant partner in the relationship; in June 1974 he was summarily dismissed from office by the newly elected President, a certain Valéry Giscard d'Estaing, for having publicly criticised the government's economic policy in a newspaper article.

Despite Giscard's publicly stated intention, the Bank's internal decision-making process after the 1973 reform was very similar to the process before the reform. (Much of the subsequent information is derived from a personal interview with a senior bank official at the time, conducted on 17 September 1996). The governor dominated the decision-making process within the Bank: 'Les décisions de politique monétaire étaient largement prises par le gouverneur' (non-attributable interview). The governor set the Conseil Général's agenda and was formally responsible for the decisions that it took. Between the two sub-governors there was a particular distribution of responsibilities: one sub-governor was responsible for the domestic aspects of monetary policy and for the management of the Bank itself, including relations with the Bank's personnel, while the other was responsible for the external aspects of monetary policy and spent much of the time abroad in this capacity. There was some delegation of the governor's powers to the sub-governors. For example, one of the sub-governors regularly took the governor's place as the president of the Commission de Contrôle des Banques. Nevertheless, despite the fact that the governor and sub-governors were bound to work very closely with each other, it is apparent that ultimate decision-making responsibility within the Bank lay with the governor personally. By contrast, the Conseil Général was little more than a talking shop. It met once a fortnight on Thursday mornings. The meetings began with an exposé of first domestic monetary events and then external matters by the respective sub-governors. The governor would then comment on the current situation before opening up the meeting for general discussion. While it is clear that Conseil's members did express their various points of view, as one official noted, 'on ne peut pas dire que c'était une institution décisionnelle' (one cannot say that it was a decision-making body) (non-attributable interview).

Just as the Bank's internal decision-making process after the 1973 reform was very similar to the process before the reform, so too was the Bank's relationship with the core executive. The governor rarely met the President of the Republic, although from 1976–9 there were weekly meetings between governor Clappier and the prime minister (Amouroux 1986: 265). Nevertheless, the keystone of the relationship between the bank and the core executive was the weekly meeting between the governor, the Directeur du Trésor, the Finance Minister and the latter's most senior personal adviser. As one official notes, 'c'est là où le gouverneur faisait valoir son point de vue et le ministre le sien' (that's where the governor put forward his own point of view and the minister did likewise) (non-attributable interview). These meetings were important because they allowed the participants to exchange technical information and to discuss matters of mutual interest, particularly concerning interest rates and commercial banking matters where their responsibilities were at least partly shared. These meetings were also important because they paved the way for the next meeting of the Conseil Général. They allowed the governor to know the Finance Minister's position and they allowed the Directeur du Trésor, who attended in his capacity as *censeur*, to know the governor's position.

As a result, therefore, one of the reasons why the Conseil Général was not a decision-making body was because most decisions had been negotiated in private between the two key parties prior to the meetings. When conflict between the Bank and the core executive did occur during these meetings, the *censeur* had the right to veto decisions and force a new deliberation which allowed time for the informal decision-making channels to be exploited further. So, the decision-making process was skewed towards the core executive. This did not mean that the Bank, most notably in the form of the governor, was absent from this process. As one former Treasury official notes: 'il y a un dialogue permanent entre les services de la Banque de France et la direction du Trésor, entre le gouverneur de la Banque de France et le ministre de l'Économie et des Finances' (there is a permanent dialogue between the Bank's services and the Treasury and between the governor and the Finance Minister) (Haberer 1990: 29). However, the same official has also noted that: 'dans un pays comme la France, où les fonctionnaires du ministre d'un côté et les dirigeants de la Banque de France de l'autre sont soumis à l'autorité du même ministre, il ne peut y avoir de très longues discussions' (in a country like France where, on the one hand, ministerial civil servants and, on the other, leaders of the Bank of France are subject to the authority of the same minister, the discussions do not last very long) (quoted in Mamou 1988: 122). As Mamou concludes, therefore, 'sous entendu: la Banque s'incline toujours devant le ministre' (in other words: the Bank always gives in to the minister) (ibid.)

In the immediate aftermath of the reform, the main period of difficulty between the Bank and the core executive occurred in 1975. At this time, the right-wing coalition government led by Jacques Chirac was faced with the prospect of important local elections in less than a year. At these elections the opposition socialist–communist alliance looked well placed to make large gains. Consequently, even though the country had already moved out of recession, the Prime Minister decided to pump an extra 30 billion francs into the system. It is clear that both Jean-Pierre Fourcade, the Finance Minister, (Goodman 1992: 117) and Renaud de la Génière, then sub-governor of the Bank of France, were opposed to this decision (*Le Monde*, 26 November 1976). Nevertheless, the Prime Minister, with the tacit consent of the President, moved ahead. Less than a year later, however, Chirac resigned because of his political differences with the President, and Giscard appointed Raymond Barre as both Prime Minister and Finance Minister. Barre, a former economist, immediately put in place a package of policies aimed at creating both exchange rate and monetary stability (Goodman 1992: 119). Needless to say, the Bank approved of the package and helped to draw it up. Goodman states that Barre personally decided many of the technical aspects of monetary policy during this period (Goodman 1992: 120), but it is apparent that these decisions were taken in concert with Bank representatives.

Overall, then, from 1973–81, and particularly from 1976–81, the level of conflict between the Bank and the core executive was minimal. This situation did not last long.

6 The core executive and the Bank of France (1981–97)

Shadowing the Bundesbank

In the period from 1981–97 the relationship between the Bank of France and the core executive was transformed. The Bank went from being the subordinate partner in the relationship to being an institution which enjoyed a considerable degree of economic and political independence. The transformation process, though, was long and complicated. Events in the period from 1981–4 created the context for the first, but aborted, proposal for greater Bank independence in 1986. It was only following the negotiation and ratification of the Maastricht Treaty on European union that the Bank's statutes were successfully reformed in 1993. Since this reform, the Bank has demonstrated that it has the capacity to shape the conduct of French monetary policy. At the same time, however, the core executive has also demonstrated that it still takes steps to influence policy in this area. In short, the 1993 reform created the conditions for a complex institutional game in which the Bank is now the key decision maker but in which the core executive is also still a principal player.

The first part of this chapter examines the troubled relationship between the Bank and the core executive from 1981–6. The second part discusses the proposed reform of the Bank in 1986 and considers why this reform was shelved. The third part then examines the growing consensus on the need for greater Bank independence that emerged in the period from 1988–93. The fourth part considers in some detail the preparation and passage of the 1993 reform. The final part analyses the relationship between the Bank and the core executive from 1994–7.

1981–6

In 1981 the Socialist party assumed office for the first time during the Fifth Republic. François Mitterrand was elected President of the Republic and the subsequent National Assembly elections returned a socialist majority. The alternation in power had profound consequences for the relationship between the Bank of France and the core executive. Whereas from 1979–81 the level of conflict between the two institutions was minimal, from 1981–6 and, in particular, from 1981–4 the relationship was highly conflictual. Speaking of the 1979–81 period, one former Bank official noted: 'tout était facile. . . . Il y avait une totale harmonie entre la politique générale et la politique du gouverneur' (everything was easy. . . . There was complete harmony between the general policy and the governor's policy) (non-attributable interview). By contrast, speaking of the 1981–4 period, the same official stated that: 'à ce moment là est venue une différence de vue totale . . .' (at this point there came to be totally different points of view) (non-attributable interview). The result of this situation was that the Bank was frozen out of the decision-making process. As another former Bank and senior governmental official stated: 'la Direction du Trésor pensait que la compétence en matière de la politique monétaire est complètement rapatriée par l'État . . . et que la Banque de France était simplement un agent d'exécution' (the Treasury thought that responsibility for monetary policy was completely taken over by the State . . . and that the Bank of France was simply an instrument of policy implementation) (non-attributable interview).

The conflict between the Bank and the core executive stemmed from the fact that the newly-elected government was committed to a reflationary economic programme based around the principles of income redistribution and public sector expansion. It was felt that this would increase both economic growth and fiscal returns, which would in turn create the conditions for a reduction in unemployment and for cuts in welfare spending. However, this programme ran counter to the prevailing international economic environment. In other countries, deflationary policies were the order of the day. Consequently, the French government was obliged simultaneously to tighten exchange controls and increase interest rates so as to try to maintain the value of the franc. There is a debate as to whether the socialists' policies cushioned the worst of the effects of the international recession on the French economy or whether they aggravated them (see for example Machin and Wright 1985). Nevertheless, it is clear that during the course of the summer of 1981 the government faced increasingly severe economic problems. The country's balance of trade deficit increased, inflation rose and the franc came under extreme pressure within the European Monetary System (EMS). In May 1981 President Mitterrand personally took the decision not to devalue the franc, but in October 1981 the inevitable could no longer be delayed.

During the course of the next eighteen months the government's economic problems worsened (for an overview of this period, see Elgie (1993: 124–30)). In June 1982 the franc was devalued within the EMS for a second time. On this occasion the devaluation was accompanied by a relatively modest package of deflationary measures. However, the beneficial effects of these measures were equally modest as well. By the end of 1982 the balance of trade deficit showed no signs of decreasing, the level of inflation was still greater than most of France's closest trading partners and the level of interest rates remained stubbornly high. Again, therefore, in early 1983 profound economic choices had to be made. This time there were two clear options. The first was to devalue the franc for the third time accompanied by a much harsher austerity programme than before. The second was to withdraw the franc from the EMS and allow it to depreciate on the open market while at the same time reflating the economy so as to boost domestic demand. The debate between the protagonists of the two options is well documented (see, for example, the bibliography in Elgie (1993) and, more recently, Cameron (1996)). Suffice to say that the President, who was initially in favour of the second option, changed his mind and chose the first. Consequently, on 21 March 1983 the franc was devalued for a third time within the EMS and a more substantial 'plan de rigueur' (austerity plan) was put in place.

In the context of the economic policy of the early years of the Mitterrand presidency, it is hardly surprising that the relationship between the Bank and the core executive was particularly difficult. On the one hand, the Bank was completely opposed to the government's policies. It was committed to defending the value of the currency and it saw that the government's policies were having the opposite effect. Consequently, it opposed economic reflation and tried to promote the virtues of a strong currency. On the other hand, however, the government, which was committed to introducing such reforms and which wanted to ensure that they were successfully implemented in time for the next set of local elections in March 1983, was unwilling to heed the Bank's advice. The result was that the Bank was sidelined from the decision-making process. For Prate, the Bank was 'isolée' (isolated) (Prate 1987: 216). Similarly, for Mamou, the Bank entered a period of 'splendide isolement' (splendid isolation) (Mamou 1988: 127). During this period the key policy choices were made by political actors, the President, Prime Minister, Finance Minister, Budget Minister and their entourages, in consultation with officials in the Direction du Trésor. Indeed, it is telling that in March 1983 the key turning point in the devaluation debate came when the Budget Minister and presidential confidante, Laurent Fabius, was persuaded to go and see the Directeur du Trésor, Michel Camdessus, who informed him of the parlous state of French currency reserves and the disastrous consequences that would ensue if the franc withdrew from the EMS (Elgie 1993: 128).

Isolated from the decision-making process, the Bank had few powers with which to influence monetary policy. In the winter of 1981–2 the governor of the Bank, Renaud de la Génière, did invoke one of his residual prerogatives and refused to agree to an increase in temporary advances to the Treasury. However, the latter circumvented this decision by simply issuing new varieties of Treasury Bonds in order to meet its short-term needs (Prate 1987: 221). Similarly, in the Bank's annual report to the President the governor did attempt to alert the public to the consequences of the government's policies. However, these reports were subject to such considerable revision (Prate 1987: 218) that their impact on public opinion was marginal and to those in the Bank it seemed as if they had even lost what little remained of their 'droit de remontrance'. In fact, during this period the one power that the Bank's governor and sub-governors did still unequivocally hold was the right to resign. This would have shocked both domestic public opinion and the wider central banking community and it might have jolted the government into changing the course of its economic policy. This option was seriously considered (non-attributable interview) but it was always rejected. Senior Bank officials believed that it would only have worsened the economic crisis and in any case it was contrary to the public service ethos with which the Bank's decision makers were imbued (non-attributable interview).

After 1984 the relationship between the Bank and the core executive improved somewhat. The first reason for the improvement in the relationship was because of the turnover in senior personnel at the Bank. When he was appointed by the right-wing government in 1979, Renaud de la Génière was given the unofficial guarantee that he would serve for a five-year term without being dismissed (non-attributable interview). Although both he and his two sub-governors frequently felt that the socialists might fail to honour this unwritten agreement (non-attributable interview), in fact it was upheld. In late 1984, however, the government did take the opportunity to appoint a new governor, Michel Camdessus. The former Directeur du Trésor was slightly more amenable to the socialists and the result of both his appointment and others was that the level of trust between the Bank and core executive increased. The second reason for the improvement in the relationship between the two institutions was because of the change in the government's economic policy. Under the guidance of the newly appointed Finance Minister, Pierre Bérégovoy, France embarked upon the 'franc fort' (strong franc/Frankfurt) policy. Otherwise known as 'competitive disinflation', the aim of this policy was to create the conditions for monetary stability so as to promote lower interest rates, which would in turn improve the conditions for economic growth. The government shadowed the deutschmark, tried to avoid inflationary devaluations, continued the policy of budgetary austerity and took the first steps to liberalise the financial and money markets. Needless to say the Bank of France was very much in favour of this policy mix, and relations with the core executive gradually improved.

Despite the improvement in the relationship between the two institutions after 1984, the experience of the early years of the Mitterrand presidency meant that the number of people calling for a greater degree of Bank independence steadily increased. For both de la Génière and his former colleague, Alain Prate, their personal experience led unequivocally to such a conclusion. De la Génière argued that 'depuis 1936 la Banque de France est trop dans la main du gouvernement' (since 1936 the Bank has been too much in the government's hand) (reported in *Le Monde*, 21–22 June 1986). For another former Bank official, this experience demonstrated that 'le statut de la Banque est apparu insuffisant' (the Bank's statutes appeared to be insufficient) (non-attributable interview). Their view was shared by that of the former governor of the Bank, Olivier Wormser. In November 1984 he argued that 'disposer d'un institut d'émission indépendant est pour une nation, grande ou petite, un indiscutable avantage' (having an independent central bank is an indisputable advantage for a country either large or small) (*L'Express*, 16 November 1984: 31). Indeed, speaking of his part in drawing up the 1973 reform, he stated that, 'grand est mon regret de n'avoir point davantage insisté pour que soit accordé à son gouverneur un statut le plaçant, pour un temps, entièrement à l'abri des aléas de la politique' (great is my regret that I did not insist more that the statutes should shelter the governor, for a time, from the ups and downs of politics) (ibid). Importantly, though, the calls for greater independence did not just emanate from former Bank officials. In one of his books, the former Prime Minister Raymond Barre argued in favour of reform (Barre 1986) as did senior Gaullist politicians such as Charles Pasqua and Philippe Auberger. By the mid-1980s, therefore, the right appeared to be won over to the idea of giving the Bank a greater degree of independence. In this way, just as the events of the 1920s and early 1930s paved the way for the reform of the Bank of France in 1936, so the experience of the early 1980s appeared to have created the conditions for another paradigm shift in the relationship between the Bank and the core executive.

1986–8

Proposals for a reform of the Bank of France began in the mid-1980s. On 10 April 1985 Charles Pasqua introduced a bill in the Senate to reform the Bank. For Pasqua, a reform of the Bank was a necessary precursor to economic recovery and he indicated that 'le redressement économique du pays ainsi que la reprise du progrès social supposent que la Banque de France recouvre la disposition de l'ensemble de ses prérogatives naturelles' (the economic upturn of the country as well the resumption of social progress assumes that the Bank of France recovers all of its natural prerogatives) (quoted in Develle 1988: 239). In fact, however, for Pasqua the Bank's 'natural prerogatives' were certainly greater than those it enjoyed at the time but in comparison to, say, the Bundesbank, they were still fairly residual. It is true that Pasqua's bill would have made it more difficult for the core executive to dismiss the governor. However, for the most part the bill would have brought about only a relatively minor shift in the balance of power between the Bank and the core executive. For example, Article 5 of the bill stated that: 'La Banque de France élabore et met en œuvre la politique monétaire propre à assurer la sauvegarde de la monnaie dans le cadre de la politique gouvernementale' (the Bank prepares and implements monetary policy appropriate to safeguarding the currency in the framework of government policy). Similarly, Articles 11 and 15 proposed that the governor and sub-governors would still be appointed in the Council of Ministers as would the members of the Conseil Général, although the latter would be nominated by various people including the Finance Minister and the Presidents of the National Assembly, the Senate and the Economic and Social Council. As Develle states about the bill: 'il ne s'agit pas à proprement parler d'établir un contre-pouvoir monétaire indépendant de l'exécutif' (it was not strictly speaking a matter of establishing a monetary counter-power independent of the executive) (Develle 1988: 239). Instead, the bill was meant to be a statement of principle which was designed to underline the economic policy differences between the right and the left in the run up to the 1986 National Assembly election.

For at least one former official, Pasqua's bill was 'pas très élaboré' (not very carefully worked out) (non-attributable interview) and in any case it was doomed to political failure. By contrast, two former Bank officials drew up a more detailed reform which aimed to give the Bank a much greater degree of independence and which was designed to be more than just a statement of good intent. Following their departure from the Bank Renaud de la Génière and Alain Prate worked together to draw up a reform proposal. As one observer stated: 'il allait au fond des choses' (it went to the bottom of things) (non-attributable interview). Indeed, it was meant to serve as a blueprint for an incoming right-wing government (non-attributable interview). In the proposal the authors stressed three particular themes (non-attributable interview). First, they wanted the Bank's decisions to be made by a collegial decision-making body rather than simply by the governor in consultation (or perhaps not) with the sub-governors. They believed that this would increase the independence of the Bank because it would allow the governor to deal with the core executive from a position of greater strength and it would also prevent a pro-core executive governor from being able to make Bank decisions unilaterally. Second, they wanted the Bank to have complete responsibility for monetary policy. To this end, they suggested that the government's representative, the *censeur*, should not even be allowed to attend Bank meetings. Third, they wanted the Bank to play a greater role in the supervision of the wider banking community. They believed that this would increase the stature of the Bank and so, again, would lead to a greater degree of independence. The de la Génière–Prate proposal was never made public, but for at least one former Bank official it contained 'une logique implacable' (an implacable logic) (non-attributable interview) which meant that reform was only a matter of time.

Apparently following this logic, the right-wing RPR–UDF coalition formally committed itself to reforming the Bank at the 1986 National Assembly election. Point 12 of the coalition's election manifesto stated the parties' aims in this domain: 'Assurer la stabilité de la monnaie, garantir l'autonomie de la Banque de France' (Assure the stability of the currency, guarantee the autonomy of the Bank of France). Moreover, following the right's victory at the election, the new Prime Minister, Jacques Chirac, announced on 15 April 1986 that the government would soon introduce a bill to give the Bank 'un statut d'autonomie' (a statute of autonomy), that is to say, 'un statut nouveau qui permettra de soustraire son action aux interventions des administrations' (a new statute which will allow its work to be shielded from the interventions of the administration) (*Le Figaro*, 16 April 1986). Adding just slightly more detail, Chirac indicated that the Bank would be charged with preserving 'la valeur interne et externe du franc' (the internal and external value of the franc) (ibid). In this context, responsibility for preparing the bill was passed to the Finance Minister, Édouard Balladur, and his set of personal advisers and officials in the Direction du Trésor.

Despite the very public commitments to reform, it soon became clear that this was not one of the Finance Minister's top priorities. In September 1986 the press reported that the bill had been delayed but that it would be ready in a few days, noting too, however, that the reform proposals were 'loin des projets "d'avant mars"' (far from the pre-March proposals). When no bill was forthcoming in October 1986 a government backbencher, Michel Pelchat, put down a written parliamentary question in which he asked the Finance Minister about the progress of the bill. The reply he received was suitably non-committal: 'il peut apparaître souhaitable de . . . consacrer [une réelle autonomie] formellement dans un texte à caractère législatif . . . une telle réforme soulève toutefois un grand nombre de questions juridiques' (it might appear desirable to set out a real autonomy for the Bank formally in a parliamentary bill . . . however such a reform raises a large number of legal questions) (Develle 1988: 302). Similar questions were asked by other government backbenchers throughout the course of 1987 and failed to receive a reply. Finally, in May 1988 one of Balladur's personal advisers let it be publicly known that 'la réforme du statut de la Banque de France n'est pas d'actualité' (the reform of the Bank's statutes is not on the cards) (*Le Monde*, 10 May 1988).

In retrospect, it is clear that the bill was never seriously considered by the government. In fact, as one of Balladur's former personal advisers noted: 'ça n'a jamais donné lieu à des débats internes au cabinet, ça n'a jamais donné lieu à des débats entre le Premier ministre et M. Balladur' (it never gave rise to an internal debate with the cabinet, it never gave rise to a debate between the Prime Minister and M. Balladur) (non-attributable interview). The bill was not forthcoming at this time because of an absence of political will. Both the Finance Minister himself and his officials in the Direction du Trésor were decidedly lukewarm to the idea of greater Bank independence. For example, as one of the former Finance Minister's advisers stated: 'ce n'est pas un secret que M. Balladur n'a jamais été un partisan acharné de l'indépendance totale de la Banque de France' (it is not a secret that Balladur has never been a firm believer in the complete independence of the Bank of France) (non-attributable interview). Indeed, Balladur himself later admitted that he did not promote the reform 'parce qu'il m'avait semblé que j'avais des choses plus urgentes à faire' (because it seemed to me that I had more important things to do) (*Le Monde*, 9 January 1993). Equally, the Direction du Trésor was also opposed to the reform. Raymond Barre accused the Direction du Trésor of deliberately shelving the reform (Barre 1988: 171), as did a former senior Bank official (non-attributable interview), and even Balladur hinted that this was one of the main reasons for the delay (*Le Monde*, 9 January 1993).

The absence of political will was the result of both economic and political factors. First, it was argued that the economic context did not favour a reform. The threat to the stability of the franc was so great just after the election that it was felt, somewhat paradoxically in the context of the 1993 debate (see below), that reforming the Bank of France might only worsen the situation (non-attributable interview). Moreover, it was then argued that the reform of the French financial markets in late 1986 made it unnecessary to proceed with a reform of the Bank. By ending the policy of 'encadrement du crédit' and by giving the Bank greater *de facto* responsibility for managing liquidity levels on a day-to-day basis through interest rate adjustments, it was felt that the arguments in favour of greater Bank independence had been undermined (*La Tribune de L'Expansion*, 10 May 1988: 6). Second, it was also argued that the political context did not favour a reform. The 1986–8 period was one of 'cohabitation' between a left-wing president and a right-wing prime minister. In this particularly sensitive period, when constitutional issues and issues concerning the division of policy responsibilities between the two main actors were so salient, the government felt that a reform of the Bank might provoke a political crisis which would benefit either the President or other political competitors (non-attributable interview). Similarly, quite apart from any problems of 'cohabitation', it is apparent that representatives of the core executive were reluctant to cede control of monetary policy to the Bank of France. Sources close to the Finance Minister rehearsed the (now) familiar argument that unelected central bankers should not be given responsibility for controlling such an important policy area (*La Tribune de L'Expansion*, 10 May 1988: 6). Finally, it is likely that Chirac and his close ally Balladur were both reluctant to go ahead with a reform because, in contrast to the situation in 1993 (see below), those who in 1986 were most keenly in favour of reform were also those who were the Prime Minister's closest political competitors. It was an open secret that Chirac would be the Gaullist candidate at the 1988 presidential election and that Barre would be the centre-right candidate. Therefore, despite Chirac's public pronouncements in favour of reform, Barre and his supporters might have made political capital from any such measure. Needless to say, this is something which Chirac and his supporters wished to avoid.

For these reasons, then, in the period from 1986–8 the economic and political environment was considered to be not right for a reform of the Bank of France. According to one person, in 1986 'le projet n'était pas vraiment mûr' (the bill was not really ready) (non-attributable interview). According to another, 'les choses n'étaient pas mûres' (things weren't ready) (non-attributable interview). Perhaps most tellingly, though, as one of Balladur's former advisers noted about the very concept of central bank independence at the time, 'personne ne savait exactement ce que cela voulait dire' (nobody really knew what it meant) (non-attributable interview). In fact, it was only during the course of the 1988–93 period, as the meaning of this concept gradually became familiar to all concerned, especially in the context of European integration, that the pressure for greater Bank independence became overwhelming.

1988–93

In 1988 Mitterrand was re-elected as President of the Republic, the National Assembly was dissolved and a minority socialist government was returned. Whereas in 1981 the advent of a socialist government caused investors to take fright and capital to be transferred abroad, in 1988 they were reassured and the stock market soared. Similarly, whereas from 1981–6 there was a considerable degree of tension between the Bank of France and the core executive, from 1988–93 relations between the two institutions were much less conflictual. For the most part this was because the Finance

Minister from 1988–92 and then Prime Minister from 1992–3, Pierre Bérégovoy, his senior monetary policy adviser, Hervé Hannoun, the Directeur du Trésor, Jean-Claude Trichet, and the governor of the Bank of France, Jacques de Larosière, all supported the same basic 'franc fort' policy. As Larosière himself stated: 'il n'[y] avait pas eu de conflits avec les ministres des Finances successifs, mais cette situation pouvait s'expliquer par le fait que tous avaient pour objectif la stabilité monétaire . . .' (there were no conflicts with successive Finance Ministers, but this situation can be explained by the fact that all of them had monetary stability as their objective) (Banque de France 1993: 85). Consequently, even though both Trichet and Larosière had been appointed by the previous government, at no point did Bérégovoy consider replacing either of them with more politically sympathetic figures.

Despite the fact that there was agreement concerning the basics of monetary policy, there were disagreements concerning the specific timing of interest rate movements. These disagreements stemmed from the fact that the pursuit of the 'franc fort' policy meant that France had to sustain relatively high levels of interest rates. In particular, it meant that French interest rates had to be higher than those in Germany. Not surprisingly, Bérégovoy was keen to see French interest rates fall; he believed that not only would this stimulate economic demand and political support at home but that it would also demonstrate to both domestic public opinion and the international financial community that French monetary policy was not simply subordinate to German monetary policy. However, Bérégovoy was regularly opposed by the other three protagonists, all of whom warned of the dangers of reducing French interest rates unilaterally. From Aeschimann's and Riché's (1996) account of this period, Bérégovoy's decision was final. If the Finance Minister insisted on an interest rate cut, especially when he had the support of the President, then such a cut did occur (see, for example, Aeschimann and Riché (1996: 102–4)). Of course, though, this is not to say that Bérégovoy could buck the market at will. Indeed, on more than one occasion, notably in October 1991, unilateral French interest rates cuts were almost immediately reversed when the value of the franc was subsequently threatened. Instead, it is simply to say that domestically in terms of the relationship between the Bank of France and the core executive the latter was still the dominant partner.

In this context it is apparent that, whereas from 1981–6 the issue of greater Bank independence was placed on the political agenda as a result of domestic conflict between the Bank and core executive, from 1988–93 this issue came to prominence as a function of other factors. During this period, two particular factors led to pressure for a reform of the Bank of France: first, the intergovernmental negotiations concerning the Maastricht Treaty on European Union and the proposals for Economic and Monetary Union; and, second, the currency crises of late 1992 and early 1993.

The issue of Bank of France independence was closely linked with negotiations concerning the Maastricht Treaty. The complexities of the bargaining process which resulted in the rules for Economic and Monetary Union are well documented elsewhere (see for example Dyson 1994). Suffice it to say here that Mitterrand promoted monetary union as early as January 1988 because he believed that it would reduce the economic influence of Germany. By contrast, the Germans were wary of monetary union because they believed that it might undermine their postwar economic strategy. Against this background, the issue of greater independence for national central banks became part of the intergovernmental bargaining process at the European level. Mitterrand came under pressure to agree to make the Bank of France more independent, both from the German Chancellor, Helmut Kohl, and from the Bundesbank President, Karl Otto Pöhl, and Jacques de Larosière in their capacity as members of the Committee for the Study of Economic and Monetary Union which was set up in June 1988 under the guidance of the President of the European Commission, Jacques Delors. Faced with this pressure, Mitterrand used the issue of Bank of France independence to forge a wider deal. He conceded on this issue in order to win German support for monetary integration (Favier and Martin-Roland 1996: 163–4). As early as the autumn of 1988, therefore, the European context meant that Mitterrand was committed to reforming the relationship between the Bank and the core executive. This commitment was then enshrined in the Treaty on European Union which was ratified in France in September 1992.

The issue of Bank of France independence was also closely linked with the currency crises in late 1992 and early 1993. In September 1992 the currencies in the European Exchange Rate Mechanism (ERM) came under speculative attack to the extent that sterling and the Italian lira were both obliged to withdraw from the system (see Chapter 4). The franc was able to remain within the system but only as a result of concerted, but reluctant, intervention on the money markets by the Bundesbank. In November 1992 pressure on the franc and other currencies in the ERM mounted once more and then in January 1993 speculation began in earnest in the run up to the National Assembly elections in March of that year. As the pressure on the franc increased during this period, so too did the prospect of greater independence for the Bank of France. In November 1992 the French Finance Minister, Michel Sapin, sought and gained permission from President Mitterrand to raise in private the question of greater Bank of France independence with the Germans (Aeschimann and Riché 1996: 158). On 21 December 1992, Sapin had a secret meeting with Helmut Schlesinger, the president of the Bundesbank, and Theo Waigel, the German Finance Minister, in which he raised the prospect of reforming the Bank of France 'rapidement' (quickly) as a way of guaranteeing Bundesbank intervention in favour of the franc if another currency crisis occurred. Although no formal agreement was reached, there was more concerted co-operation between the two governments thereafter and it is hardly a coincidence that during the next wave of speculative attacks in early January 1993 Sapin stated publicly for the first time that he was in favour of reforming the Bank's statutes (*Le Monde*, 12 January 1993: 18).

As a result of both factors, whereas the issue of greater Bank of France independence was absent from the 1988 elections, it was very much back on the agenda at the 1993 legislative election. For example, in addition to Sapin's commitment other leading Socialist party members such as the Industry Minister, Dominique Strauss-Kahn, also publicly argued in favour of reforming the Bank's statutes (Aeschimann and Riché 1996: 164). Similarly, Édouard Balladur announced that he had made a mistake in not reforming the Bank in 1986 and stated that, 'aujourd'hui, cela correspond pour moi à une volonté tout à fait claire' (today it represents for me a very clear commitment) (*Le Monde*, 9 January 1993: 18). Equally, in December 1992 the former President of the Republic and leading centre-right figure, Valéry Giscard d'Estaing, announced that he was in favour of reform and in January 1993 the UDF confederation of parties over which he presided proposed a private members bill to this effect. Article 1 of this bill was a very clear signal of its intention: 'La Banque de France est l'institution qui détermine et conduit la politique monétaire de la France. Elle veille au maintien de la valeur de la monnaie' (The Bank of France is the institution which determines and conducts French monetary policy. It ensures that the value of the currency is maintained) (UDF 1993). Overall, therefore, by early 1993 it appeared as if the economic and political environment was indeed ready for a fundamental reform of the relationship between the Bank of France and the core executive.

1993

The right-wing coalition won a spectacular victory in the legislative election of March 1993. Between them, the RPR and UDF controlled 485 out of 577 National Assembly seats, whereas the Socialist party returned fewer than 70 deputies. The result was another period of 'cohabitation'. This time, though, the political environment was very different to the one seven years previously. In 1993, President Mitterrand was both physically and politically weak and the government was largely free from presidential interference. Moreover, the focus of presidential competition at this time was between two

Gaullist party figures, the newly-appointed Prime Minister, Édouard Balladur, and the former Prime Minister and leader of the RPR, Jacques Chirac. It was in this context that the government prepared the reform of the Bank of France.

In 1993, and in contrast to the situation in 1986, the right was clearly serious about reforming the Bank. In the RPR–UDF joint election manifesto the promise of reform was unequivocal. Under the section entitled 'Assurer la stabilité de la monnaie' (Guaranteeing currency stability), the two parties pledged that: 'Dès la session de printemps 1993, sera votée une loi assurant l'indépendance de la Banque de France' (Right at the start of the 1993 spring session a law guaranteeing the independence of the Bank of France will be passed) (*Le Monde*, 10 February 1993). Then, at the first meeting of the new Council of Ministers at the beginning of April Balladur formally presented the Finance Minister, Edmond Alphandéry, with three legislative priorities, one of which was to reform the Bank. Furthermore, on 8 April during his first speech to the newly-elected National Assembly Balladur reaffirmed his government's intention: 'Une loi sera déposée dans les prochaines semaines pour mettre en œuvre [l'autonomie de la Banque de France]' (A law will be tabled in the next few weeks to bring about the autonomy of the Bank of France) (*Le Monde*, 10 April 1993). Finally, on 18 April Balladur publicly stated that the first draft of the reform was ready and that he would be examining it in two days time (*Le Monde*, 20 April 1993). Indeed, such was the contrast with the situation in 1986 that some fears were expressed that this time the government was being too hasty (ibid).

Ostensibly the main difference between the 1986 and 1993 situation was the commitment to central bank independence contained in the Maastricht Treaty. Indeed, in personal interviews various protagonists attested to this fact. France had ratified the Treaty and so the government was under a moral and legal obligation to introduce legislation to reform the Bank. However, despite this general commitment, the government was under no obligation to introduce such legislation immediately. Point 5 of Article 109e of the Maastricht Treaty simply stated that 'each member state shall, as appropriate, start the process leading to the independence of its central bank' during the second stage of European Monetary Union (EMU), which would commence on 1 January 1994. Moreover, Article 108 merely noted this process had to be completed by the start of the third stage of EMU, which would come into force no earlier than 1 January 1997 and no later than 1 January 1999. Consequently, had it so wished, the government could have introduced legislation as late as 1996 or, as it turned out, even later still. In this context, it is somewhat misleading to argue that the reform was introduced in 1993 because of the Maastricht Treaty. Instead, as Alphandéry himself stated, the Treaty only provided the 'toile de fond' (backdrop) (*La*

Tribune Desfossés, 12 May 1993: 2) to the reform. Why, then, did the government rush to reform? It did so for both short-term economic and political reasons.

The government felt that there were short-term economic gains to be had from a quick reform. Repeatedly, Alphandéry stated that the reform would bring about a greater degree of confidence in the franc (see for example the interview in *Le Monde*, 24 April 1993: 1). As a result, he believed that the reform would increase the likelihood of rapid interest rate cuts and, in particular, that the differential between French and German interest rates would be reduced or even eliminated (*Le Monde*, 24 April 1993). Indeed, this was also the position of one of the most senior parliamentary proponents of the reform (non-attributable interview). Moreover, Alphandéry also believed that the reform would reduce the level of inflation (see, for example, his evidence to the National Assembly Finance Commission in Auberger (1993: 60)). Alphandéry was trained as an economist; as a student he had worked on the issue of central bank independence, and he was well aware of the academic literature that suggested a link between central bank independence and low inflation (*Le Monde*, 13 May 1993). Overall, the Finance Minister was keen to argue that the reform was not simply motivated by Maastricht commitments but that it was an integral part of the government's overall economic strategy and, in particular, its policies to reduce unemployment (*Le Monde*, 24 April 1993).

The government also felt that there were short-term political gains to be had from a quick reform. Needless to say, Alphandéry, Balladur, the government and the right generally hoped, and perhaps even expected, that the economic benefits outlined above would be felt in time for the 1995 presidential election contest. More particularly, the decision to reform the Bank so quickly may be seen as part of Balladur's own presidential strategy (personal interviews). In the contest for the 1995 election, Balladur was aware that Chirac was his main right-wing competitor. Because Chirac controlled the RPR political machine, Balladur was also aware that, despite being a member of the Gaullist party, he had to find political allies elsewhere. Consequently, his strategy was to win the support of the centre-right UDF confederation. As one part of this strategy, UDF representatives were given a disproportionately large number of senior posts in the new government; as another part, reforms to which the UDF were most committed were carefully promoted. As a result of the UDF's pro-European stance, it suited Balladur to signal that a reform of the Bank of France was one of his top legislative priorities. By promoting the reform, when it was common knowledge that in the past he had been sceptical of the benefits that might accrue from it, Balladur increased his pro-European credentials and reinforced the likelihood that the UDF would support him at the election, as it eventually did.

Whatever the motivations for the speed of the reform, the bill itself was prepared in the usual manner. The Service des Affaires Monétaires et Financières (Monetary and Financial Section) of the Direction du Trésor was given the responsibility for drafting the wording of the bill in conjunction with representatives of both the Finance Minister's and the Prime Minister's personal staffs (non-attributable interview). In contrast to the situation in 1986, this time the Direction du Trésor was in no position to shelve the reform and, building on the work that it had already done prior to the election (Aeschimann and Riché 1996: 164), a draft was soon ready. This draft was then passed on to the Bank of France for its comments and, according to one observer, 'il y a eu des discussions extrêmement viriles entre le gouverneur et le directeur du Trésor' (there were some extremely virile discussions between the governor and the head of the Treasury) (non-attributable interview) especially concerning the issue of whether the government or the Bank should determine the external parity of the franc (see p. 133). Faced with unresolved issues in this area and others, the Prime Minister was then called upon to arbitrate. Indeed, despite the fact that the Finance Minister was responsible for the overall preparation and presentation of the bill, the Prime Minister 's'est plus qu'intéressé au texte . . .' (took more than just a passing interest in the bill) (non-attributable interview). He personally wrote perhaps the most key article, Article 1, of the bill (non-attributable interview) and he also took the slightly unusual step of personally presenting the bill to the constitutional lawyers in the Council of State. Following the Prime Minister's arbitrations, the bill was finally discussed in the Council of Ministers on 10 May, where President Mitterrand formally (and quite presciently as it transpired) expressed some doubts as to its constitutionality (*Le Figaro*, 12 May 1993).

Parliamentary discussion of the bill lasted from mid-May to early July. The National Assembly Finance Commission proposed a considerable number of amendments, the most important of which concerned the composition of the Bank's future decision-making institution, the Conseil de la Politique Monétaire (Monetary Policy Council), or CPM. The government wanted nominations to the CPM to be made by a large number of public institutions, including members of the most senior administrative bodies such as the Council of State and the Court of Auditors. The Finance Commission, however, proposed that these bodies should be excluded from the list of nominees. The government accepted this amendment but in return insisted that other aspects of the bill, including Article 1 (see p. 133), would remain unaltered. The Senate Finance commission also proposed a large number of amendments, some of which threatened to change the initial text of the bill quite considerably. Most notably, the Senate proposed that the CPM's role should be more clearly defined (to the detriment of the core executive) and that the Finance Minister should not be allowed to send a representative to attend its meetings. The government felt unable to accept these amendments and the Finance Minister threatened to use his constitutional powers to overturn these and all other Senate amendments if some compromise was not reached (*Le Monde*, 4/5 July 1993). Needless to say, this was sufficient for a mutually acceptable agreement to be found.

The government's overwhelming majority in the National Assembly meant that there was no possibility of the bill being defeated. However, there were some objections to the reform. First, the Communist party voted against the bill. This position was consistent with its opposition to the Maastricht Treaty and was also motivated by the party's refusal to support a bill which overturned one of the Popular Front's major pieces of legislation. Second, the Socialist party also voted against the bill. This was seemingly inconsistent with its pro-Maastricht position; however, the party justified its stance by arguing that the EMU timetable did not necessitate reform at this time. It might also be added that the party's stance helped to disguise the divisions within its own ranks between those who were pro-Maastricht and pro-reform and those who were anti-Maastricht and anti-reform. Third, over fifty majority deputies also either abstained or refused to take part in the vote. This was meant to show that they supported the government generally but were opposed to this particular text (*Le Monde*, 16 June 1993: 2). Almost without exception, this group of deputies had opposed the Maastricht Treaty the previous year. Now, they argued that the reform would amount to a 'dénationalisation de la monnaie' (denationalisation of the currency) and that it would 'confie un pouvoir exorbitant à un clan de technocrates et de notables . . .' (give an exorbitant amount of power to technocrats and notables) (*Le Monde*, 16 June 1993: 2). In the early stages of the bill's preparation, Balladur tried to balance the pro-European wishes of his centrist allies with the anti-European concerns of his Gaullist colleagues. He did so by saying that the reformed Bank would not be 'independent' but 'autonomous'. Indeed, the leader of the anti-Maastricht faction in the RPR, Philippe Séguin, welcomed this semantic change of heart (*Le Figaro*, 6 April 1993). By contrast, the UDF was opposed to this terminology, fearing that it signalled a weakening of the reform proposal (*Libération*, 15 April 1993). Faced with losing the support of centrists on this key issue, the Prime Minister quietly dropped this debate. Consequently, the anti-Maastricht Gaullists were isolated within the majority in their opposition to the bill. Although their opposition was somewhat embarrassing for the Prime Minister, they threatened neither the passage of the bill nor his political prospects and so no concessions were made to them.

All told, the 1993 reform brought about a significant change in the relationship between the Bank of France and the core executive. During the preparation of the bill Alphandéry frequently stressed that the government was proposing a French model of central bank independence. (See, for example, *Le Monde*, 24 April 1993; and Auberger (1993: 60)). Such statements were clearly designed to placate both public and right-wing party political opinion. Nevertheless, it is also apparent that the government was strongly influenced both by the Bundesbank model and by the experience of the US Federal Reserve. What is more, in a number of places the text of the law does not simply approximate the wording of, for example, Articles 105–107 of the Maastricht Treaty concerning the future status of the European Central Bank, it actually copies the wording *verbatim*. Notwithstanding these points, it is apparent that the 1993 reform significantly affected both the economic and political indicators of independence.

With regard to economic independence, there are several key articles. Article 1 states that the Bank 'définit et met en œuvre la politique monétaire dans le but d'assurer la stabilité des prix' [formulates and implements monetary policy with the aim of ensuring price stability]. It then goes on to say that members of the Bank 'ne peut ni solliciter ni accepter d'instructions du Gouvernement ...' [can neither request nor accept instructions from the government]. Similarly, Article 7 states that the CPM is 'chargé de définir la politique monétaire' [responsible for formulating monetary policy]. Furthermore, Article 3 states: 'Il est interdit à la Banque de France d'autoriser des découverts ou d'accorder tout autre type de crédit au Trésor public ... L'acquisition directe par la Banque de France de titres de leur dette est également interdite' [The Bank of France is prohibited from authorising credit or granting any form of debt facility to the Treasury ... The direct acquisition of government debt is also prohibited]. These provisions represent innovations which make the Bank considerably more independent of the core executive. Moreover, as before, the Bank still sets interest rates and jointly supervises the regulation of the wider banking sector. It must be noted, though, that Article 2 states that the government is still responsible for fixing exchange rate parities and the Bank still plays no part in the governmental budgetary process. Nevertheless, despite these last two provisions, the 1993 reform resulted in a significant increase in the level of economic independence.

With regard to political independence there are several key articles. For example, Article 13 states that the governor and the two sub-governors are appointed for a six-year, once-renewable term, while Article 10 states that they have security of tenure and makes it difficult for them to hold any other posts simultaneously. These provisions are consistent with a relatively independent central bank. However, it should be noted that there is no official nomination procedure (in other words the Finance Minister, Prime Minister and President maintain control of the appointment process) and appointees do not need professional qualifications. These provisions are consistent with a relatively dependent central bank. The conditions concerning the composition of the Bank's main decision-making body, the CPM, and the rules governing its procedures are less equivocal. In addition to Article 10 above, Article 8 states that the CPM's members are appointed on a staggered basis for a nine-year, non-renewable term from a list of nominations made by the presidents of the National Assembly, the Senate and the Conseil Économique et Social (Economic and Social Council). Moreover, those nominated must have professional experience and competence in monetary, financial or economic domains. Furthermore, although Article 9 states that the Prime Minister and the Finance Minister (or his/her representative) are allowed to attend meetings of the CPM, it also states they are not allowed to vote and that decisions are made collectively by the Council's members. Finally, the possibility of other office-holding is restricted. All of these provisions correspond to a politically independent central bank.

In these ways, the 1993 law greatly increased the level of political independence. As the figures in Appendix 3 show, the 1993 reform increased the overall level of Bank independence from the core executive from 0.18 to 0.59. Clearly, the precise figures have no meaning in themselves; it is not reasonable to conclude from them that the Bank was nearly three-fifths independent compared with only one-fifth independent previously. However, it is reasonable to conclude that the Bank was significantly more independent under its 1993 statutes than it was under its 1973 statutes, and that the overall increase in independence was a result of increases in both political and economic indicators.

1994–7

During the course of the 1993 reform, it was reiterated that central bank independence could not simply be decreed; it also had to be won through practical experience. In this context the implementation of the reform and the actual transfer of monetary policy-making power from the core executive to the Bank of France was eagerly anticipated. In the three years since the reform of the Bank the CPM has demonstrated its independence, but events have also shown that the process of monetary policy making is still quite complex and that the Bank of France and the core executive are still involved in, an albeit discrete, bargaining game.

The first meeting of the CPM took place on 5 January 1994 amidst considerable media attention. Present at the meeting were the Prime Minister and the Finance Minister and the nine members of the CPM. The CPM consisted of the governor, Jean-Claude Trichet, the former Directeur du Trésor who was appointed in September 1993, and the two sub-governors, Hervé Hannoun, the former head of Bérégovoy's personal staff who was appointed in September 1993, and Denis Ferman, a Bank official who was appointed in 1990. The other six members of the CPM were appointed in the days just before the first meeting. The composition of these appointments reflected the political realities of the nomination process. First, President Mitterrand insisted that the former socialist Finance Minister, Michel Sapin, be appointed. The Prime Minister was opposed to this idea but the unwritten rules of 'cohabitation' meant that he had to acquiesce to the President's demand (*Libération*, 5 January 1994). Second, the Prime Minister was also obliged at least to acknowledge the demands of both the pro- and anti-European lobbies. The appointments of Jean Boissonat, Bruno de Maulde and, particularly, Michel Albert pleased the pro-European centrist lobby, whereas the appointments of Denise Flouzat and Jean-Pierre Gérard, both of whom were proposed by Philippe Séguin, pleased the anti-European lobby. In all, the CPM was by no means a politically or economically homogeneous organisation (which, it might be argued, was a good thing) but there was, at least initially, a pro-'franc fort' majority.

Since its first meeting, the CPM established for itself very clear routines and standard operating procedures. These are derived in part from the contents of the August 1993 law and the December 1993 decree (no. 93–1278), which gave more detail about the CPM's functioning, and in part from the CPM's own official 'règlement intérieur' (internal rules) and the unofficial practices which have developed over time. For example, Article 3 of the December 1993 decree states that each meeting of the CPM officially approves the minutes of the last meeting. These minutes are then stored in the official archives. Similarly, the members of the CPM formally agreed that they were bound by the principle of collective responsibility (non-attributable interview), that the governor was the official spokesperson for CPM decisions and that in the days immediately prior to CPM meetings no one would comment on the measures that might or might not be taken (*Les Echos*, 27–28 January 1995).

CPM meetings take place every other Thursday morning from 10.00 a.m. to no later than 1.15 p.m. These meetings are preceded the day before by an unofficial preparatory meeting 'pour qu'on puisse échanger nos informations' (so that we can exchange information) (non-attributable interview). In addition, there may also be extraordinary meetings (see p. 139) should the need arise. By virtue of the fact that CPM members have no other professional commitments, with the exception of one who is a university lecturer, all nine members regularly attend official meetings. However, the degree of core executive representation varies. According to the 1993 law, the Prime Minister and Finance Minister both have the right to attend CPM meetings and if the Finance Minister cannot attend he or she has the right to send a representative. Since January 1994, attending the CPM has not been a prime ministerial priority. Balladur only attended the first ever meeting and his successor, Alain Juppé, had failed to attend any meeting by the end of 1996 more than eighteen months after his appointment. By contrast, Finance Ministers have attended more frequently but somewhat unevenly. Edmond Alphandéry turned up with 'une grande régularité' (great regularity); his short-lived successor, Alain Madelin, showed up only once; and his successor, Jean Arthuis 'vient mais sans régularité' (comes but not regularly) (non-attributable interview). More often than not, then, the only core executive representation at CPM meetings comes in the form of the Directeur du Trésor who is the Finance Minister's officially designated delegate.

There are two parts to CPM meetings (the information in the next two paragraphs is derived from personal interviews except where indicated). The first part lasts until around 11.30 a.m. It begins with presentations by the governor and/or the sub-governors on the state of the markets and the general economic situation. CPM meetings are also held just after Bundesbank meetings, so its most recent decisions are also open to discussion. There is then a general discussion about monetary policy and, in particular, interest rate policy in which the representative of the core executive is free to take part. As one protagonist noted: 'Ces échanges sont des échanges assez libres dans lesquelles chacun exprime son point de vue et naturellement explique sa position' (these exchanges are quite open in which everyone states their point of view and of course explains their position). At 11.30 a.m. there is then a coffee break and the core executive representatives leave the room. There is no legal obligation for them to do so, but this is the practice that has been established. The nine CPM members then reconvene and, in the absence of core executive representation, take the necessary decisions concerning interest rate policy.

According to one protagonist, 'aucune décision aussi minime soit-elle n'est prise sans un vote' (no decision however small is taken without a vote). Each member has one vote, and in the case of a tie the governor has the casting vote. It is clear that there are differences of opinion among the various members of the CPM. Indeed, the resignation of Michel Sapin in June 1995 and the replacement of both Jean Boissonat and Bruno de Maulde in January 1997 has weakened the pro-'franc fort' component of the CPM. Their successors, Paul Marchelli, Jean-René Bernard and Pierre Guillen respectively, are reputed to be more 'Eurosceptical' than those they replaced. Nevertheless, to date at least, the CPM has not simply been split into two factions. According to Boissonat, 'les majorités . . . ont été fluctuantes' (majorities have fluctuated) (*Les Echos*, 27–28 January 1995). Indeed, protagonists took great pains to indicate that the CPM was a highly collegial institution. According to one CPM member, this was because the governor allowed everyone to state their opinion, because the number of CPM members was sufficiently large to permit debate but sufficiently small for decisions to be made, and because CPM members themselves were from highly diverse professional backgrounds. It might also be added that CPM members have offices which are next to each other in the same building. Consequently, they see each other extremely frequently and members have established good working relationships.

It is apparent, therefore, that since January 1994 the CPM has demonstrated qualities which are consistent with a central bank which is independent not just in theory but also in practice. As noted above, the 1993 law states that the CPM formulates monetary policy and that its members can neither request nor accept instructions from the government. Evidence clearly indicates that these statutes have been upheld since 1994. CPM members proudly state that they are responsible for deciding monetary policy (personal interviews). In this sense, therefore, the Bank of France is now independent. Trichet himself observed that in terms of the CPM's relationship with the Finance Ministry 'le cordon ombilical est rompu' (the umbilical cordon is cut) (*Les Echos*, 10 January 1994) and the governor has frequently stated that the CPM is both apolitical and transpartisan (see for example *Le Monde*, 17 December 1994).

At the same time, however, there is still a close relationship between the Bank and the core executive. As Alphandéry stated at the time of the first meeting of the CPM, 'les ponts avec le ministre ne seront pas coupés' (the links with the Minister will not be cut off) (*Libération*, 5 January 1994). Indeed, as one member of the CPM stated: 'on n'a pas intérêt à ce que les ponts soient coupés. . . . La politique monétaire dépend tellement des choix budgétaires et des choix européens que nous ne pouvons pas être absents du monde politique' (it is not in our interest that links are cut off. . . . Monetary policy is so dependent on budgetary and European choices that we cannot be absent from the political process' (non-attributable interview). This point is fundamental. Monetary policy, and the ability to fix short-term interest rates, cannot be dissociated from more general economic policies. Despite the Bank's prerogatives in the area of monetary policy, it still has to operate not just in a global economic context and a European economic context but also in a context that is in part determined by the government's budgetary, fiscal, industrial, financial and general European policies. Consequently, while there is no question that the CPM has been freely responsible for taking monetary policy decisions since January 1994, there is also no question that it has had to do so in a context from which the core executive has been far from absent. Therefore, the core executive has remained an important actor in the formulation of monetary policy.

Since January 1994 there have been several significant aspects to the relationship between the Bank and the core executive. First, the core executive has been able to influence the monetary policy-making process through the CPM's appointment procedure. By virtue of the fact that appointments are made in the Council of Ministers and that the President chairs the Council of Ministers, there is no doubt that the head of state is in a position to shape the composition of the CPM. Since his election in May 1995, President Chirac has used his position to appoint three people with whom he is well acquainted and who, as noted above, do not necessarily share the general 'franc fort' consensus. Indeed, the appointments that the President made in January 1997 were extremely controversial. The centrist President of the Senate, René Monory, publicly criticised the appointments of Bernard and Guillen, indicating that he intended to propose a reform of the nomination procedure so as to put an end to the President's ability to influence the appointment procedure (*Le Monde*, 5–6 January 1997).

Second, the core executive maintains an influence through its official and unofficial direct contacts with members of the CPM. The official contacts come in the form of core executive representation at CPM meetings. This representation allows the government's priorities to be expressed and made known to the meeting. No orders are given but there is still a sense in which an environment can be created which helps to shape the course of the CPM's internal decision-making process. The unofficial contacts come in two forms. There are institutionalised unofficial contacts in the shape of the meeting between the governor, the Finance Minister and the Directeur du Trésor which still takes place each week at Bercy, the home of the Finance Ministry. As with the situation prior to 1994, these meetings allow information to be exchanged and different viewpoints to be expressed on a regular basis. There are also uninstitutionalised unofficial contacts in the shape of telephone calls, chance encounters and meetings at receptions, dinner parties and the like. Members of the CPM are not isolated from the political world; their personal address books will often include the names of senior government officials, and it is natural that from time to time they should meet. As one CPM member acknowledged, 'Je suis, moi, un ami personnel du Premier ministre et je trouve aussi que le Président de la République a de l'amitié pour moi' (I am a personal friend of the Prime Minister and I also find that the President is fond of me) (personal interview). These formal and informal, institutionalised and uninstitutionalised, contacts help to regulate the decision-making process and they also allow the core executive to have access to that process.

Third, the core executive maintains an influence through indirect public communication. The government will use the media to put across its point of view. The Finance Minister may make a statement to the press which calls into question the CPM's policy (see, for example, the report in *Le Monde*, 20

October 1995). The President may surreptitiously promote the publication of a newspaper article presenting a scarcely veiled personal criticism of the governor (Aeschimann and Riché 1996: 303–4). In turn, of course, members of the CPM will also use the media to communicate their own preferences. The governor has given a large number of high profile interviews since the beginning of 1994. Other members of the CPM have been less forthcoming but, perhaps increasingly, they have also put pen to paper (see, for example, the articles by Marchelli and Gérard in *Le Monde*, 27 November 1996 and 29 November 1996, respectively). This indirect communication helps to shape public opinion and market opinion, and also helps to pave the way for the more direct contacts that take place between representatives of the two institutions.

Since January 1994, certain events have clearly demonstrated the nature of the relationship between the Bank and core executive. For example, one of the controversial issues during the preparation of the 1993 reform concerned the question of the relationship between external and internal monetary policy. In the end, the law stated that the government fixed the parity of the franc (i.e. external monetary policy), whereas the Bank determined and implemented policy within this general framework (i.e. internal monetary policy). In fact, the distinction between the two areas is not always clear. For example, in March 1995 the franc came under considerable speculative attack. Although the franc was still within the specified limits of the reformed European exchange rate system, the issue of the proper parity of the franc began to be raised. Consequently, while the CPM was still responsible for intervening on the markets and for manipulating interest rates so as to redress the situation, the Finance Minister also began to be drawn into these discussions in the context of the possible need for a parity revision. In fact, speculation ended following an extraordinary meeting of the CPM at 7.30 in the morning on 8 March 1995. The Finance Minister personally attended this meeting and, significantly, this was the only meeting at which the Minister remained in the room (with the blessing of the CPM) when policy decisions were actually made (personal interviews). This example demonstrates the sometimes fuzzy margins of monetary policy. Even though a clearer division of responsibilities for external and internal monetary policy was subsequently restored, this was the occasion when the core executive was most closely involved in the direct formulation of monetary policy since the 1993 reform.

A further indication of the nature of the relationship between the Bank and the core executive can be found in the debate over interest rate policy in the autumn of 1995. At this time, the government was becoming increasingly impatient because interest rates were not coming down as quickly as it would have liked. The government wanted a reduction in interest rates so as to boost growth and lower the cost of debt, whereas the Bank feared that such a reduction would only threaten the value of the franc. In October 1995, matters came to a head. Representatives of the governing majority, including the Finance Minister, Jean Arthuis, publicly criticised the Bank. Indeed, the Prime Minister's office was forced to issue a statement stating that its relations with the Bank were excellent (*Le Monde*, 26 October 1995), a sure sign that something was wrong. During this time a subtle bargaining process was taking place. The Bank indicated, both publicly and privately, that the government's and, in particular, the President's economic policies were not sufficiently clear to permit interest rates to fall (see Aeschimann and Riché 1996: 305–8). It argued that only if the President unequivocally committed himself to EMU and to meeting the convergence criteria would the conditions for a fall in interest rates be possible. On 26 October on the 8.00 p.m. news, Chirac did just that. In the next few days the value of the franc increased markedly, and on 1 November a member of the CPM stated publicly that the President's declaration had paved the way for a reduction in interest rates (*Le Monde*, 3 November 1995). This episode demonstrates the subtlety of the relations between the reformed Bank and the core executive. There was no formal deal; there were no demands made or instructions given. Instead, there was a period during which each side let the other know what it wanted and what it was willing to do in order to bring it about. From the perspective of the CPM: 'nous avons insisté lourdement sur la nécessité de réaliser des économies et, par conséquent, nous avons pesé sur la politique du gouvernement' (we strongly insisted on the need for spending cuts and, as a result, we were able to influence the government's policy) (non-attributable interview). From the perspective of the government, political pressure had been applied to accelerate a cut in interest rates which otherwise might not have been forthcoming.

Finally, the 1995 presidential election provides a good indication of the contemporary relationship between the Bank and the core executive. The election is the most significant event in French political life. It occurs once every seven years and it provides the opportunity for candidates to put forward their competing visions of France and for voters to decide which one they prefer. Needless to say, monetary policy is central, directly or indirectly, to the promises that candidates make. Yet, monetary policy is now in the purview of the CPM. Therefore, there is the incentive for candidates to bring the Bank into the political debate and for the Bank to respond to that incentive. In 1995, Chirac criticised Trichet's comments about the state of the French economy (*Le Monde*, 15 April 1995); by so doing, he was publicly reaffirming his belief that technocrats had too much power and was indirectly signalling that an alternative economic policy was possible. In the context of the 'morosity' which surrounded the 1995 election campaign,

Chirac believed that this would be a popular strategy (Elgie 1996). Soon after, however, Chirac's main rival, Balladur, criticised his competitor's outburst, stating that 'on ne polémique pas avec la Banque de France' (one does not get involved in an argument with the Bank of France) (*Le Monde*, 20 April 1995). Balladur thought that this was a good strategy because it would demonstrate that the hot-headed RPR leader was not presidential material, whereas he himself was. The next day, Chirac appeared on the main television news and produced a letter which Trichet had sent him in which the governor wrote, 'je tiens à ce que vous le sachiez que vous avez toujours exprimé votre très ferme attachement à la stabilité du franc . . .' (I want you to know that you have always indicated your very firm attachment to the stability of the franc) (*Le Monde*, 21 April 1995). Trichet's letter was confidential but Chirac seized upon it to reaffirm his presidential stature. It is no coincidence that this is the first time that the Bank of France has ever been drawn into an electoral campaign in this way. Instead, it is simply a reflection of the changing relationship between the Bank and the core executive.

All these examples demonstrate that the Bank is now a much more important actor than it used to be. However, they also demonstrate that the core executive is still inextricably involved in the general process of monetary policy making. At times, this means that there is a certain degree of confusion as to the respective responsibilities of representatives of the two institutions. At other times, it means that a subtle bargaining game is being played out both publicly and privately by players on both sides. At yet other times, it means that the core executive is seeking to draw the Bank into the electoral and political arena, and that representatives of the Bank will be unable to avoid being drawn in. In short, the Bank is more independent than before but it is still locked into a decision-making process which is just as much political as it is economic and monetary.

7 The political control of economic life

At the heart of the most fundamental questions about the relations between core executives and central banks is the issue of control: whether core executives can, or wish to, exercise control over central banks in terms of either the aims and the substance of monetary policy, or over the appointments of senior personnel to central banks. Obviously, as the previous chapters have demonstrated, at different historical junctures core executives have seen these questions in very different ways, depending on the interaction of the domestic environment in which they were operating, the political objectives and electoral and governing strategies of politicians and the prevailing international economic setting. Clearly, the question of whether, and how, core executives wish to control central banks cannot be separated from the larger economic and political world in which core executives govern. As the historical record repeatedly illuminates, monetary policy does not take place in a vacuum. The aim of this chapter is to examine the questions of control by core executives over central banks, and hence, the variations in levels of economic and political independence of the latter, within an appropriately broad political and economic context. The first part of the chapter explains the general difficulties which core executives, and politicians in particular, face in confronting economic life, and places the recent move towards the abdication of political control of monetary matters by core executives within this context. The second and third parts, primarily using the examples of the British and French experiences, explain the chronological development of political control by core executives over central banks through an analysis of the historical change in the broad trends in the political control of economic life. The final part assesses the imminent creation of a European Central Bank beyond the political control of the core executives of the European Union, or any other supra-national site of political authority, in the light of the particular political and economic context in which European core executives now operate.

The problem of control

For core executives across the world the international economy is an inherently complicated space in which to operate, whatever the particular domestic complexities that press upon them. As Keynes insisted, economic life is most fundamentally characterised by uncertainty. Faced with the opacity of economic causality, economic agents, including governments, must make choices about how to act with regard to an unknown future. In this context, economic decision making can rarely be more than the assessment of the comparative risk of alternatives in relation to circumstances which are at least partially cognitively hidden from those who must exercise their judgment. For example, even if it is possible to identify the abstract circumstances in which a devaluation might effectively stimulate an economy without causing inflation, it is an extremely difficult practical judgment for policy makers to decide if those circumstances at any particular political juncture have been met, especially as circumstances in regard to the foreign exchange markets can change so quickly.[1]

Given the precariousness of their ability to keep even a minimal grip over the general setting in which they must operate, core executives, and politicians in particular, have considerable incentives, at least in the first instance, to apply as much control over economic life as is at all beneficial. In the words of John Dunn, 'both for private citizens and for rulers, accordingly, the choice of effective economic policies is, under normal conditions, the most important and permanent of political needs' (Dunn 1990: 35). To win votes, politicians must use their political power to try to deliver, or promise for the future, particular economic benefits to at least a sizeable section of the electorate. For the same reason, they must claim that general economic outcomes are the direct result of their actions whatever the frequent implausibility of the claimed causal relationships (Butler 1995). To refuse to act in any kind of economic terms, or to present government as if this were the case, would be for politicians everywhere an act of electoral suicide.

At the same time, however, the exercise of political control in economic policy is deeply problematic for politicians. Of course, there are many factors that in the final instance politicians can do absolutely nothing about, from the micro level, such as the performance of individual domestic firms, to the international level, such as the behaviour of economic agents in other nation-states. But, just as crucially, even if politicians could act for themselves more effectively with regard to other sites of agency, they are frequently not in a position to know which policies are most likely to win the approval of the electorate. The only firm conclusions of the best empirical evidence are that a macroeconomic downturn is associated with a fall in government support and that voters choose between parties according to a complicated mix of retrospective and prospective judgments about economic performance (Lewis-Beck 1988; for more determinate conclusions see Grier 1991; Hibbs 1977; Nordhaus 1975; Alt 1985; Beck 1984; Williams 1980). As Schumpeter argued, citizens of modern representative democracies tend to think about politics with less responsibility and ability than they display in other aspects of their lives (Schumpeter 1994). On economic matters, the most pressing of political issues, this is without doubt particularly true. Most citizens are economic agents but they are far more likely to see themselves as fundamentally dependent on the political agency of others to meet their economic needs and aspirations. Similarly their understanding of even relatively simple economic causality is often poor. For example, electorates tend to welcome the short-term benefits of an expansionary monetary policy, whatever the economic circumstances, without considering the often potentially greater long-term costs. Politicians will always be tempted, therefore, to give visible priority to the most politically salient economic issues out of all proportion to their actual economic utility, even if to do so damages their longer term ability to try to control the economy to their own ends.

The general move towards central bank independence has been in the final instance a response to these dilemmas. After the collapse of Bretton Woods and the American-driven march towards financial liberalisation, politicians found monetary policy too difficult a piece of comparative risk assessment to trust themselves to carry out with enough reasonable hope for success. Politically, they faced the constant temptation to satisfy the desire of electorates for short-term economic benefits, whatever the potentially more destructive long-term consequences. Externally, they were confronted with the massive uncertainties generated by the financial and, in particular, foreign exchange markets which raised the direct economic cost of attempting to satisfy those desires. Politicians hoped that if central banks were made responsible for judging monetary policy within a statutory framework defined by the pursuit of price stability, then they themselves could preside over the delivery of a set of particular anti-inflationary benefits without risking the economic and political pitfalls inherent in more ambitious projects of political control over economic life.

The historical development of political control

In the eighteenth and nineteenth centuries, core executives saw no need to exercise political control over what we would now describe as macroeconomic life. Indeed, they did not see that there was a macroeconomic problem. At the same time, even where some limited form of representative democracy had taken hold, as in Britain and France, politicians saw little need to think about how to deliver economic services to their electorates and did not encourage public expectations of government as a site of economic agency. Neither the questions of how to create wealth nor how to distribute it really featured in political life; the terms of politics, or at least those of high politics, were essentially defined outside the economic sphere. What mattered in Britain politically were constitutional questions and foreign policy, for example, while French politics was dominated by the struggle between secular republicanism and Catholic conservatism in the long aftermath of the Revolution. Even when economic crisis did threaten after 1873, those governments that felt compelled to act resorted to protectionism, a form of political control over economic life which was inherently tied to strategic foreign policy considerations and which in its essence predated the modern state.

Consequently, so far as core executives did wish to control central banks during the nineteenth century, in particular, it was not to exercise any political control over economic life. For their part, during the first half of the century, British governments wanted to control the commercial gains of the Bank of England and, just as significantly, its capacity to create credit. What these governments were defending was an ideological idea about how economic life normatively should work. From this vantage point institutions vested with legal authority, such as central banks, were a potentially poisonous and corrupting influence and needed to be kept in check. More generally core executives, as demonstrated both in France and Britain, primarily sought control over their central banks to ensure that their military purposes would not be compromised by the absence of funds on conducive terms. In part, this meant that governments were keen to establish a firm grip on their own financial resources, most significantly through the creation of income tax. More directly, they tried to exercise some control over the appointment and dismissal of central bank personnel. In France, at the beginning of the nineteenth century, Napoleon wanted to protect his military efforts by creating an at least partially politically dependent Bank of France. In Britain over a century later, the Coalition government's anxiety about the critical state of British war finances led to the first dismissal of a Governor of the Bank of England.

It was during the interwar years, as macroeconomic policy became politicised, that economic life began to take on its contemporary problematic form for core executives (for a discussion of the international economic and financial context, see League of Nations (1944)). Both the expansion of representative democracy after 1918 and the external threat posed to its continuance meant that politicians, in particular, faced considerable incentives to exercise some political control over economic matters. By the mid-1920s, politicians were deeply aware that decisions taken by central banks had fundamental consequences in terms of the structural conditions in which they had to act. By using its own unrestrained judgment, the Bank of France effectively precipitated the downfall of two centre-left governments; in Britain, the Conservative government, led by Stanley Baldwin that lost power in 1929 over the issue of unemployment, believed itself grievously damaged by the Bank of England's conduct of monetary policy after the return to the gold standard at the prewar parity. More generally, if elected governments themselves could not exercise power in a way that could make a difference to the economic lives of their enlarged electorates, then it was quite possible that citizens would turn away from representative democracy. In this context, for politicians to be seen not to be governing but rather accepting the authority of unelected and seemingly economically privileged central banks was clearly profoundly dangerous.

Yet, however strong the need and desire for political control, achieving it required a new *modus vivendi* for core executives. As Winston Churchill so wretchedly discovered, politicians could not act differently unless they acquired better cognitive knowledge about how economic life actually worked. Just as significantly, they needed to find a means of insulating their domestic economies from some of the massive volatility of the international economy, particularly with regard to capital flows across national borders. Consequently, it was only after the collapse of the gold standard in 1930–2 and the subsequent penetration of some of Keynes' ideas about the impact of monetary policy on economic life that the French and British core executives exercised any enduring control over the operation of monetary policy by their respective central banks. In Britain, the Chancellor simply asserted the authority to judge interest rates for himself and bureaucratised the formal consideration of monetary policy in the Treasury. In France, the Popular Front government used the legislative process to gain full control of the personnel at the centre of the Bank of France and create a *de facto* far more unified site of political agency over monetary policy. Strikingly, however, in both cases core executive control over central banks was not matched by any real effort to exercise greater control over other aspects of economic life outside the traditional realm of international trade. The British government steadfastly refused to match an expansionary monetary policy with any move to develop an active fiscal policy, while in France the Popular Front government eschewed exchange controls, in practice the necessary condition for their preferred monetary policy, until it was too late to save itself.

After the Second World War, still mindful of the failures of the interwar years and their ultimately terrible cost in terms of representative democracy and security, Western European core executives created for themselves a far more ambitious and comprehensive project for the political control of significant parts of economic life. In pure monetary terms, politicians in both France and Britain institutionalised their existing control over central banks through nationalisation. Against the backdrop of exchange controls, for the duration of the Bretton Woods era they not only controlled interest rates but decided, according to their own judgment, for what purposes monetary policy would be used and who, in central banks, would at any particular time have responsibility for policy implementation. In the larger economic realm, governments used an array of different policies and policy instruments to try to secure particular productive and distributional outcomes, according to their own preferences (Shonfeld 1965). To a lesser or greater degree in particular cases, they nationalised significant parts of the industrial sector of the economy, allowing both some direct control over both industrial production and strategy and the setting of prices and employment conditions in politically charged areas of economic life. More critically, many sought to increase the supply-side rationality and productivity of the private sector through either corporatism or indicative planning. On occasion, in relation to both the public and private sectors, these governments looked to achieve some control over the business cycle through a discretionary fiscal policy. At the same time, as Alan Milward has persuasively argued, the governments that committed themselves to the Treaties of Paris and Rome in the 1950s saw in economic integration a means to strengthen their capacity to politically act in an economically interdependent world (Milward 1992). In this context, politicians across Western Europe trumpeted their new assumed ability to control economic life, promising their electorates that they could deliver ever higher levels of growth, employment and expenditure on the welfare state, and asked to be judged accordingly.

Unsurprisingly, the reality of postwar economic life, and the causality of West European success, was far more complicated than the picture painted in the prevalent political discourse. Certainly it was not simply political control that was yielding all the economic benefits that most citizens enjoyed. In the words of Peter Gourevitch: 'Prosperity reinforced the economic policies thought to have caused it. The mixed economy and demand management coincided with prosperity. Public debate attributed causality to the linkage' (Gourevitch 1989: 270). At least part of Western Europe's economic success was rooted in particular dynamics of economic activity over which core executives could either exercise no control, or from which they could simply contingently benefit. Whatever particular policies core executives pursued, and some, most notably in West Germany (Katzenstein 1987), reaped significant rewards from their corporatist endeavours, the Western European economies benefited from the growth of opportunities offered by postwar reconstruction, technological advancement and the external supply of cheap commodities. What certainly did not particularly matter in economic terms was Keynesianism. After all, Keynes' General Theory was in the first instance a prescription for how governments could stimulate recovery from a depression. Nonetheless, in many ways it was the fundamental political assumption of Keynesianism, the idea that government could manage economic life to the greater collective good, which politicians presented to electorates as the intellectual framework for the whole postwar project of political control (Milward 1992: chapter 2). By contrast, exchange controls, which were ironically part of Bretton Woods at the insistence of Keynes himself and the necessary international condition for domestic economic control according to the tastes of particular core executives (Ruggie 1982), rarely featured in postwar political discourse. Consequently, once exchange controls were abolished and Keynesianism was discredited, core executives would find it far more difficult both to achieve practical political control over economic life and to convince their electorates that they could be a site of reasonably useful economic agency.

The contradictions inherent in the postwar political project began to be exposed in the 1970s. In the wake of the collapse of Bretton Woods and the oil price shock it was clear that economic life, both at the international and domestic levels, had profoundly changed. Led by the United States, which was forced to confront the consequences of its own economic profligacy during the Cold War, governments gradually responded by divesting themselves of exchange controls in a bid to attract footloose capital for their domestic purposes (see Helleiner 1994). In abolishing exchange controls, governments increased the uncertainty of the economic environment in which they had to operate. In particular, they massively increased the uncertainty generated by the foreign exchange markets. Consequently, they made it even more difficult for themselves to make prudent judgments about the comparative risk of alternative policy options. Matters were made still worse when certain governments responded to the recession and inflation of the 1970s by pumping ever higher levels of demand into their economies. Somewhat unsurprisingly in this context, the idea took hold in the foreign exchange and financial markets that politicians and bureaucrats would always look to maximise a political utility, not an economic and social welfare function. Through ridding themselves of the means of politically controlling international capital flows, governments had made the exercise of their own judgment a deeply dangerous enterprise.

In this context, financial liberalisation redefined the possibilities of politics in the postwar world. From the 1970s, domestic projects centred around the political control of parts of economic life became increasingly untenable. As both the Mitterrand and Thatcher governments discovered painfully, politicians could no longer decide for themselves on some aspect of the economy which they wished to control – whether that be aggregate domestic demand, key sectors of the industrial economy or the domestic money supply – because the overall economic cost transmitted through the exchange rate and the balance of payments was too high. In particular, financial liberalisation mitigated against any effort to exercise political control over economic life for the kind of social democratic purposes which lay at the heart of the postwar political project (Thompson 1997). Governments that needed to keep a firm grip on public expenditure and budget deficits, even in times of recession, to try to maintain credibility in the foreign exchange markets could not but seek to reduce their expenditure on the welfare state. Governments that desired to compete for international investment for domestic growth needed to remain competitive in terms of their taxation structure with other states (Lee and McKenzie 1989). With the concurrent further liberalisation of world trade and the economic rise of East Asia producing gainers and losers in Western Europe, according to wage and skill competitiveness (Wood 1994), governments increasingly came to operate in an economic world in which it made little sense to try to exercise political control according to the idea that citizens have a collective interest in the collective performance of the national economy.

Yet, whatever the enormity of change, in terms of the relationship between politicians and the electorate the incentives for core executives, and politicians in particular, to exercise political control over economic life remained relatively undiminished. Crucially, public expectations, encouraged at least in part by the continuity in the political discourse of core executives, were still defined by the experience of the first postwar era (Clarke *et al.* 1993). The public realism attributed to the fictional Bill Clinton in *Primary Colours* – 'no politician can make it be the way it used to be. Because we're living in a new world now. . . . You've got to do the heavy lifting your own selves. I can't do it for you' (Anonymous 1996: 161) – has not as a rule permeated political life. Unsurprisingly, public attitudes towards agency for economic life have been unstable. For example, while an exit poll conducted during the British general election of 1992 showed that almost half of those questioned blamed 'world economic conditions' for the depressed state of the British economy (Crewe 1993) – an attribution not at all causally plausible (see Smith 1992) – the British Conservative government was never able to recover politically from the fall of the sterling parity in September 1992. Practically, governments cannot simply try to pursue the most optimal policies in the context of economic liberalisation without regard for political considerations. The most economically productive response to trade liberalisation, for example, would be a large-scale reassignment of labour. But, since this raises fundamental questions of equity which strike at the heart of citizens' normative ideas about representative democracy, it would be an extraordinarily difficult task for governments to achieve.

Reassigning labour may be in the final instance the only practically useful response to a particular set of circumstances that may be deemed unfair by abstract considerations of justice, but it also appears to privilege the interests of some parts of the electorate over others. This is, of course, particularly apparent when governments, through their own choices, have helped to shape the boundaries of competitiveness. In the same context, although the EU has offered European governments the means to control some of the consequences of economic interdependence more effectively, politicians must justify integration to increasingly Eurosceptic electorates who, at least on occasion, seem anxious to see some demonstration of national political control (Gamble 1995).

In terms of particular relationships with central banks, this new world created a particularly complicated set of incentives for core executives. Both the French and British governments, after some initial hesitation by the former, responded to the early economic crisis of the 1970s by trying to strengthen their existing grip on their respective central banks. In France, the government used legislation to place more dependable personnel in the Bank of France. Meanwhile, British politicians simply reiterated their authority to decide interest rates for themselves, however injudiciously. In the early 1980s both the Mitterrand and Thatcher governments found themselves in deep conflict with their respective central banks as, in different political spaces, they tried to implement economic policies contrary to the constraints of the international setting in which they needed to operate. In this context, maintaining core executive control over central banks meant fierce confrontation. In the case of Britain, where the government under Nigel Lawson's chancellorship came to treat the Bank of England with complete disregard, the confrontation lasted for the best part of a decade and spilled out into the public domain. The dilemma, unsurprisingly, was that such confrontation ultimately produced political and economic costs for both governments. Core executive control of central banks was made into a salient political issue in itself. The more heavy-handed political control became, the more difficult it became to justify.

Contemporary central bank independence and political control

By committing itself in March 1983 to anti-inflationary policies to defend the franc in the ERM, the French government took its first decisive step away from the political control of monetary policy. While the French Finance Minister and Treasury still formally set the level of interest rates for the next decade, and the idea floated in 1986 to make the Bank of France independent failed to gather political support, in practical terms French monetary policy was now, in the final instance at least, being decided by the Bundesbank. In effect, the French government was choosing the way of exchange rate stability and long-term credibility, in the hope that this would eventually yield real economic benefits for the electorate, over the unpredictable economic consequences of continuing political control in the prevailing international setting. Yet, there was no necessary reason why either shadowing the Bundesbank through the ERM or finally giving greater autonomy to the Bank of France was the only practical option for the French government. The British Conservative government demonstrated during the 1980s and the 1990s that political control over monetary policy can still be possible. The consequences may at times be extremely damaging, as borne out by the frequent interest rate premiums and sterling crises of the 1980s and their deflationary aftermath. But, in first pursuing an independent monetary policy after sterling's departure from the ERM and then persistently defying the Bank of England over the level of interest rates from 1995, John Major and Kenneth Clarke, in particular, proved that in certain circumstances political control could still yield substantive economic benefit, despite the free movement of capital across national borders. The choice confronting governments with open medium-sized economies, after the Mitterrand and Thatcher experiments, was whether to gamble on a high-risk strategy of political control, or opt for prudence.

The manner in which particular EU governments responded to this dilemma was in practice determined by their attitude towards European integration, mitigated by domestic political considerations. Certainly, it was the intense desire to participate in the single currency project that created the strongest and most direct incentive in the 1990s for most governments to cede formal control over monetary policy to central banks. By 1997, most EU governments were working with independent central banks on the terms required by the Maastricht Treaty. For its part, the French government not only made the Bank of France independent to comply with the treaty but used this legislative action to help itself qualify for entry to monetary union in 1999. By granting central bank independence relatively early, French ministers hoped to gain anti-inflationary credibility in the foreign exchange markets so as to keep its interest rates as close as possible to those in Germany and, therefore, make it easier for themselves to reduce the budget deficit and meet the Maastricht convergence criteria. By contrast, even when the British Conservative government reassessed the risk of returning to political control in 1992–3, its European policy provided no incentive to make the Bank of England independent. The dramatic exit from the ERM and the ferocious spill-over in terms of Maastricht ratification killed any realistic hope within the British government that it could utilise its 'opt-in' to the single currency later in the decade. Unsurprisingly in this context, the

British Conservative government chose to forge a new relationship with the Bank of England and a new framework for a domestically oriented monetary policy well outside the EU mainstream.

Domestically, all the EU governments operated in a very particular set of political circumstances that inevitably had some bearing on how they managed the independence issue, especially in terms of implementing change. In France the Gaullist government, led by Balladur, chose to act quickly because the Prime Minister wanted both to minimise as far as possible the economic cost of defending the franc in 1993 and to further his own presidential ambitions. Meanwhile, British governments could not, even if they had wished to pursue a different EU policy, have escaped the conundrum of how to reconcile an independent Bank of England on the terms demanded by the Maastricht Treaty with the constitutional principle of parliamentary sovereignty. When the incoming Labour government in 1997 took the radical decision to give the Bank greater autonomy, it explicitly kept for itself both the authority to set an inflation target and to give the Bank instructions in circumstances of its own consideration. Abdicating formal political control on the German model was not something any British government could contemplate without a far more radical change in political and institutional structures.

Nonetheless, if the monetary union project created the general momentum in the EU towards central bank independence during the 1990s, it also gave core executives, with newly established autonomous central banks, a continuing means of access – albeit partial – to monetary decision making. In France, for example, an intense desire to qualify for monetary union has dominated both the core executive and the Bank of France. This shared objective has effectively restricted the space for substantial disagreement about monetary matters. The imperatives in policy have been towards maintaining the franc parity within the ERM, interest rate convergence with Germany and reducing the budget deficit. In these circumstances, French ministers have been able to bargain discretely with the Bank of France to ensure that their concerns are at least tacitly considered when decisions on interest rates are made. Consequently, to the extent that certain French ministers have on occasion articulated misgivings about their lack of political control, they have effectively been expressing reservations about their own exchange rate and European policies. So far as the French government has remained firmly committed to monetary union, it was not likely to perceive the Bank of France as a forcible constraint on its ability to manage the economy according to its own preferences.

Evidently, in general terms and different circumstances, as the German experience indicates, the price for foregoing political control either over a central bank or monetary policy itself can be far higher. Unlike its French counterpart, the German government cannot control the appointment of the majority of key personnel to the central bank. The Central Bank Council of the Bundesbank is dominated by the Presidents of the regional branches of the Bundesbank, who are appointed by the Bundesrat, acting on the *de facto* binding suggestions of the Länder (Katzenstein 1987: 64). On significant occasions, notably in times of recession, the German government and the Bundesbank have been deeply divided about fundamental economic priorities. While the legitimacy of the authority of the Bundesbank certainly depends to some extent on the central bank's practical flexibility in the final instance (Marsh 1992), for the most part German governments have had to accept that, even in what are for them exceptionally dangerous electoral circumstances, their will cannot prevail. Three postwar Chancellors – Ludwig Erhard in 1966, Kurt George Kiesinger in 1969 and Helmut Schmidt in 1982 – saw their tenure in office abruptly terminated by the consequences of the Bundesbank's pursuit of a particular monetary policy (Marsh 1992: 170). In this sense, giving up political control, even when its direct economic utility has been mitigated, creates dangers of a kind to which the French core executive has thus far not really been exposed.

At the same time, the German experience demonstrates that to reap the available rewards from an independent central bank core executives must, if they cannot rely on the self-control of other economic agents, exercise political control over some non-monetary aspects of economic life (Hall 1994). As Keynes argued in the first chapter of the General Theory, if politics is to be relatively inflation-free without high levels of involuntary unemployment, then money wage rates need to be kept depressed. (Given that workers are more usually concerned with relative than absolute real wages, in a decentralised and uncontrolled economy the only method for real wages to fall without impairing the relative status of any particular set of workers is a general rise in prices. For further discussion, see Tobin (1972)). For the most part, successive German governments during the postwar era, at least until the aftermath of reunification, used their authority and Germany's social market economic structures to encourage, and if necessary enforce, effective wage restraint (for the contribution of the organisation and political strategies of German trade unions to this outcome, see Markovits (1986)). If the economically active electorate and organised economic interest groups rarely challenged the doctrinal importance of wage restraint in regard to export competitiveness, then this was in part because German governments saw the defence of this consensus as part of their political project (Kreile 1978). The only real rebellion from either a German government or the electorate in this area came in 1973–4. Against an inflation rate of only 7 per cent, and encouraged by the expansionary rhetoric of the social democratic government, employees negotiated wage increases for themselves averaging between 12 and 15 per cent. Unsurprisingly, the Bundesbank responded by tightening an already restrictive monetary policy. In the wake of the severe unemployment that ensued, the general commitment to wage restraint was restored. In 1980, when inflation again rose to 6 per cent, all economic agents adjusted their economic expectations to limit the likely restrictiveness imposed by the Bundesbank (Thiel 1989). Crucially, core executives, by divesting themselves of political responsibility for monetary policy, cannot provide themselves with an automatic pilot for economic management even given the limited political possibilities in economic policy defined by financial liberalisation.

The European Central Bank and the future of political control

It is within this ultimately complicated political context that the core executives of the European Union states will wrestle with the question of control in relation to the European System of Central Banks (ESCB). Given the overwhelming need for German consent to a single currency, it would have been practically impossible for the EU governments not to have committed themselves to the principle of central bank independence, both for the European Central Bank (ECB) and the national central banks, in creating the single currency. In January 1991 the French Finance Ministry suggested that the Council of Economic and Finance Ministers (ECOFIN) should be strengthened into a 'gouvernement économique' (Dyson 1994: 147). Around the same time, the French government submitted a draft treaty to the Inter-Governmental Conference (IGC) on Monetary Union which would have established some political control over monetary matters. In particular it proposed that ECOFIN and the European Council be given a role in drawing up the broad guidelines for economic policy as well as the power to introduce minimum reserve requirements (Italianer 1993: 69). The former, of course, would have posed an implicit challenge to the authority of any European Central Bank, statutorily required to pursue price stability as its prime economic objective. Unsurprisingly the German government, backed by the Benelux states and Denmark (Garrett 1993: 55), quickly rebuffed most of the French plan and the independence of the European Central Bank was uncontested for the remainder of the IGC.

The final Treaty on European Union offers no substantive means for either ECOFIN and the European Council, or individual governments, to exercise any political control over monetary policy. In terms of economic independence, the European Central Bank will be at least as autonomous as the Bundesbank with a single stated mission to maintain price stability and the sole authority to decide monetary policy. In the words of the Treaty:

> The primary objective of the ESCB shall be to maintain price stability. Without prejudice to the objective of price stability, the ESCB shall support the general economic policies in the Community. . . . When exercising the powers and carrying out the tasks and duties conferred upon them by this Treaty and the Statute of the ESCB, neither the ECB, nor a national central bank, nor any members of their decision-making bodies shall seek or take instructions from Community institutions or bodies, from any government of a Member State or from any other body. The Community institutions and bodies and governments of the Member-States undertake to respect this principle and not to seek to influence the members of the decision-making bodies of the ECB or of the national central banks in the performance of their tasks.
>
> (European Communities 1992, Articles 105 and 107)

This formal guarantee of a high level of economic independence is unlikely to be effectively challenged in day-to-day practical terms once a single currency is created. Given the strictness of the convergence criteria, and the sure insistence of the German Constitutional Court and Bundestag that they shall be adhered to, the monetary union that is likely to emerge in 1999 may consist in the first instance of only a minority of EU states. Since those which will have qualified to participate will *de facto* be those states that have been most successful in maintaining low inflation and fiscal discipline, there is unlikely to be a majority who wish to dilute the commitment to price stability as the primary objective of monetary policy. At the same time, in all probability it will be more difficult within a diffuse supra-national site of monetary authority for either ECOFIN or individual governments to exercise the kind of informal influence that the French core executive has retained within the Bank of France.

In terms of political independence, the European Central Bank will probably be more autonomous than any other central bank in the world (Crawford 1993: 195). There will not be any real opportunity for individual governments to control the personnel of the central bank through appointments (see Appendix 4). The Governing Council of the ECB will be composed of a six-person Executive Board (a president, vice-president and four other members) and the governors of each national central bank participating in the single currency. Members of the Executive Board will be appointed for eight-year non-renewable terms by common accord of the governments of the member states at the level of heads of state or government, at the recommendation of ECOFIN, after consultation with the

European Parliament and the Governing Council of the ECB (European Communities 1992, Article 109a).[2] Any individual government will, therefore, be able to control one appointment to the Governing Council and have one vote around the table in the appointment of six others. Even with regard to appointing the governor of its own national central bank, each government will be constrained. The Treaty stipulates that all members of the monetary union must provide that the term of office of a governor shall be no less than five years. In practice this means that no term can be shorter than electoral cycles for national legislatures in any member-state. Any national governor who is dismissed will have the right of appeal to the European Court of Justice (European Communities 1992, Article 14). For its part, ECOFIN, even it managed to act with a single will, could only control the appointment of half of the Council if no more than six states joined monetary union. The larger the union grows, the less opportunity there will be for ECOFIN to exert collective influence. Only in the somewhat improbable circumstances that the individual governments represented in ECOFIN acted collectively at the EU level and then co-ordinated their respective appointments of national central bank governors could politicians exercise any kind of political control over the ECB. Neither will the ECB be held to account for its performance by any other site of political authority. It will need only to draw up quarterly reports and address an annual report on the activities of the ECSB and on the monetary policy of both the previous and current year to the attention of the European Parliament, ECOFIN, the Commission and the European Council (European Communities 1992, Protocol on the Statutes of the European System of Central Banks and of the European Central Bank, Article 15; for further discussion of the independence of the ECB, see Crawford (1993: chapter 14)). Overall, the ECB scores 0.68 on a scale from 0.00 for complete dependence to 1.00 for complete independence (see Appendix 4).

At the same time, exercising control over wages as a counterpart to an independent central bank will have particular complications for governments within a European monetary union. Clearly, the EU not only does not possess the same kind of institutions for the co-ordination of wage bargaining that existed in Germany, but member states have shown no inclination to create such a framework for the future. The regulation of labour markets affecting the rights of collective organisations of workers and wage negotiation are explicitly excluded from the Social Chapter Protocol of the Maastricht Treaty (see Lange 1993). Given the difficulties in sustaining national corporatist structures during the 1990s and the mutual incompatibility of existing national industrial relations systems, there is little reason to presume that an EU system of collective bargaining will emerge in the foreseeable future (Streeck and Schmitter 1991). The effective pursuit of wage restraint within the single currency area will, therefore, be dependent on the continuing viability of national structures and the efforts of national governments. Those governments that qualify for monetary union in the first instance will obviously have been sufficiently successful at encouraging wage restraint to have maintained a low level of inflation. Indeed in 1995, of all the EU states, only Greece, Sweden and Denmark recorded an annual increase in unit labour costs above 3 per cent (*Economic Outlook*, June 1996, A16). The question for participating states will be whether success in this regard has been primarily causally dependent on high levels of unemployment, or if, as they aspire to higher levels of growth and employment within the single currency project, more direct political control than hitherto deployed by most governments will be required to squeeze wage expectations.

Outside the direct monetary realm, there are likely to be very few alternative means for exercising any direct political control over economic life in the context of monetary union. Fiscally, governments will from the outset be very constrained, and will remain so unless unemployment within the European Union, and hence demands on the welfare state, are dramatically reduced. In September 1995 the German government called for 'the installation of additional measures [beyond those stipulated in the Treaty on European union] to secure budget discipline' (*Financial Times*, 12 September 1995). Fifteen months later, in December 1996, after extremely fraught negotiations between Germany and France, the EU Heads of Government agreed to a Stability and Growth Pact which will impose virtually automatic penalties on member states running budget deficits above 3 per cent. Only in the event of either a natural disaster, or if they experience a fall in Gross Domestic Product (GDP) of at least 2 per cent over a year, will member states automatically be exempt from penalties. (During the last thirty years, such a severe recession has only occurred thirteen times in any of the fifteen EU states). In cases where GDP falls between 0.75 and 2.0 per cent, EU finance ministers will be able to use political discretion in deciding whether to impose penalties, taking into account factors such as the abruptness of the downturn (*Financial Times*, 14 December 1994).[3] Given the difficult experience that almost all the EU governments have faced in achieving the same target for budget deficits set in the Maastricht convergence criteria, governments that participate in the single currency will be committing themselves to enduring fiscal austerity. Even more critically, they effectively will prevent themselves from dealing with rising unemployment during a recession through the existing structures of their welfare states. If the French government began the drive towards monetary union in 1988 hoping that a European Central Bank, in which Germany occupied simply one more seat around the table, would create an international setting in which co-ordinated fiscal expansion could be used as a tool for economic growth (see Kennedy 1991), it successors will find little space to exercise political judgement over broad fiscal questions.

Even in terms of exchange rate management, where formal authority for deciding policy in relation to non-Community currencies will lie with the Council of Ministers (Council of the European Communities, 1992, Article 109), governments will in practice be able to exercise limited political control. Although authority in Germany over exchange rate policy similarly lies with the federal government, the Bundesbank has never shown itself willing simply to allow the politicians to decide German exchange rate policy without fiercely pressing its own preferences (Marsh 1992: chapter 6). Of course on several important occasions, most dramatically over the terms of German monetary reunification in 1990, the Bundesbank has been forced in the final instance to accept the will of the politicians (Marsh 1992: chapter 8). Nevertheless, in terms of the routine dilemmas posed by exchange rate management, any relatively independent central bank, like the Bundesbank, is in a strong position to constrain the options open to governments. If, for example, a government wishes to devalue its currency against that of a major competitor, then an independent central bank, which judges that such an action would jeopardise price stability, can simply raise interest rates so as to strengthen the currency. While the consequences of a fall in the Euro against the dollar will, by virtue of the size and trading patterns of the EU economy, be less inflationary than a similar depreciation of the deutschmark, there is no good reason to suppose that an independent European Central Bank committed to price stability will not be anxious to preserve some measure of exchange rate stability.

More radically, the efforts by the French government to try to use European integration itself as a means for the strong currency states to exercise some political control over the economic policies of the other member states have so far reaped little reward. After the devaluations by a succession of member states, both inside and outside the ERM in 1992–3, the French government pushed hard for what would have amounted to the imposition of some kind of supra-national authority over individual governments' exchange rate policies. In 1996 French ministers requested on several occasions that member states that engaged in what they deemed, 'competitive devaluations' should receive reduced regional aid, only for the proposals to be blocked by the European Commission (*Financial Times*, 31 July 1996). Neither, in the same year, was the French government able to convince a sufficient number of its partners to make membership of a new Exchange Rate Mechanism compulsory for those states not participating in the single currency. As events presently stand, therefore, EU governments outside the single currency area will be able to judge economic policy for themselves, as far as their own preferences on joining monetary union and the constraints of the foreign exchange and financial markets allow.

Palpably, anxiety is mounting within the French core executive over the prospective lack of any substantial political control over macroeconomic life within monetary union. In June 1996 the French Finance Minister, Jean Arthuis, publicly suggested that the single currency states should form a G7 style club to co-ordinate policy on such issues as setting budgetary targets, implementing budgetary policy and exchange rate matters (*Financial Times*, 18 June 1996). Five months later, Alain Juppé told the French National Assembly that it was time to discuss growth and employment in the planned monetary union and that the future European Central Bank should be held to account by governments (*Financial Times*, 28 November 1996). Most dramatically, Jacques Chirac, just prior to the European Council held in Dublin in December 1996 at which the Stability and Growth Pact was due to be finalised, declared that members of the single currency needed to turn themselves into a 'political power', capable of 'indicating to the European Central Bank what are the limits of its action and giv[ing] it general orientations' (*Financial Times*, 14 December 1996). Unsurprisingly, however, Germany has thus far done no more than pay lip service to French worries. In March 1997 Germany did agree to the creation of a symbolic Council for the single currency states but insisted that the new institution would have no substantive powers (*Financial Times*, 13 March 1997). Quite simply, the German government cannot, for constitutional and electoral reasons, be seen to be diluting the principle of non-political control effectively embodied in both the Treaty of European Union and the Stability and Growth Pact.

In a historical context, the creation of a European Central Bank represents the most complete departure in Europe from the idea, dating from the interwar years, that politicians can and should exercise political control over monetary policy. This can be clearly seen in Appendices 2–4 by comparing the figures for political and economic independence. Even following the most recent reforms of the Bank of England and the Bank of France, the British and French core executives still retain the capacity to exert a degree of political control over their respective central banks. Whereas both the Bank of England and the Bank of France currently enjoy a considerable degree of economic independence (with unweighted scores of 0.50 and 0.64 respectively), both are also still subject to a certain not insignificant amount of political control, notably concerning bank appointments and the internal decision-making process (with unweighted scores of 0.46 and 0.53 respectively). By contrast, unless the Treaty is revised, the European Central Bank will benefit from a considerable degree of both economic and political independence (with unweighted scores of 0.64 and 0.72 respectively). Moreover, the figures for the European Central Bank are measuring the degree of independence not from national governments, replete with their own direct popular legitimacy, but from the Commission and/or the Council of Ministers, both of which themselves only enjoy a limited amount of indirect political legitimacy.

Put simply, under the proposed European System of Central Banks politicians will not decide interest rates for themselves and they will not be in a position to control the people who will. During the interwar years governments became increasingly desperate, under pressure generated by the expansion in democratic representation and the internal and external threat to the legitimacy of democracy, to bring monetary policy and central banks into representative democratic life. Confronted, in circumstances of economic collapse after 1929, with a choice between representative democratic responsiveness and the international financial structures which significantly legitimised the depoliticisation of monetary policy by virtue of the operation of a partial automatic pilot for judgments about interest rates, most governments across Europe prioritised the former. Now, the EU governments have judged that in the international setting they have helped to create, it is too dangerous in economic, and sometimes political, terms to make monetary policy responsive to the dynamics of representative democracy. Interest rates are again a matter of technocratic judgment because politicians have concluded that for the sake of long-term practical benefit monetary policy should only be directed towards an objective, namely price stability, that will often clash with the expressed preferences of electoral majorities. If, therefore, a European Central Bank does what politicians would want to do, but often feel tempted not to, the greater the practical economic returns for governments.

Nonetheless, there is no good reason to suppose that the issue of political control over macroeconomic life, including monetary policy, has been historically buried. In the long term the incentives to find new means to exercise practical political control are likely to persist because of the ultimately entrenched dilemmas in regard to economic life created by the particular relationship between politicians and electorates in representative democracies. Certainly economic life will continue to be the most salient aspect of European politics. Since monetary policy will remain, in whatever setting, a judgment about the comparative risk of alternatives, the European Central Bank will almost certainly at times judge unfortuitously, or at least be widely perceived to have done so, given the opaqueness of economic causality. For electorates to accept that mistakes in judgment are simply an inevitable hazard of economic decision making will require not only an enduring consensus about the value of price stability but also about the authority of the EU as a site of political agency. If, as John Dunn has argued, 'a *demos* which can only be prevented from maiming its own future interests by being purposefully excluded from decision-making . . . is likely to prove too greedy, too myopic and too impatient to put up with being governed, over questions which it seems to be important, in the teeth of its own will' (Dunn 1996b: 521), politicians across the EU would need to remain collectively committed to the proposition that 'there is no alternative' for the independence of the ECB to remain unquestioned. Given that the value of European integration, and monetary integration in particular, is far from an uncontested public good across the EU, such a consensus is extremely unlikely to emerge at either elite or electoral level. Whatever its practical economic benefits for core executives, permanently foresaking political control for central bank independence at the supra-national level cannot in the final instance immunise politicians from the pressures to exercise political judgment over economic life.

Appendix 1

Calculating Central Bank independence

Political independence (overall weighting 0.50)

1) *Governor* (weighting 0.30)

a) Appointment	1.00	Appointments made by the bank itself
	0.50	Appointments made with some bank involvement
	0.00	Appointments made by government
b) Nomination	1.00	Nominations made by the bank itself
	0.50	Nominations made with some bank involvement
	0.00	Nominations made by government
c) Qualifications	1.00	Some professional qualifications are necessary
	0.00	No professional qualifications are necessary
d) Term of office	1.00	Over eight years
	0.50	Between five and eight years
	0.00	Below five years
e) Dismissal	1.00	Complete security of tenure
	0.50	Dismissal with some bank involvement
	0.00	No security of tenure
f) Renewability	1.00	Not renewable
	0.50	Renewable once
	0.00	Renewable
g) Other posts	1.00	Other office-holding not permitted
	0.00	Other office-holding permitted

2) *Sub-governors* (weighting 0.20)

a) Appointment	1.00	Appointments made by the bank itself
	0.50	Appointments made with some bank involvement
	0.00	Appointments made by government
b) Nomination	1.00	Nominations made by the bank itself
	0.50	Nominations made with some bank involvement
	0.00	Nominations made by government
c) Qualifications	1.00	Some professional qualifications are necessary
	0.00	No professional qualifications are necessary
d) Term of office	1.00	Over eight years
	0.50	Between five and eight years
	0.00	Below five years

e) Dismissal	1.00	Complete security of tenure
	0.50	Dismissal with some bank involvement
	0.00	No security of tenure
f) Renewability	1.00	Not renewable
	0.50	Renewable once
	0.00	Renewable
g) Other posts	1.00	Other office-holding not permitted
	0.00	Other office-holding permitted
h) Staggering	1.00	Staggered appointments
	0.00	Appointments made simultaneously

3) *Board of governors* (weighting 0.20)

a) Government reps.	1.00	There are no government representatives on the board
	0.75	There are a minority of government representatives on the board
	0.25	There are a majority of government representatives on the board
	0.00	There are only government representatives on the board
b) Appointment	1.00	Appointments made by the bank itself
	0.50	Appointments made with some bank involvement
	0.00	Appointments made by government
c) Nomination	1.00	Nominations made by the bank itself
	0.50	Nominations made with some bank involvement
	0.00	Nominations made by government
d) Qualifications	1.00	Some professional qualifications are necessary
	0.00	No professional qualifications are necessary
e) Term of office	1.00	Over eight years
	0.50	Between five and eight years
	0.00	Below five years
f) Dismissal	1.00	Complete security of tenure
	0.50	Dismissal with some bank involvement
	0.00	No security of tenure
g) Renewability	1.00	Not renewable
	0.50	Renewable once
	0.00	Renewable
h) Other posts	1.00	Other office-holding not permitted
	0.00	Other office-holding permitted
i) Staggering	1.00	Staggered appointments
	0.00	Appointments made simultaneously

4) *Decision-making process* (weighting 0.30)

a) Policy-making	1.00	Collective
	0.00	Not collective
b) Instructions	1.00	The board does not accept government instructions
	0.00	The board accepts government instructions

c) Veto	1.00	Government representatives do not have a veto
	0.00	Government representatives do have a veto
d) Salary	1.00	The bank fixes its own salaries
	0.00	The government fixes board members' salaries
e) Capital	1.00	100 per cent private capital
	0.50	Some private capital
	0.00	No private capital
f) Legislature	1.00	Bank does not have to report periodically to the legislature
	0.00	Bank must report periodically to the legislature

For each of the four sets of indicators of political independence, the mean is calculated and then the weighted mean is derived by taking these figures and multiplying each one by the appropriate weighting. The sum of weighted means is then calculated and this figure is multiplied by 0.5 to give the overall total for weighted political independence.

Economic independence (overall weighting 0.50)

a) Mission	1.00	A single stated mission to guarantee price stability
	0.50	A plurality of missions
	0.00	No mission statement at all
b) Monetary policy	1.00	The bank determines monetary policy
	0.50	Some degree of bank involvement in monetary policy
	0.00	The government determines monetary policy
c) Interest rates	1.00	The bank decides key interest rate movements
	0.00	Government decides key interest rate movements
d) Exchange rates	1.00	The bank determines exchange rate parities
	0.00	The government determines exchange rate parities
e) Regulation	1.00	The central bank regulates the wider banking sector
	0.50	Central bank is jointly responsible for regulation
	0.00	The government is the chief regulator
f) Government lending	1.00	Bank is prohibited from lending to the government
	0.50	Some limits to bank's obligation to lend to the government
	0.00	The bank is obliged to lend to the government
g) Budget	1.00	The bank plays a part in the budgetary process
	0.00	The budget is the government's sole responsibility

The mean figure is calculated. This figure is then multiplied by 0.5 to give the overall total for weighted economic independence.

The sum of weighted political independence and weighted economic independence is the figure for overall central bank independence.

Appendix 2

Bank of England independence, 1694–1997[1]

	1694	1931	1946	1997
Political independence (overall weighting 0.5)				
Governor (weighting 0.3)				
Appointment	1.00	1.00	0.00	0.00
Nominations	1.00	1.00	0.00	0.00
Qualifications[2]	1.00	1.00	0.00	0.00
Term[3]	0.00	1.00	0.50	0.50
Dismissal	1.00	1.00	1.00	1.00
Renewability	1.00	0.00	0.00	0.00
Other posts	0.00	0.00	1.00	1.00
Total	5.00	5.00	2.50	2.50
Mean	0.71	0.71	0.36	0.36
Weighted mean	0.21	0.21	0.11	0.11
Sub-governors (weighting 0.2)				
Appointment	1.00	1.00	0.00	0.00
Nominations	1.00	1.00	0.00	0.00
Qualifications	1.00	1.00	0.00	0.00
Term	0.00	0.50	0.50	0.50
Dismissal	1.00	1.00	1.00	1.00
Renewability	1.00	1.00	0.00	0.00
Other posts	0.00	0.00	1.00	1.00
Staggering[4]	–	–	–	1.00
Total	5.00	5.50	2.50	3.50
Mean	0.71	0.79	0.36	0.44
Weighted mean	0.14	0.16	0.07	0.09
Board of governors (weighting 0.2)[5]				
Government representatives	1.00	1.00	0.25	0.25
Appointment	1.00	1.00	0.00	0.50
Nominations	1.00	1.00	0.00	0.00
Qualifications	1.00	1.00	0.00	1.00
Term	1.00	1.00	0.00	0.00

Dismissal	1.00	1.00	0.00	1.00
Renewability	0.00	0.00	0.00	0.00
Other posts	0.00	0.00	0.00	1.00
Staggering	1.00	1.00	1.00	1.00
Total	7.00	7.00	1.25	4.75
Mean	0.78	0.78	0.14	0.53
Weighted mean	0.16	0.16	0.03	0.11
Decision-making process (weighting 0.3)				
Decisions	0.00	0.00	0.00	1.00
Instructions	1.00	1.00	0.00	1.00
Government veto	1.00	1.00	0.00	1.00
Salary	1.00	1.00	0.00	0.00
Capital	1.00	1.00	0.00	0.00
Legislature	1.00	1.00	1.00	0.00
Total	5.00	5.00	1.00	3.00
Mean	0.83	0.83	0.17	0.50
Weighted mean	0.25	0.25	0.05	0.15
Sum of weighted means	0.76	0.78	0.26	0.46
Weighted political independence	0.38	0.39	0.13	0.23
Economic independence (overall weighting 0.5)				
Mission	0.00	0.00	0.00	1.00
Monetary policy	1.00	0.00	0.00	0.50
Interest rates	1.00	0.00	0.00	1.00
Exchange rates	0.00	0.00	0.00	0.00
Bank regulation	0.50	0.50	1.00	0.00
Government lending	0.50	0.50	0.00	1.00
Budget	0.00	0.00	0.00	0.00
Total	3.00	1.00	1.00	3.50
Mean	0.43	0.14	0.14	0.50
Weighted economic independence	0.21	0.07	0.07	0.25
Overall independence	**0.59**	**0.46**	**0.20**	**0.48**

Notes:

[1] Unlike the Bank of France, the Bank of England was primarily governed by precedent rather than statute until 1946. The codings reflect this situation.

[2] Until 1946, the Bank's Court of Directors was composed mainly of 'merchants' of the City of London (Hennessy 1995: 200). Consequently, although formally no professional qualifications were needed to serve on the Court, in practice this was a requirement. This has implications for codings relating to the governor, deputy governor and the Court and is reflected in the calculations.

[3] For all governor, sub-governors and board of governors calculations, the figure for the term of office is the average of actual terms rather than the legal term.

[4] Until 1997, there was only one deputy governor. Calculations are adjusted accordingly.

[5] For all figures until 1997, the board of governors is deemed to be the Court of Directors. For 1997 figures, the board of governors is deemed to be the Monetary Policy Committee.

Appendix 3

Bank of France independence, 1800–1997

	1800	1808	1936	1945	1973	1993
Political independence (overall weight 0.5)						
Governor (weighting 0.3)[1]						
Appointment	1.00	0.00	0.00	0.00	0.00	0.00
Nominations	1.00	0.00	0.00	0.00	0.00	0.00
Qualifications	1.00	0.00	0.00	0.00	0.00	0.00
Term[2]	0.50	0.50	0.50	0.50	0.50	0.50
Dismissal	1.00	0.00	0.00	0.00	0.00	1.00
Renewability	0.00	–[3]	0.00	0.00	0.00	0.50
Other posts	0.00	0.00	1.00	1.00	1.00	1.00
Total	4.50	0.50	1.50	1.50	1.50	3.00
Mean	0.64	0.08	0.21	0.21	0.21	0.43
Weighted mean	0.19	0.03	0.06	0.06	0.06	0.14
Sub-governors (weighting 0.2)						
Appointment	1.00	0.00	0.00	0.00	0.00	0.00
Nominations	1.00	0.00	0.00	0.00	0.00	0.00
Qualifications	1.00	0.00	0.00	0.00	0.00	0.00
Term	0.50	0.50	0.50	0.50	0.50	0.50
Dismissal	1.00	0.00	0.00	0.00	0.00	1.00
Renewability	0.00	–	0.00	0.00	0.00	0.50
Other posts	0.00	0.00	1.00	1.00	1.00	1.00
Staggering	1.00	1.00	0.00	0.00	0.00	0.00
Total	5.50	1.50	1.50	1.50	1.50	3.00
Mean	0.69	0.21	0.19	0.19	0.19	0.38
Weighted mean	0.14	0.04	0.04	0.04	0.04	0.08
Board of governors (weighting 0.2)[4]						
Government representatives	1.00	0.75	0.25	0.00	0.00	0.75
Appointment	1.00	1.00	0.00	0.00	0.00	0.00
Nominations	1.00	1.00	0.00	0.00	0.00	0.50
Qualifications	1.00	1.00	0.00	0.00	1.00	1.00
Term	0.50	1.00	0.50	0.50	0.50	1.00

Dismissal	1.00	0.00	0.00	0.00	0.00	1.00
Renewability	0.00	0.00	0.00	0.00	0.00	1.00
Other posts	0.00	0.00	0.00	0.00	0.00	1.00
Staggering	1.00	1.00	1.00	0.00	1.00	1.00
Total	6.50	5.75	1.75	0.50	2.50	7.25
Mean	0.72	0.64	0.19	0.06	0.28	0.81
Weighted mean	0.14	0.13	0.04	0.01	0.06	0.16
Decision-making process (weighting 0.3)						
Decisions	1.00	1.00	0.00	0.00	1.00	1.00
Instructions	1.00	1.00	0.00	0.00	0.00	1.00
Government veto	1.00	0.00	0.00	0.00	0.00	1.00
Salary	–[5]	1.00	0.00	0.00	0.00	0.00
Capital	1.00	1.00	1.00	0.00	0.00	0.00
Legislature	1.00	1.00	0.00	0.00	0.00	0.00
Total	5.00	5.00	1.00	0.00	1.00	3.00
Mean	1.00	0.83	0.17	0.00	0.17	0.50
Weighted mean	0.30	0.25	0.05	0.00	0.05	0.15
Sum of weighted means	0.77	0.45	0.19	0.11	0.21	0.53
Weighted political independence	0.39	0.23	0.10	0.06	0.11	0.27
Economic independence (overall weight 0.5)						
Mission	0.00	0.00	0.00	0.00	0.00	1.00
Monetary policy	1.00	1.00	0.00	0.00	0.00	1.00
Interest rates	1.00	1.00	0.00	0.00	0.00	1.00
Exchange rates	0.00	0.00	0.00	0.00	0.00	0.00
Bank regulation	0.00	0.00	0.00	0.50	0.50	0.50
Government lending	0.50	0.50	0.50	0.50	0.50	1.00
Budget	0.00	0.00	0.00	0.00	0.00	0.00
Total	2.50	2.50	0.50	1.00	1.00	4.50
Mean	0.36	0.36	0.07	0.14	0.14	0.64
Weighted economic independence	0.18	0.18	0.04	0.07	0.07	0.32
Overall independence	**0.57**	**0.42**	**0.13**	**0.13**	**0.18**	**0.59**

Notes:

[1] For 1800 figures, the president of the *comité central* is deemed to be the governor and the other two posts on the *comité central* are deemed to be the sub-governors.

[2] For all governors, sub-governors and board of governors calculations, the figure for the term of office is the average of actual terms rather than the legal term.

[3] For 1808 figures, the governor's and sub governors' terms of office were unlimited and so the renewability figure is left blank.

[4] For all figures until 1993, the board of governors is deemed to be the *conseil général*. For 1993 figures, the board of governors is deemed to be the *Conseil de la politique monétaire*.

[5] For 1800 figures, the law stated that Bank members would not be remunerated and so the salary figure is left blank.

Appendix 4

European Central Bank independence

	Code	Treaty/Protocol article[1]
Political independence (overall weight 0.5)		
Governor (weighting 0.3)[2]		
Appointment	0.00	P 11.2
Nominations	–[3]	–
Qualifications	1.00	P 11.2
Term	0.50	P 11.2
Dismissal	1.00	P 11.4
Renewability	1.00	P 11.2
Other posts	1.00	P 11.1
Total	4.50	
Mean	0.75	
Weighted mean	0.23	
Sub-governors (weighting 0.2)[4]		
Appointment	0.00	P 11.2
Nominations	–	–
Qualifications	1.00	P 11.2
Term	0.50	P 11.2
Dismissal	1.00	P 11.4
Renewability	1.00	P 11.2
Other posts	1.00	P 11.1
Staggering	1.00	P 50
Total	5.50	
Mean	0.79	
Weighted mean	0.16	
Board of governors (weighting 0.2)[5]		
Government representatives	0.75	T 109b 1
Appointment	0.50	–
Nominations	0.50	–
Qualifications	1.00	–
Term	0.50	(P 14.2)
Dismissal	1.00	P 14.2

Renewability	0.50	–
Other posts	1.00	–
Staggering	1.00	–
Total	6.75	
Mean	0.75	
Weighted mean	0.15	
Decision-making process (weighting 0.3)		
Decisions	1.00	P 10.2
Instructions	1.00	P 7
Government veto	1.00	T 109b 1
Salary	1.00	P 11.3
Capital	0.00	–
Legislature	0.00	–
Total	4.00	
Mean	0.67	
Weighted mean	0.20	
Sum of weighted means	0.72	
Weighted political independence	0.36	
Economic independence (overall weight 0.5)		
Mission	1.00	P 2
Monetary policy	1.00	P 3.1
Interest rates	1.00	P 12.1
Exchange rates	0.00	T 109.1
Bank regulation	0.50	P 25.1
Government lending	1.00	P 21.1
Budget	0.00	–
Total	4.50	
Mean	0.64	
Weighted economic independence	0.32	
Overall independence	0.68	

Notes:

1 P: Protocol on the Statute of the European System of Central Banks and the European Central Bank. T: Treaty on European Union. The relevant Protocol article is indicated unless reference is made only in the Treaty.

2 The governor is deemed to be the President of the European Central Bank.

3 No reference is made to nomination procedures for either the President, the Vice-President or the members of the Executive Board.

4 The sub-governors are deemed to be the Vice-President of the European Central Bank and the members of the Executive Board.

5 The board of governors is deemed to be the Governing Council. As a result of the overall composition of the Governing Council (P 10.1), except where indicated national legislation is the primary source of information for each coding in this section. The coding figure is an estimated average of the appropriate national legislation.

Notes

3 The core executive and the Bank of England (1694–1987)

1 From the beginning of the eighteenth century, England was involved in the War of Spanish Succession (1701–13), the War of Austrian Succession (1739–48), the Seven Year War (1756–63), the American War of Independence (1775–83) and the War Against Revolutionary France (1792–1802, 1802–15). The Bank's operations, as government debt servicer, allowed Britain, with a substantially smaller population, to defeat France in war throughout the eighteenth century and contributed to the eventual emergence of Britain as an imperial power (Dickson 1967; Brewer 1989).

2 In practice, for all the moral fervour which ministers brought to the task – Gladstone: '[t]he expenses of a war are a moral check which it has pleased the Almighty to impose on the ambition and lust of conquest that are inherent in so many nations' – debt still eventually played an important part in financing the Crimean War (see Anderson, 1963–4).

3 In a sequel William Gladstone in his second tenure as Chancellor, fuming at what he saw as the Bank's profiteering through the timing of dividend payments on the national debt, set up the Post Office Savings Bank as an alternative source of credit.

4 The Bank Rate originated in the aftermath of a monetary crisis in 1836–7 when the Usury Laws were repealed. Under the Usury Laws, the rate of interest was subject to a legal maximum of 5 per cent. From 1822 to 1839 the level fluctuated between 4 and 5 per cent. Only in June 1839 did the official rate at which the Bank of England supplied credit rise above 5 per cent, establishing the modern Bank Rate (Moggridge 1971: 167).

5 It is by no means clear that the Bank's operation of the Bank Rate during this period did in practice damage the domestic economy. Concluding his seminal empirical study covering the subject, Charles Goodhart wrote:

> the great years of the Gold Standard (1890–1914) were remarkable *not* because the system enforced discipline and fundamental international equilibrium on this country [Britain] by causing variations in the money supply but because the system allowed for the development of such large-scale, stabilising and equilibrating, short term, international capital flows, that

> autonomous domestic expansion was rarely disrupted by monetary or balance of payments disturbances.
>
> (Goodhart 1986: 219)

6 For his part, Chamberlain was highly critical of the City in general, believing that it lived off the wealth-creating capacity of industry, but he emphatically placed tariff reform in the imperial context at the heart of his practical agenda.
7 Of course, the broader questions about the relationship between the end of the war and the means to prosecute it were a source of deep conflict between ministers, eventually leading to the replacement of Asquith by Lloyd George as head of the Coalition government.
8 Keynes was certainly setting himself up against an orthodoxy of which the Bank stood at the heart. The Tract was dedicated to the Bank and the preface declared that 'nowhere is the need of innovation more urgent [than in questions of currency]' (Skidelsky 1992b: 154).
9 It was in this context that Keynes made his famous remark: 'But this *long run* is a misleading guide to current affairs. *In the long run* we are all dead. Economists set themselves too easy, too useless a task if in tempestuous seasons they can only tell us that when the storm is long past the ocean is flat again' (Skidelsky 1992b: 156).
10 Inspired by Keynes, the Macmillan Report (House of Commons 1931a) did eventually offer an alternative framework which would have involved staying on the gold standard but using monetary policy to regulate the volume and price of bank credit 'so as to maintain output and employment at the maximum compatible with adherence to the international gold standard and with the maintenance of the stability of the international price level' (para. 303). At the same time, the Bank Rate would have been used to try to contract credit either at home, or in the world at large, rather than for attracting foreign funds, even if this meant accepting greater fluctuations in the gold reserves (paras. 352–3). But the report's recommendations were engulfed in the sterling crisis of July–September 1931.
11 The first step towards cheaper money was taken by the Bank in February 1931, but thereafter the Bank was generally opposed to lower interest rates (Howson 1975: 87).
12 Since taxation had financed only 50 per cent of expenditure on the war, monetary policy was used during the war to facilitate government borrowing at low nominal interest rates.
13 This is not to suggest that the new government was indifferent to the old problem of debt management. Indeed, it introduced a special rate of rediscount on Treasury bills, meaning that its operative rate of lending, as formal lender of last resort to the discount market, was actually reduced by 0.5 per cent after the Bank Rate was raised (House of Commons 1959: 406).
14 In his memoirs, Butler states that he saw decontrol of the currency as the first step towards decontrol of the economy (Butler 1973: 160).
15 In the words of Bruce-Gardyne and Lawson, 'the Bank *did* resist the pressures to float, and continued to do so right up to the morning of the day the Chancellor's decision was announced. Its advice was simply brushed aside' (Bruce-Gardyne and Lawson 1970: 171).
16 Internally, in 1959 the Court delegated to the Governor formal standing authority to settle changes in the Bank Rate with the Chancellor (Fforde 1992: 692).
17 In 1972 the Bank Rate was replaced by the Minimum Lending Rate.

18 Sterling was floated in June 1972 after a six-week membership of the European snake.
19 For example, the day after sterling started falling rapidly in March 1976, interest rates were reduced. While Healey clearly must have sanctioned the move, he was later scathing about it, blaming the Bank as if it had nothing to do with him (Dell 1991: 207).

4 The core executive and the Bank of England (1988-97)

1 In 1994, for example, fixed rate loans stood at around 21 per cent of outstanding mortgages in Britain compared to 90 per cent in France and over 60 per cent in Germany.
2 The notable exception in the government's attitude came during the Delors Committee on monetary union. Although the central bank governors were appointed to this committee, which met during 1988–9, in their personal capacity, other EC governments, most strikingly the French, saw their respective governors as the means to push their views on the subject within the committee. Thatcher and Lawson, refusing to take the monetary union debate seriously anyway, left Leigh-Pemberton to his own devices, realising only when it was too late that this would produce a report deeply inimical to their judgment on the subject (Thompson 1996: 125–30).
3 In the aftermath of the hearings, in January 1994, one of the members of the committee, the Conservative backbencher Nicholas Budgen, unsucessfully introduced a private members bill into the House of Commons to create an autonomous Bank along the lines set out in the report.
4 The six-week gap between the meeting and the publication of minutes was the same time period used in the United States by the Federal Open Market Committee for this purpose. In the words of Terence Burns:

> We took the decision in the case of the monthly monetary meetings that the detail of that should only be released six weeks after the event, because it would then be sufficiently distanced from the point of decision-making, so that people would not immediately draw implications about what might be going to happen tomorrow and the day after. We were trying to have our cake and eat it; to release the information but do it in a way that was not too market sensitive and would not handicap the ability of the Bank of England to do their normal business.
>
> (House of Commons 1995: 403)

5 The increase in rates on 7 December came the day after the government had been defeated in the House of Commons on the budget provision to increase VAT on fuel. As such it raised suspicion in the financial markets and the media that Clarke was prepared to disregard the new formal rules for monetary decision-making when the going got tough (*Financial Times*, 8 December 1994).

7 The political control of economic life

1 For a discussion which sees economic policy making by politicians and bureaucrats generally in this context but which argues that ideas are the main mediators from the complexities of reality to political choices, see Goldstein (1993).

2 Unless Britain notifies the Council of its wish to move to Stage Three of monetary union, it will be excluded from the right to participate in appointments to the Executive Board.

3 For Germany, automatic penalties for 'excessive' budget deficits were non-negotiable. On several occasions German officials threatened to abandon discussions on the Stability Pact with the fourteen other EU states and negotiate a separate stability pact with those states participating in the first wave of monetary union in 1999 (*Financial Times*, 11 November 1996).

Bibliography

Aeschimann, Éric, and Riché, Pascal (1996), *La guerre de sept ans. Histoire secrète du franc fort 1989–1996*, Paris: Calmann-Lévy.

Alesina, Alberto, and Gatti, Roberto (1995) 'Independent Central Banks: Low Inflation at No Cost?', in *American Economic Review*, vol. 85, no. 2, pp. 196–200.

Alesina, Alberto, and Roubini, Nouriel (1992) 'Political Cycles in OECD Economies', in *Review of Economic Studies*, vol. 59, pp. 663–88.

Alesina, Alberto, and Summers, Lawrence H. (1993) 'Central Bank Independence and Macroeconomic Performance: Some Comparative Evidence', in *Journal of Money, Credit and Banking*, vol. 25, no. 2, pp. 151–62.

Alt, James E. (1985) 'Political Parties, World Demand, and Unemployment: Domestic and International Sources of Economic Activity', in *American Political Science Review*, vol. 79, no. 4, pp. 1016–40.

Amouroux, Henri (1986) *Monsieur Barre*, Paris: Robert Laffont.

Anderson, Olive (1963–4) 'Loans versus Taxes: British Financial Policy in the Crimean War', in *Economic History Review*, vol. 16, no. 2, pp. 314–27.

Anonymous (1996) *Primary Colours*, London: Vintage.

Auberger, Philippe (1993) *Rapport fait au nom de la commission des finances, de l'économie générale et du plan sur le projet de loi (no. 158) relatif au statut de la Banque de France et au contrôle des établissements de crédit*, Paris: National Assembly, no. 270.

Aubin, Christian (1985) 'Les changements du gouverneur de la Banque de France: une perspective historique', in *Chroniques d'Actualité de la S.E.D.E.I.S.*, vol. 32, no. 3, pp. 131–4.

Banaian, King, Laney, Leroy O., and Willett, Thomas D. (1983) 'Central Bank Independence: An International Comparison', in *Federal Reserve Bank of Dallas. Economic Review*, March, pp. 1–13.

Banque de France (1993) *Bulletin mensuel*, June.

Barre, Raymond (1986) *Réflexions pour demain*: Paris, Flammarion.

—— (1988) *Questions de confiance*, Paris: Flammarion.

Barro, Robert J., and Gordon, David B. (1983) 'Rules, discretion and reputation in a model of monetary policy', in *Journal of Monetary Economics*, vol. 12, July, pp. 101–22.

Bayley, David (1975) 'The Police and Political Development in Europe', in Charles Tilly (ed.), *The Formation of the National States in Western Europe*, London, Princeton University Press, pp. 328–79.

Beaverbrook, Lord (1966) *Politicians and the War 1914–1918*, London: Collins.

Beck, Nathaniel (1982) 'Presidential Influence on the Federal Reserve in the 1970s', in *American Journal of Political Science*, vol. 26, no. 3, pp. 415–45.

—— (1984) 'Domestic Political Sources of American Monetary Policy: 1955–1982', in *Journal of Politics*, vol. 46, pp. 786–817.

Bénassy, Agnès, and Pisani-Ferry, Jean (1994) 'Indépendance de la banque centrale et politique budgétaire', in *Revue française des finances publiques*, no. 46, pp. 81–92.

Bloch-Lainé, François (1976) *Profession: fonctionnaire*, Paris: Seuil.

Bon-Garcin, Isabelle (1994) 'La Banque de France de 1800 à nos jours', in *Les petites affiches*, vol. 383, no. 73, pp. 4–7.

Bouvier, Jean (1973) *Un siècle de banque française*, Paris: Hachette.

—— (1987) 'Les relations entre l'État et la Banque de France depuis les années 1950', in *Vingtième Siècle*, no. 13, January–February, pp. 23–33.

—— (1988) 'The Banque de France and the State from 1850 to the Present Day', in Gianni Toniolo (ed.), *Central Banks' Independence in Historical Perspective*, Berlin: de Gruyter, pp. 73–103.

Bowen, H.V. (1995) 'The Bank of England During the Long Eighteenth Century', in Richard Roberts and David Kynaston, *The Bank of England: Money, Power and Influence 1694–1994*, Oxford: Clarendon Press, pp. 1–18.

Brewer, John (1989) *The Sinews of Power: War, Money and the English State 1688–1783*, London: Unwin Hyman.

Brittan, Samuel (1971) *Steering the Economy: The Role of the Treasury*, Harmondsworth: Penguin.

Bruce-Gardyne, Jock, and Lawson, Nigel (1970) *The Power Game*, London: Macmillan.

Bulpitt, Jim (1986) 'The Discipline of the New Democracy: Mrs Thatcher's Domestic Statecraft', in *Political Studies*, vol. 34, no. 1, pp. 19–39.

Burdekin, Richard C.K., Wihlborg, Clas, and Willett, Thomas D. (1992) 'A Monetary Constitution Case for an Independent European Central Bank', in *The World Economy*, vol. 15, no. 2, pp. 231–49.

Burns, Terence (1995) *Managing the Nation's Economy: The Conduct of Monetary and Fiscal Policy*, Treasury Occasional Paper 5, London: H.M. Treasury.

—— (1996) *Speech to the 25th Annual Conference of Economists*, London: H.M. Treasury.

Busch, Andreas (1994) 'Central Bank Independence and the Westminister Model', in *West European Politics*, vol. 17, no. 1, pp. 53–72.

Butler, Anthony (1995) 'Unpopular Leaders: The British Case,' in *Political Studies*, vol. 43, no. 1, pp. 48–65.

Butler, Lord (1973) *The Art of the Possible*, Harmondsworth: Penguin.

Cairncross, Alex (1995) 'The Bank of England and the British Economy', Richard Roberts and David Kynaston, *The Bank of England: Money, Power and Influence 1694–1994*, Oxford: Clarendon Press, pp. 56–82.

Cameron, David R. (1996) 'Exchange Rate Policies in France, 1981–1983: The Regime-Defining Choices of the Mitterrand Presidency', in Anthony Daley (ed.), *The Mitterrand Era. Policy Alternatives and Political Mobilization in France*, London: Macmillan, pp. 56–82.

Cerny, Philip (1990) *The Changing Architecture of Politics: Structure, Agency and the Future of the State*, London: Sage.

Clarke, Harold *et al.* (1993) 'The Political Economy of Attitudes Towards Polity and Society in West European Democracies', in *Journal of Politics*, vol. 55, no. 4, pp. 98–109.

Conseil Économique et Social (1993) *Les implications d'un statut rénové de la Banque de France*, Paris: Direction des Journaux officiels.

Coudé de Foresto, Yvon (1972) *Rapport no. 36 sur la Banque de France*, Paris: Sénat.

Cowling, Maurice (1971) *The Impact of Labour 1920–1924*, Cambridge: Cambridge University Press.

Crawford, Malcolm (1993) *One Money for Europe?*, London: Macmillan.

Crewe, Ivor (1993) 'Voting and the Electorate', in Patrick Dunleavy, Andrew Gamble, Ian Holliday and Gillian Peele (eds), *Developments in British Politics 4*, London: Macmillan, pp. 92–122.

Crossman, Richard (1972) 'Introduction', in Walter Bagehot, *The English Constitution*, London: Collins/Fontana, pp. 1–57.

Cukierman, Alex, Webb, Steven B., and Neyapti, Bilin (1992) 'Measuring the Independence of Central Banks and Its Effect on Policy Outcomes', in *World Bank Economic Review*, vol. 6, no. 3, pp. 353–98.

Dalton, Hugh (1959) *Principles of Public Finance*, 4th edn, London: Routledge.

—— (1962) *High Tide and After: Memoirs 1945–1960*, London: Frederick Miller.

Dauphin-Meunier, A. (1936) *La Banque de France*, Paris: Gallimard.

Deane, Marjorie, and Pringle, Robert (1994) *The Central Banks*, London: Hamish Hamilton.

Debelle, Guy, and Fischer, Stanley (1994) 'How Independent Should a Central Bank Be?', in Jeffrey Fuhrer (ed.), *Goals, Guidelines and Constraints Facing Monetary Policy-makers*, Boston: Federal Reserve Bank of Boston Conference Series No. 38, pp. 195–221.

Dell, Edmund (1991) *A Hard Pounding: Politics and Economic Crisis 1974–1976*, Oxford: Oxford University Press.

de Kock, M.H. (1974) *Central Banking*, 4th edn, London: Crosby, Lockwood, Staples.

De Long, J. Bradford, and Summers, Lawrence H. (1992) 'Macroeconomic Policy and Long-Run Growth', in *Federal Reserve Bank of Kansas. Economic Review*, vol. 77, no. 4, pp. 5–26.

Desaunay, François (1956) 'L'État centralisé de l'An VIII et la fondation de la Banque de France', in *La Revue Administrative*, vol. 5, no. 52, pp. 471–8.

Develle, Michel (1988) *Vive le Franc!*, Paris: Olivier Orban.

Devine, Fiona (1995) 'Qualitative Analysis', in David Marsh and Gerry Stoker (eds), *Theory and Methods in Political Science*, London: Macmillan, pp. 137–53.

Dickson, P.G.M. (1967) *The Financial Revolution in England: A Study in the Development of Public Credit 1688–1756*, London: St Martin's Press.

Dowd, Kevin, and Baker, Simon (1994) 'The New Zealand Monetary Policy Experiment – A Preliminary Assessment', in *The World Economy*, vol. 17, no. 6, pp. 855–67.

Dunleavy, Patrick (1995) 'Estimating the Distribution of Positional Influence in Cabinet Committees under Major', in R.A.W. Rhodes and Patrick Dunleavy (eds), *Prime Minister, Cabinet and Core Executive*, London: Macmillan, pp. 298–321.

Dunleavy, Patrick, and Rhodes, R.A.W. (1990) 'Core Executive Studies in Britain', in *Public Administration*, vol. 68, no. 1, pp. 3–28.

Dunn, John (1990) *The Economic Limits to Modern Politics*, Cambridge: Cambridge University Press.

—— (1996a) *The History of Political Theory and Other Essays*, Cambridge: Cambridge University Press.

—— (1996b) 'How Democracies Succeed', in *Economy and Society*, vol. 25, no. 4, pp.511–28.

Duprat, J-P. (1976) 'La situation juridique de la Banque de France après la réforme de ses statuts', in *Revue de Science Financière*, no. 2, April–June, pp. 369–474.

Dyson, Kenneth (1994) *Elusive Union: The Process of Economic and Monetary Union in Europe*, London: Longman.

Eijffinger, Sylvester, and Schaling, Eric (1993) 'Central Bank Independence in Twelve Industrial Countries', in *BNL Quarterly Review*, no. 184, March, pp. 49–89.

Elgey, Georgette (1968) *Histoire de la IVe République. La République des Contradictions, 1951–1954*, Paris: Fayard.

Elgie, Robert (1993) *The Role of the Prime Minister in France, 1981–91*, London: Macmillan.

—— (1996) *Electing the French President. The 1995 Presidential Election*, London: Macmillan.

Epstein, G.A. (1992) 'Political economy and comparative central banking', in *Review of Radical Political Economics*, vol. 24, no. 1, pp. 1–30.

European Communities (1992) *Treaty on European Union*, Luxembourg: Office for Official Publications of the European Communities.

Fair, Don (1979) 'The Independence of Central Banks', in *The Banker*, vol. 129, no. 644, pp. 31–41.

Favier, Pierre, and Martin-Roland, Michel (1996) *La Décennie Mitterrand. 3. Les défis*, Paris: Seuil.

Fay, Stephen (1987) *Portrait of an Old Lady: Turmoil at the Bank of England*, London: Viking.

Fforde, John (1992) *The Bank of England and Public Policy 1941–1958*, Cambridge: Cambridge University Press.

Finer, S.E. (1970) *Comparative Government*, Harmondsworth: Penguin.

Flora, Peter, and Alber, Jens (1995) 'Modernisations, Democratisation and the Development of the Welfare States in Western Europe', in Peter Flora and Arnold J. Heidenheimer (eds), *The Developments of Welfare States in Europe and America*, London: Transaction Publishers, pp. 37–80.

Flora, Peter, and Heidenheimer, Arnold J. (1995) *The Developments of Welfare States in Europe and America*, London: Transaction Publishers.

Fuhrer, Jeffrey C. (1997) 'Central Bank Independence and Inflation Targeting: Monetary Policy Paradigms for the Next Millenium', in *New England Economic Review*, Federal Reserve Bank of Boston, January–February, pp. 19–36.

Gamble, Andrew (1995) 'Economic Recession and Disenchantment with Europe', in *West European Politics*, vol. 18 no. 3, pp. 158–74.

Garrett, Geoffrey (1993) 'The Politics of Maastricht', in Barry Eichengreen and Jeffry Frieden (eds), *The Political Economy of European Monetary Unification*, San Francisco: Westview Press, pp. 47–64.

Gleske, Leonhard (1995) 'Bundesbank Independence, Organisation and Decision-making', in *Central Banking*, vol. 6, no. 1, pp. 21–7.

Goldstein, Judith (1993) *Ideas, Interests and American Trade Policy*, Ithaca: Cornell University Press.

Goodhart, C.A.E. (1995) *The Central Bank and the Financial System*, London: Macmillan.

Goodhart, Charles (1986) *The Business of Banking 1891–1914*, Aldershot: Gower.

—— (1991) *The Evolution of Central Banking*, London: The MIT Press.

Goodhart, Charles, Capie, Forrest, and Schnadt, Norbert (1994) 'The Development of Central Banking', in Forrest Capie, Charles Goodhart, Stanley Fischer and Norbert Schnadt (eds), *The Future of Central Banking*, Cambridge: Cambridge University Press, pp. 1–112.

Goodman, John B. (1991) 'The Politics of Central Bank Independence', in *Comparative Politics*, vol. 23, April, pp. 329–49.

—— (1992) *The Politics of Central Banking in Western Europe*, London: Cornell University Press.

Gourevitch, Peter (1989) 'The Politics of Economic Policy Choice in the Post-War Era', in Paolo Guerrieni and Pier Carlo Padoan (eds), *The Political Economy of Integration: States, Markets and Institutions*, Brighton: Harvester Wheatsheaf.

Greider, William (1987) *Secrets of the Temple: How the Federal Reserve Runs the Country*, New York: Simon and Schuster.

Grew, Raymond (ed.) (1978) *Crises of Political Development in Europe and the United States*, Princeton: Princeton University Press.

Grier, K. (1991) 'On the Existence of a Political Monetary Cycle,' in *American Journal of Political Science*, vol. 33, pp. 376–89.

Grilli, Vittorio, Masciandro, Donato, and Tabellini, Guido (1991) 'Political and Monetary Institutions and Public Financial Policies in the Industrial Countries', in *Economic Policy*, no. 13, pp. 342–92.

Guerrieri, Paolo, and Padoan, Pier Carlo (1989) *The Political Economy of Integration: States, Markets and Institutions*, Brighton: Harvester Wheatsheaf.

Haas, Peter M. (1992) 'Introduction: Epistemic Communities and International Policy Coordination', in *International Organization*, vol. 46, no. 1, pp. 1–36.

Haberer, Jean-Yves (1990) 'Le ministère de l'Économie et des Finances et la politique monétaire', in *Pouvoirs*, no. 53, pp. 27–36.

Hall, Peter (1994) 'Central Bank Independence and Co-ordinated Wage Bargaining: The Interaction of Germany and Europe', in *German Politics and Society*, vol. 31, pp. 1–23.

Harris, José (1972) *Unemployment and Politics: A Study in English Social Policy 1886–1914*, Oxford: Clarendon Press.

Hayward, J.E.S. (1997) 'Finer's Comparative History of Government', in *Government and Opposition*, vol. 32, no. 1, pp. 114–31.

Held, David (1995) *Democracy and the Global Order: From the Modern State to Cosmopolitan Governance*, Cambridge: Polity Press.

Helleiner, Eric (1994) *States and the Re-Emergence of Global Finance: From Bretton Woods to the 1990s*, Ithaca: Cornell University Press.

Hennessy, Elizabeth (1995) 'The Governors, Directors and Management', in Richard Roberts and David Kynaston (eds), *The Bank of England: Money, Power and Influence 1694–1994*, Oxford: Clarendon Press, pp. 185–216.

Henning, C. Randall (1994) *Currencies and Politics in the United States, Germany and Japan*, Washington DC: Institute for International Economy.

Hetzel, Robert L. (1990) 'Central Banks' Independence in Historical Perspective: A Review Essay', in *Journal of Monetary Economics*, vol. 25, pp. 165–76.

Hibbs, Douglas (1977) 'Political Parties and Macro-Economic Policy', in *American Political Science Review*, vol. 71, no. 4, pp. 1467–87.

Hilton, Boyd (1980) *Corn, Cash, Commerce: The Economic Policies of the Tory Government, 1815–1830*, Oxford: Oxford University Press.

—— (1988) *The Age of Atonement: The Influence of Evangelicalism on Social and Economic Thought 1785–1865*, Oxford: Clarendon Press.

Hirst, Paul, and Thompson, Graham (1996) *Globalisation in Question: The International Economy and the Possibility of Governance*, Cambridge: Polity Press.

House of Commons (1931a) *The MacMillan Report*, London: HMSO.

—— (1931b) *The MacMillan Report, Minutes of Evidence*, London: HMSO.

—— (1959) *Committee of the Working of the Monetary System, Report*, London: HMSO.

—— (1992) *Select Committee on the Treasury and the Civil Service: Appendices to First Report, Minutes of Evidence*, London: HMSO.

—— (1993a) *Treasury and Civil Service Select Committee Report: The Role of the Bank of England*, London: HMSO.

—— (1993b) *Minutes of Evidence Taken Before the Treasury and Civil Service Select Committee, 7 July 1993*, London: HMSO.

—— (1993c) *Minutes of Evidence Taken Before the Treasury and Civil Service Select Committee, 21 July 1993*, London: HMSO.

—— (1993d) *Minutes of Evidence Taken Before the Treasury and Civil Service Select Committee, 2 November 1993*, London: HMSO.

—— (1993e) *Minutes of Evidence Taken Before the Treasury and Civil Service Select Committee, 30 June 1993*, London: HMSO.

—— (1995) *Minutes of Evidence Taken Before the Select Committee on the Parliamentary Commissioner for Administrations, 13 December, 1995*, London: HMSO.

Howson, Susan (1975) *Domestic Monetary Management in Britain 1919–38*, Cambridge: Cambridge University Press.

—— (1993) *British Monetary Policy 1945–51*, Oxford: Clarendon Press.

Hughes, J.R.T. (1960) *Fluctuations in Trade, Industry and Finance*, Oxford: Oxford University Press.

Ingham, Geoffrey (1984) *Capitalism Divided: The City and Industry in Britain's Social Development*, London: Macmillan.

Italianer, A. (1993) 'Mastering Maastricht: EMU Issues and How They Were Settled', in K. Gretschmann (ed.), *Economic and Monetary Union: Implications for National Policy-Makers*, Maastricht: EIPA.

Johnson, Christopher (1992) *The Economy Under Mrs Thatcher 1979–1990*, Harmondsworth: Penguin.

—— (1996) *In with the Euro, Out with the Pound: The Single Currency for Britain*, Harmondsworth: Penguin.

Katzenstein, Peter (1987) *Policy and Politics in West Germany: The Growth of a Semi-Sovereign State*, Philadephia: Temple University Press.

Keegan, William (1984) *Mrs Thatcher's Economic Experiment*, Harmondsworth: Penguin.

Kennedy, Ellen (1991) *The Bundesbank: Germany's Central Bank in the International Monetary System*, London: Pinter.

Kennedy, William (1987) *Industrial Structure, Capital Markets and the Origins of British Economic Decline*, Cambridge: Cambridge University Press.

King, Anthony (1994) ' "Chief Executives" in Western Europe', in Ian Budge and David McKay (eds), *Developing Democracy: Comparative Research in Honour of J.F.P. Blondel*, London: Sage, pp. 150–63.

Koch, Henri (1983) *Histoire de la Banque de France et de la Monnaie sous la IVe République*, Paris: Bordas.

Kooiman, Jan (1993) 'Governance and Governability: Using Complexity, Dynamics and Diversity', in Jan Kooiman (ed.), *Modern Governance: New Government–Society Interactions*, London: Sage, pp. 35–48.

Krause, George A. (1994) 'Federal Reserve Policy Decision Making: Political and Bureaucratic Influences', in *American Journal of Political Science*, vol. 38, no. 1, pp. 124–44.

Kreile, Michael (1978) 'West Germany: The Dynamics of Expansion', in Peter Katzenstein (ed.), *Between Power and Plenty: Foreign Economic Policies of Advanced Industrial States*, Madison: University of Wisconsin Press, pp. 191–224.

Labour Party (1997) *New Labour: Because Britain Deserves Better*, London: Labour Party.

Lane, Jan-Erik, and Ersson, Svante O. (1991) *Politics and Society in Western Europe*, London: Sage.

Lange, Peter (1993) 'Maastricht and the Social Protocol: Why Did They Do It?', in *Politics and Society*, vol. 21, no. 1, pp. 5–36.

Lawson, Nigel (1992) *The View from No. 11: Memoirs of a Tory Radical*, London: Bantam Press.

League of Nations (Ragnar Nurkse) (1944) *International Currency Experience: Lessons of the Inter-war Period*, League of Nations, Economic, Financial and Transit Department.

Lee, Dwight, and McKenzie, Richard (1989) 'The International Political Economy of Declining Tax Rates', in *National Tax Journal*, vol. 42, pp. 79–83.

Lévy, Raphael-Georges (1911) *Banques d'Émission et Trésors Publics*, Paris: Hachette.

Lewis-Beck, Michael (1988) *Economics and Elections: The Major Western Democracies*, Ann Arbor: University of Michigan Press.

Ludlow, Peter (1982) *The Making of the EMS: A Case Study of the Politics of the EC*, London: Butterworth Scientific.

Machin, Howard, and Wright, Vincent (1985) *Economic Policy and Policy Making under the Mitterrand Presidency*, London: Pinter.

Mackintosh, John P. (1968) *The British Cabinet*, 2nd edn, London: Methuen.

Mamou, Yves (1988) *Une machine de pouvoir. La Direction du Trésor*, Paris: La Découverte.

Markovits, Andrei (1986) *The Politics of West German Trade Unions: Strategies of Class and Interest Representation in Growth and Crisis*, Cambridge: Cambridge University Press.

Marsh, David (1992) *The Bundesbank: The Bank that Rules Europe*, London: Mandarin.

Marsh, Peter (1978) *The Discipline of Popular Government: Lord Salisbury's Domestic Statecraft 1881–1902*, Aldershot: Gregg Revivals.

Masciandro, Donato, and Spinelli, Franco (1994) 'Central Banks' Independence: Institutional Determinants, Rankings and Central Bankers' Views', in *Scottish Journal of Political Economy*, vol. 41, no. 4, pp. 434–43.

Masciandro, Donato, and Tabellini, Guido (1988) 'Monetary Regimes and Fiscal Deficits: A Comparative Analysis', in Heng-Sheng Cheng (ed.), *Monetary Policy in Pacific Basin Countries*, Boston, Kluwer Academic Publishers.

Maxfield, Sylvia (1994) 'Financial Incentives and Central Bank Authority in Industrializing Nations', in *World Politics*, vol. 46, July, pp. 556–88.

Milward, Alan (1992) *The European Rescue of the Nation-State*, London: Routledge.

Milward, Alan, Lynch, Frances, Romero, Federico, Ranieri, Ruggero, and Sörensen, Vibeke (1993) *The Frontier of National Sovereignty: History and Theory 1945–1992*, London: Routledge.

Moggridge, D.E. (1971) *The Collected Writings of John Maynard Keynes, vol. V: A Treatise on Money*, London: Macmillan.

—— (1972) *British Monetary Policy 1924–1931: The Norman Conquest of $4.86*, Cambridge: Cambridge University Press.

—— (1980) *The Collected Writings of John Maynard Keynes, vol. XXV: Activities 1940–1944 Shaping the Post-War World: The Clearing Union*, London: Macmillan.

Moran, Michael (1986) *The Politics of Banking: The Strange Case of Competition and Credit Control*, Oxford: Blackwell.

Moreau, Émile (1954) *Souvenirs d'un Gouverneur de la Banque de France. Histoire de la Stabilisation du Franc (1926–1928)*, Paris: Éditions M.-Th. Génin.

Morgan, Kenneth (1979) *Consensus and Disunity: The Lloyd George Coalition Government 1918–1922*, Oxford: Clarendon Press

—— (1984) *Labour in Power 1945–1951*, Oxford: Clarendon Press.

Mount, Ferdinand (1992) *The British Constitution Now: Recovery or Decline?*, London: Heinemann.

Noël, Octave (1888) *Les Banques d'Émission en Europe*, vol. 1, Paris: Berger-Levrault.

Nordhaus, William (1975) 'The Political Business Cycle', in *Review of Economic Studies*, vol. 142, no. 2, pp.169–98.

North, Douglass and Weingast, Barry (1980) 'Constitutions and Commitment: The Evolution of Institutions Governing Public Choice in Seventeenth Century England', in *Journal of Economic History*, vol. 49, pp. 802–32.

Parkin, Michael (1978) 'In Search of a Monetary Constitution for the European Communities', in M. Frattiani and Theo Peters (eds), *One Money for Europe*, New York: Praeger, pp. 167–95.

Parkin, Michael (1987) 'Domestic Monetary Institutions and Deficits', in James M. Buchanan, Charles K. Rowley and Robert D. Tollison, *Deficits*, Oxford: Basil Blackwell, pp. 310–327.

Pennant-Rea, Rupert (1995) 'The Bank of England: Yesterday, Today, Tomorrow', in Richard Roberts and David Kynaston (eds), *The Bank of England: Money, Power and Influence 1694–1994*, Oxford: Clarendon Press, pp. 217–224.

Pierson, Christopher (1991) *Beyond the Welfare State? The New Political Economy of Welfare Policy*, Cambridge: Cambridge University Press.

Plessis, Alain (1985) *La politique de la Banque de France de 1851 à 1870*, Geneva: Dalloz.

Plihon, Dominique (1994) 'Indépendance ou autonomie de la Banque de France', in *Regards sur l'actualité*, no. 204, pp. 3–23.

Polanyi, Karl (1944) *The Great Transformation: The Political and Economic Origins of Our Times*, Boston: Beacon Press.

Pollard, Sydney (1970) *The Gold Standard and Employment Policies Between the Wars*, London: Methuen.

—— (1982) *The Wasting of the British Economy: British Economic Policy 1945 to the Present*, London: Croom Helm.

Prate, Alain (1987) *La France et sa monnaie. Essai sur les relations entre la Banque de France et les gouvernants*, Paris: Julliard.

Redon, Michel, and Besnard, Denis (1996) *La Banque de France*, Paris: Presses Universitaires de France.

Reid, Margaret (1982)*The Secondary Banking Crisis 1973–1975*, London: Macmillan.

Rhodes, R.A.W. (1995) 'From Prime Ministerial Power to Core Executive', in R.A.W. Rhodes and Patrick Dunleavy (eds), *Prime Minister, Cabinet and Core Executive*, London: Macmillan, pp. 11–37.

Rhodes, R.A.W., (1996) 'The New Governance: Governing without Government', in *Political Studies*, vol. 44, no. 4, pp. 652–67.

Rhodes, R.A.W. and Dunleavy, Patrick (eds) (1995) *Prime Minister, Cabinet and Core Executive*, London: Macmillan.

Roberts, Richard, and Kynaston, David (eds) (1995) *The Bank of England: Money, Power and Influence 1694–1994*, Oxford: Clarendon Press.

Rogoff, Kenneth (1985) 'The Optimal Degree of Commitment to an Intermediate Monetary Target', in *Quarterly Journal of Economics*, vol. 100, no. 4, , pp. 1169–90.

Rose, Richard (1985) 'The Job at the Top: The Presidency in Comparative Perspective', in George C. Edwards, Steven A. Schull and Norman C. Thomas (eds), *The President and Public Policy Making*, Pittsburgh, University of Pittsburgh Press, pp. 3–21.

Rosenau J., and Czempiel, E.O. (1992) *Governance without Government: Order and Change in World Politics*, Cambridge: Cambridge University Press.

Ruggie, John (1982) 'International Regimes, Transactions, and Change: Embedded Liberalism in the Postwar Economic Order', in *International Organisation* vol. 36, no. 2. pp. 379–415.

Sabatier, Guy (1972) *Rapport no. 2680 sur la Banque de France*, Paris: Assemblée Nationale.

Saint-Geours, Jean (1979) *Pouvoir et Finance*, Paris: Fayard.

Sayers, R.S. (1970) 'The Return to Gold 1925', in Sydney Pollard (ed.), *The Wasting of the British Economy: British Economic Policy 1945 to the Present*, London: Croom Helm.

Sayers, R. (1976) *The Bank of England 1891–1944, vol. 1*, Cambridge: Cambridge University Press.

Schumpeter, Joseph (1994) *Capitalism, Socialism and Democracy*, London: Routledge.

Secrétariat d'État à la Présidence du Conseil et à l'Information (1946) *Évolution du Statut de la Banque de France*, Paris: Notes Documentaires et Études, no. 292.

Semler, Dwight (1994) 'Focus: The Politics of Central Banking', in *East European Constitutional Review*, vol. 3, nos. 3–4, pp. 48–52.

Shonfeld, Andrew (1965) *Modern Capitalism: The Changing Balance of Public and Private Power*, Oxford: Oxford University Press.

Simmons, Beth A. (1994) *Who Adjusts? Domestic Sources of Foreign Economic Policy during the Interwar Years*, Princeton: Princeton University Press.

Skidelsky, Robert (1967) *Politicians and the Slump: The Labour Government 1929–1931*, London: Macmillan.

—— (1992a) *John Maynard Keynes, Hopes Betrayed 1883–1920*, London: Macmillan.

—— (1992b) *John Maynard Keynes, vol. II, The Economist as Saviour*, London: Macmillan.

Skinner, Quentin (1989) 'The State', in Terence Ball, James Farr and Russell Hanson (eds), *Political Innovation and Conceptual Change*, Cambridge: Cambridge University Press.

Skowronek, Stephen (1982) *Building the New American State*, Cambridge: Cambridge University Press.

Smith, David (1987) *The Rise and Fall of Monetarism*, Penguin: Harmondsworth.

—— (1992) *From Boom to Bust: Trial and Error in British Economic Policy*, Penguin: Harmondsworth.

Stephens, Philip (1996) *Politics and the Pound: The Conservatives' Struggle with Sterling*, London: Macmillan.

Strange, Susan (1996) *The Retreat of the State: The Diffusion of Power in the World Economy*, Cambridge: Cambridge University Press.

Streeck, Wolfgang, and Philippe Schmitter (1991) 'From National Corporatism to Transnational Pluralism', in *Politics and Society*, vol 19. no 2. pp. 133–64.

Sturm, Roland (1989) 'The Role of the Bundesbank in German Politics', in *West European Politics*, vol. 12, no. 2, pp. 1–11.

Sykes, Alan (1979) *Tariff Reform in British Politics 1903–1913*, Oxford: Clarendon Press.

Thatcher, Margaret (1993) *The Downing Street Years*, London: Harper Collins.

Thiel, Elke (1989) 'Macroeconomic Policy Preferences and Co-ordination: A View From Germany', in Paolo Guerrieni and Pier Carlo Padoan (eds), *The Political*

Economy of Integration: States, Markets and Institutions, Brighton: Harvester Wheatsheaf, pp. 202–30.

Thompson, Helen (1996) *The British Conservative Government and the European Exchange Rate Mechanism*, London: Pinter.

—— (1997) 'The Nation-State and International Capital Flows in Historical Perspective', in *Government and Opposition*, vol. 32, no. 1, pp. 84–113.

Tilly, Charles (ed.) (1975) *The Formation of the National States in Western Europe*, London: Princeton University Press.

Tobin, James (1972) 'Inflation and Unemployment,' in *American Economic Review*, vol. 62, no. 1, pp. 1–18.

Toniolo, Gianni (1988) *Central Banks' Independence in Historical Perspective*, Berlin: de Gruyter.

UDF (1993) *Proposition de loi sur l'indépendance de la Banque de France*, Paris: National Assembly.

Walker, Patrick Gordon (1970) *The Cabinet*, London: Jonathan Cape.

Wallace, Helen (1993) 'European Governance in Turbulent Times,' in *Journal of Common Market Studies*, vol. 31, no. 3, pp. 293–303.

Wood, Adrian (1994) *North-South Trade, Employment and Inequality: Changing Fortunes in a Skill-Driven World*, Oxford: Oxford University Press.

Williams, John T. (1980) 'The Political Manipulation of Macroeconomic Policy', in *American Political Science Review*, vol. 84, pp. 767–96.

Williamson, Philip (1992) *National Crisis and National Government: British Politics, the Economy and Empire 1926–1932*, Cambridge: Cambridge University Press.

Woolley, John T. (1984) *Monetary Politics: The Federal Reserve and the Politics of Monetary Policy*, Cambridge: Cambridge University Press.

—— (1994) 'The Politics of Monetary Policy: A Critical Review', in *Journal of Public Policy*, vol. 14, no. 1, pp. 57–85.

Index

For Product Safety Concerns and Information please contact our EU representative GPSR@taylorandfrancis.com Taylor & Francis Verlag GmbH, Kaufingerstraße 24, 80331 München, Germany